D0572905

Chef Paul Prudhomme's
Louisiana Tastes

Also by
Chef Paul Prudhomme

Chef Paul Prudhomme's Louisiana Kitchen

Chef Paul Prudhomme's Family Cookbook
(with the Prudhomme Family)

Chef Paul Prudhomme's Seasoned America

Chef Paul Prudhomme's Fork in the Road

Chef Paul Prudhomme's Pure Magic

Chef Paul Prudhomme's Fiery Foods That I Love

Chef Paul Prudhomme's Kitchen Expedition

Chef
Paul
Prudhomme's
Louisiana
Tastes

Exciting Flavors from

the State That Cooks

William Morrow and Company, Inc.   New York

Copyright © 2000 by Paul Prudhomme

All rights reserved. No part of this book may be reproduced or utilized in any form or by any means, electronic or mechanical, including photocopying, recording, or by any information storage or retrieval system, without permission in writing from the Publisher. Inquiries should be addressed to Permissions Department, William Morrow and Company, Inc., 1350 Avenue of the Americas, New York, N.Y. 10019.

It is the policy of William Morrow and Company, Inc., and its imprints and affiliates, recognizing the importance of preserving what has been written, to print the books we publish on acid-free paper, and we exert our best efforts to that end.

Library of Congress Cataloging-in-Publication Data

Prudhomme, Paul.
Chef Paul Prudhomme's Louisiana tastes. —1st ed.
　　p.　　cm.
　　Includes index.
　　ISBN 0-688-12224-8
　　1. Cookery, American—Louisiana style.　I. Title.
TX715.2.L68P76　2000
641.59763—dc210　　　　　　　　　　　99–35611
　　　　　　　　　　　　　　　　　　　　　CIP

Printed in the United States of America
First Edition
1　2　3　4　5　6　7　8　9　10

BOOK DESIGN BY RALPH FOWLER

www.williammorrow.com

641.59763
PRU
2000

Contents

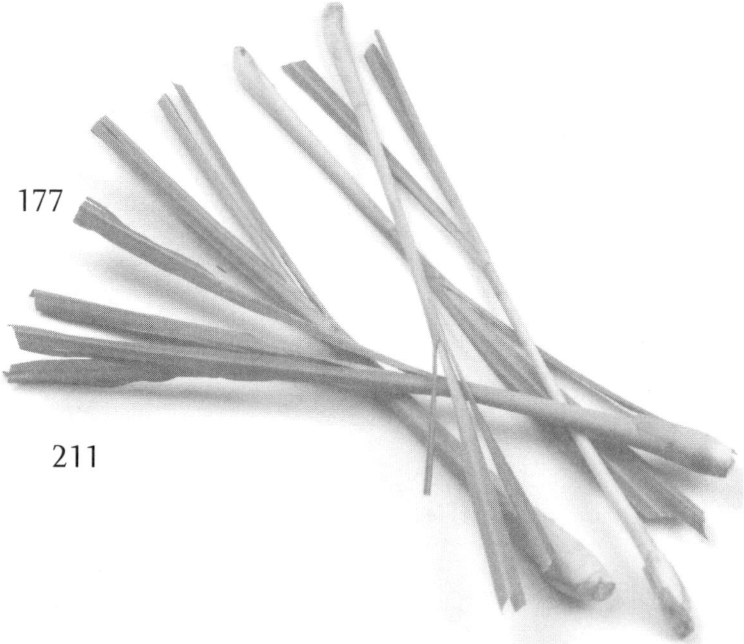

Acknowledgments

A project as complicated as a cookbook could never be completed without the assistance of many people, and although I've thanked everyone in person, I want to thank them in these pages so you'll know who they are and how much they helped.

Pam Hoenig, our editor at William Morrow, guided all of us through the various stages of producing this book, from its initial concept to the final revisions, and we are grateful for her patience and creativity. All the staff at Morrow have, in fact, been extremely helpful and supportive during all the years we've worked together.

We refer to Patricia Kennedy Livingston as our "New Orleans editor," but her contributions encompass so much more than editing. She cooked each and every one of these dishes in her own kitchen, made notes at every step to make the techniques easier to understand, and suggested content for the recipe headnotes. Patricia also organized all the recipes into categories, prepared the manuscript, proofread the galleys, designed many of the photos, and generally stepped in wherever needed.

All these recipes were born in my Research and Development Kitchen. In that exciting setting, Sean O'Meara, Director of the R & D Kitchen, with a permanent crook in his neck from looking over his shoulder toward the stove and me, tirelessly entered the ingredients, amounts, and procedures into the computer as I worked. He watched the clock so we'd know how long a certain step took. I rely heavily on Sean's sense of taste to verify my own impressions, and he often suggests options I hadn't thought about. If we decided to adjust a seasoning, he'd refigure it, and he made any other changes that our tasting indicated. Sean also shopped for the food and was a whiz at ferreting out unusual ingredients. As our resident computer expert, he was called on to solve any problems with equipment or programs.

Chef Chris Pasia, Corporate Executive Chef of the R & D Kitchen, who is a talented chef in his own right, was my right arm in the kitchen—a truly valuable assistant. He efficiently prepped all the ingredients, offered numerous suggestions for taste combinations, and shared his wonderful ideas for presentations. Because Chris has culinary experience gained from working around the world, his knowledge of unusual ingredients and cooking techniques is invaluable.

We certainly couldn't have managed in the kitchen nearly as well without the four beautiful Pasia ladies—Chris's wife, Choleta, and their daughters, Charyn, Cherriepin, and Cherrielet—who volunteered their time, talents, and taste buds. Choleta's help was especially appreciated, for she painstakingly measured out each component of the seasoning blend for every recipe.

You know what they say about the worth of a picture! Paul Rico's sumptuous studio photographs of the finished dishes, and the out-of-doors shot for the jacket, with the help of landscape architect David

Henrique, enable us to show you just how appealing these recipes are. Chef Marty Cosgrove added immensely to the photography sessions, with his sure knowledge of my cooking style, his good eye for design, and his ability to implement whatever plans we placed before him.

Shawn Granger McBride, the Magic Seasonings Blends President and CEO, deserves not only gratitude but some kind of trophy for unerringly charting the best and quickest course through the multitude of problems, setbacks, and complications that inevitably occur during the lengthy endeavor of writing a book. I've found it works best to have one person who knows what the entire team is doing, and Shawn is that person. Thanks are also offered to the staff at MSB, who shared their ideas and opinions during necessary but long meetings pertaining to the book.

Finally, I owe an enormous thank-you to all of you across the country who read cookbooks for fun, enjoy trying new recipes, and share your delight in wonderful flavors with your friends and families. I'm grateful that you buy my books, eat at my restaurant, and buy my spices, for these ventures give me the means to do the charity work that I love and to teach and spend time with culinary students across the country. Without you I'd be just another fat man with a beard! So please know that when I include you in my thanks—I really mean it. You make it all possible and worthwhile.

Introduction

Hi! It's great to be invited into your kitchen again—together we can make some fantastic meals! To my way of thinking, fantastic meals and great cooking are about more than just putting nourishment into your body, although, of course, that was food's first purpose. Although flavor is incredibly important to me (and to you too, I'm sure, or you wouldn't have this book in your hands), good food means more than that—to me, it's very emotional and means sharing love and friendship. Let me explain.

I was the youngest of thirteen children, and when my last sister got married I was appointed to help Mother in the kitchen, so I've been around cooking since I was just a child. I saw firsthand how Mother used her skills and knowledge to express her love for her family, and some of my happiest memories are of all of us sitting around the table, laughing and talking and sharing the day's events. If one of us had a hard day or wasn't feeling well, the sight of a favorite dish and the concern of other family members couldn't help but make that person feel better.

The kitchen table was where we got to really know one another, where we learned about family history, the give-and-take of relationships, manners, and how to hold a conversation. It was where we learned how precious life and family are, and what being a family really means.

I'm pretty sure that people have been eating together since long before we could talk. As hunters and gatherers settled down and became farmers, it took the entire family to raise the food and prepare the meals, so, of course, they all stopped to eat at the same time. There weren't any books, televisions, or schools, so people talked about crops, weather, and family matters, and these conversations further strengthened their sense of family.

We Prudhommes weren't the only ones who regularly gathered around the table to feed body and spirit—up until the 1960s or so, most families across the country would never have thought of eating separately. But we lost something very precious when other activities became more important—committee meetings, working late, classes, social events, and sports. I don't pretend to be a sociologist, but I think there must be some connection between the loss of the daily family meal and the fracturing of families and their traditional values. I think that, as a nation, we're nearing a crisis with our children because many of them don't know who they are or what their heritage is.

I wish I could say something like "Use this cookbook and it'll bring your family back together," but there's no magic in the pages themselves. What I can say, though, is "Use this book and your emotions to create some wonderful dishes, and make the effort to bring your family together for a meal." Maybe you can't count on all family members to be at the table every night, but perhaps you can begin with two or three nights a week. And if you're a family of one, then think close friends when I refer to family members. We all need love and fellowship, even if we don't have children or a spouse.

Another example of how important food is to us is the fact that when we want to impress someone, the first thing we do is feed them. Think about it. A young man wants to impress a date—he takes her out to dinner. A lady wants to impress a gentleman—she invites him over for a home-cooked meal. A businessperson needs the goodwill of a client—he or she takes that person to lunch. The highest compliment we can pay a new friend or acquaintance is to invite him or her home for dinner.

The ideas for many recipes in this book were inspired by the wealth of new, and in some cases unusual, foods that are available today in our grocery stores, supermarkets, and ethnic markets. For example, yucca, mango, papaya, Japanese eggplant, balsamic vinegar, chipotle chile peppers, and tilapia are just a few of the delicious ingredients that I've learned to use.

Look at the recipe for Chicken with a Green and White Taste on page 186 and you'll see what I mean. The "green" comes from sugar snap peas, similar to snow peas, and when lightly cooked and combined with the right seasonings, they are a highlight of this chicken dish. Notice, too, that it's got three kinds of chile peppers—fresh jalapeños and ground dried New Mexico and ancho peppers—which we certainly didn't have when I was growing up.

Although not every recipe in this book contains a newly discovered ingredient, I was able to create these dishes with far greater freedom and excitement than when I put my first cookbook together. The methods used are mostly traditional Louisiana ones, similar to the way

I cooked as a youngster, although I constantly learn new techniques from professionals and home cooks as I travel around the country and the world. I've always said my main mission in life is to make your dinner better, and all these recipes were created around the idea of making you happy. Another one of my goals is to help you become a better cook. I try to explain "why" whenever I do anything unusual, and, for the first time, in many of these recipes I've included "tasting notes" so you can follow and understand how the flavor, smell, color, and texture of an ingredient or a dish will develop as it browns and as you add other ingredients. You don't have to eat much of the food—just rub the back of a spoon on the ingredient and you can taste the intensity of the browning or seasoning. In a couple of instances we even talk about the color of the smoke, for that can be important, too. I hope you'll think about what you're doing, and maybe even make notes to yourself in the margins of the book.

You'll notice that the layout of each recipe is a bit different from my previous books. We've separated the seasoning mix from the main part of the recipe, so it stands out and you can easily make it up anytime. Store the mixes in a plastic zipper bag or small jar in your pantry and they'll be there whenever you're ready to cook.

Please read through "Notes from My Kitchen" because it contains useful information that is too lengthy to include with each recipe. And right now I'm going to give you a really important suggestion: Carefully read the entire recipe before starting to cook it; you don't want to get halfway through and discover that the garlic you're about to add should have been fire-roasted.

If this is the first of my cookbooks you've used, I'd like to suggest a good order in which to proceed. The secret of success in cooking is the same as the secret of success in life: Pay attention! First, read the recipe and make your shopping list. When you're ready to cook, read the recipe again. Start the stock if indicated, make the seasoning mix, prep the vegetables, then get out measuring cups, bowls, pots and pans, thermometer if needed, and check to see if any ingredients need to be cold or at room temperature when added to the dish.

In line with what I said earlier, as wonderful as it is for a family to eat together, it's even better when family members cook together! One person can start the stock and prepare the seasoning mix, another can chop the vegetables, and if there's a third person to help, he or she can get out all the staples—vinegar, oil, sugar, and so forth. Turn off the television, for you'll have a lot more fun talking and laughing as you cook. Before you know it, you'll have a wonderful dinner and a closer family.

To sum up, this book is about making people happy. When I sign off as I do below, it's because I firmly believe that cooking, eating, and loving are very closely related.

Let's get started!

Good cooking,

Good eating,

Good loving,

Chef
Paul
Prudhomme's
Louisiana
Tastes

Appetizers to Start Things Off Right!

Most families in the rural part of Louisiana where I grew up didn't have anything so formal as an "appetizer," although once restaurants began serving food to visitors the idea was incorporated into the menu. Most of the dishes that eventually ended up as appetizers could just as easily have been the main course of a meal, assuming the quantity was large enough, or in small portions, a light lunch or supper.

Crab Claws Vinaigrette with Fire-Roasted Mayonnaise

Makes 8 appetizer servings

Crab claws aren't an unusual appetizer, but fire-roasting the onion and garlic for the mayonnaise gives it a unique flavor that adds a whole new dimension to this favorite. When you go to the little bit of trouble to use the optional squash and eggplant for your presentation, you're giving your guests notice that you're serving something very special!

Vinaigrette

1½ cups seafood stock
¼ cup chopped onions
¼ cup chopped celery
¼ cup seeded and chopped red bell peppers
¼ cup seeded and chopped green bell peppers
¼ cup seeded and chopped yellow bell peppers
1 teaspoon minced fresh garlic
1 tablespoon cane vinegar, or your favorite vinegar
1 tablespoon white balsamic vinegar
3 tablespoons apple cider vinegar
1 tablespoon rice vinegar
1 tablespoon mirin (sweet rice wine)
1 tablespoon lightly packed light brown sugar

1 pound cooked crab claws with meat (about 50 pieces)

Fire-Roasted Mayonnaise

2 large eggs
2 tablespoons chopped fire-roasted onions
5 cloves garlic, fire-roasted
1 cup vegetable oil

Seasoning Mix

1½ teaspoons salt
1¼ teaspoons paprika
1 teaspoon dill weed
¾ teaspoon cayenne
¾ teaspoon ground cumin
¾ teaspoon dry mustard
¾ teaspoon onion powder
¾ teaspoon dried thyme leaves
½ teaspoon garlic powder
½ teaspoon black pepper
½ teaspoon ground dried chipotle chile peppers
¼ teaspoon white pepper

* * * * *

2 medium-size white squashes or bell peppers (optional)
Lettuce leaves
1 medium-size Japanese eggplant (the cylindrical variety), or a
    long, narrow squash such as zucchini (optional)

1. Combine the seasoning mix ingredients in a small bowl. Reserve 1 tablespoon of this mixture for the Fire-Roasted Mayonnaise.

2. Make the vinaigrette: In a large saucepan, combine the remaining seasoning mix with all the vinaigrette ingredients and place over high heat. Cook until the liquid is reduced to about ½ cup after straining, about 20 minutes. Remove from the heat, let cool to room temperature, then strain through a fine-mesh strainer. Discard the vegetables and combine the liquid with the crab claws in a medium-size bowl or a plastic zipper bag. Toss well (or, if using a zipper bag, close securely and turn upside down a few times) to coat. Marinate in the refrigerator, tossing (or turning) every 20 minutes, for at least 1 hour.

3. Make the mayonnaise: Process the reserved 1 tablespoon seasoning mix with the eggs, onions, and garlic in a blender or food processor until they are light and frothy, about 30 seconds. With the appliance running, add the vegetable oil in a very thin stream until the oil is absorbed and a thick mayonnaise consistency is reached, about 2 to 3 minutes. Cover and refrigerate until ready to serve.

4. For assembly: If you're using the squashes or bell peppers as containers for the vinaigrette, cut a shallow hole, 2 inches in diameter, into the center of the stem end of each one. If desired, make notches around the edge of the hole for decoration. Using a melon baller, scoop out the meat of the squash and discard it, leaving a shell about ¼ inch thick. Parboil the squashes in a large pot of boiling water for 10 minutes, then drain and let cool.

5. Arrange the lettuce leaves on a serving platter. Fill the cooled squashes or peppers with the Fire-Roasted Mayonnaise and place them on the platter. If you're using the eggplant to display the crab claws, cut it in half and place it, flat side down, on the platter. Poke the sharp tips of the claws into the eggplant so that they are all standing upright, and serve to your very impressed guests. If you prefer, you can serve the vinaigrette in a small bowl and the claws directly on the platter.

Crabmeat au Gratin

Makes 6 servings

The use of chipotle chile peppers (smoked dried jalapeño peppers) and the fact that the corn is roasted before being combined with the other ingredients give this casserole a subtle but distinctive smoky flavor. Wonderful! Carefully checking the crabmeat to remove any bits of shell and cartilage is a tedious, time-consuming chore, but it's necessary, so get comfortable and just do it. By the way, the cheese will be easiest to grate if it's very cold. If you can't find large ears of corn, you'll probably need to roast 4 or 5 ears to get the amount needed—at least 2 cups.

3 large ears fresh corn, still in their husks, or
    frozen ears of corn if you prefer
2 tablespoons olive oil
½ cup chopped onions
¼ cup chopped celery
¼ cup seeded and chopped red bell peppers
¼ cup seeded and chopped yellow bell peppers
2 tablespoons unsalted butter
2 medium-size eggs
1 tablespoon white balsamic vinegar
¾ cup vegetable oil
1 pound lump crabmeat, picked over to remove
    all bits of shell and cartilage
10 ounces Muenster cheese, in all, freshly
    grated

Seasoning Mix

1¼ teaspoons ground dried
    chipotle chile peppers

1 teaspoon salt

¾ teaspoon paprika

½ teaspoon dried basil

½ teaspoon garlic powder

½ teaspoon dry mustard

½ teaspoon dried oregano

¼ teaspoon onion powder

¼ teaspoon black pepper

¼ teaspoon white pepper

1. Combine the seasoning mix in a small bowl.

2. Leave the husks on the corn and roast the ears in a preheated 375°F oven until the husks are dry and browned in places and the corn produces a roasted aroma, 15 to 20 minutes. If you're using frozen ears of corn, defrost them completely and pat dry. Wrap loosely in aluminum foil, punch a few holes in the foil (so the corn will roast, not steam), and proceed as instructed above. Remove from the oven. When cool enough to handle, cut the kernels from the cobs, getting as much of the juice from the cobs as possible. You should have about 2¼ cups. Set aside. Reduce the oven temperature to 325°F.

3. Heat the olive oil in a 10-inch skillet over high heat until it is very hot, about 3 to 4 minutes. Add the onions, celery, bell peppers, and 1 tablespoon of the seasoning mix. Cook, stirring occasionally, until the colors of the bell peppers brighten noticeably and the onions begin to darken around the edges, about 4 to 5 minutes. *During this time you will taste the distinctive flavors of the herbs in the seasoning mix as they begin to attach themselves to the vegetables.* Add the remaining seasoning mix, stir well, and cook, stirring occasionally, until the mixture is well browned (but be careful not to let it burn!), about 3 to 4 minutes. *While the vegetables are caramelizing, you will be able to taste the increasing sweetness in the browned parts.* Add the butter and stir until it melts *(taste the wonderful richness now!)*, then remove from the heat.

4. Process the eggs in a food processor until they're fluffy, about 45 seconds. Add the vegetable mixture from the skillet and the vinegar and process for 20 seconds. With the machine running, slowly add the vegetable oil, then process just until well blended, about 1 minute. You should have about 1¾ cups of this mixture. Now transfer it to a bowl and add the crabmeat and roasted corn. Stir gently but thoroughly to distribute the ingredients evenly.

5. Sprinkle half the grated cheese evenly over the bottom of a 9 × 13-inch baking pan or casserole dish. Spoon the crab/vegetable mixture over the cheese, then sprinkle the remaining cheese evenly on top. Bake until the cheese is browned around the edges and the crabmeat mixture is heated through, about 35 to 40 minutes. Remove from the oven and let sit for about 5 to 10 minutes before serving, as the flavor of the crab is best if it's allowed to cool slightly.

Crawfish-Stuffed Mushrooms

Makes 12 mushroom caps; 4 appetizer servings

You can use 1 color of bell pepper, instead of the 3 colors, if you prefer. We used varieties of chile peppers that were available in our local supermarkets at the time we shopped, and you should use whatever chiles are fresh and available in your area. Always test the heat of chiles before you use them—an easy way to do this is to cut the top off of the chile and touch it to the tip of your tongue. If it's too hot on your tongue, it will be too hot in your dish. If you prefer a mild flavor, use a smaller quantity or a mild variety. As with any crawfish recipe, you can use shrimp if you prefer.

12 mushroom caps, about 2½ to 3 inches in diameter
Vegetable oil or vegetable oil cooking spray
½ cup unseasoned dried bread crumbs
¼ cup finely chopped fresh cilantro leaves
4 tablespoons (½ stick) unsalted butter
2 tablespoons olive oil
¾ cup finely chopped shallots
½ cup finely chopped celery
½ cup seeded and finely chopped green bell peppers
½ cup seeded and finely chopped red bell peppers
½ cup seeded and finely chopped yellow bell peppers
2 tablespoons seeded and finely chopped fresh poblano chile peppers
2 tablespoons seeded and finely chopped fresh red, preferably, or green jalapeño chile peppers

Seasoning Mix

2 teaspoons salt
1 teaspoon cayenne
1 teaspoon dry mustard
1 teaspoon onion powder
1 teaspoon paprika
¾ teaspoon garlic powder
½ teaspoon black pepper
½ teaspoon rubbed sage
¼ teaspoon white pepper

2 tablespoons finely chopped fresh fennel leaves

½ cup all-purpose flour

1 to 1½ cups seafood stock

½ cup plain yogurt

1 pound peeled Louisiana crawfish tails

1½ cups heavy cream

1. Combine the seasoning mix ingredients in a small bowl.

2. Cut a very thin slice off the tops of the mushroom caps, so that they can sit flat in the pan. Using a melon baller or a sharp spoon, remove the soft, spongy parts from inside the mushroom caps. Finely chop the trimmings—you should have about 1 cup. Brush the caps lightly with vegetable oil on all sides or spray lightly with vegetable oil cooking spray.

3. In a small bowl, combine the bread crumbs, cilantro, and 2 teaspoons of the seasoning mix.

4. Place the butter and olive oil in a 5-quart saucepan over high heat. When the butter sizzles, add the shallots, celery, all the bell peppers, both the chile peppers, the reserved mushroom trimmings, and the remaining seasoning mix. Stir well, then cover and cook, uncovering to stir twice, until the vegetables are golden brown, about 8 to 10 minutes. Reduce the heat to medium, uncover, add the fennel, stir well, recover, and continue to cook until the onions are dark golden brown, about 2 to 4 minutes. *The vegetables will retain a light crunch and a faint sweetness, followed by a strong brown taste from the brown bits on the bottom of the pan and a strong herb and spice finish.*

5. Uncover the pan, sprinkle the flour over the vegetables, and stir until the white of the flour is no longer visible, then spread the mixture evenly over the bottom of the pan. Re-cover and cook until a brown crust forms on the bottom of the pan, about 1 to 3 minutes. Uncover and add 1 cup of the stock and scrape the bottom of the pan until the brown crust is completely dissolved into the mixture. Add the yogurt and crawfish and stir well. Re-cover and cook until the mixture reaches at least 200°F on an instant-read thermometer, about 2 to 3 minutes. Stir in about ½ cup of the bread crumb mixture and remove from the heat. Set aside 1 cup of this mixture for making the sauce.

6. Preheat the oven to 350°F.

7. Fill each mushroom cap with a generous 2 tablespoons of the stuffing, pressing it in as you work, then mound an additional 2 tablespoons on top. A small ice

cream scoop works well, or you can use a soupspoon and your hands. Press the stuffing into a dome shape, making sure it is firmly packed. Sprinkle the tops and sides of the mounded filling lightly with the remaining bread crumb mixture—easy to do if you pick up the mushroom caps and turn them as you sprinkle. Place the mushrooms in a large baking pan. Bake until the tops of the stuffing are golden brown, about 15 to 20 minutes. (Mushrooms can behave very differently during cooking, sometimes becoming either very dry or very soggy. If they become too dry during cooking, add the additional ½ cup of stock to the pan. If the caps begin to collapse, reduce the cooking time and increase the oven temperature to 400°F.)

8. While the mushrooms are baking, make the sauce. Combine the reserved stuffing and the heavy cream in a blender and process until smooth, about 1 minute. The cream will thicken during this process. Transfer the mixture to a 10-inch skillet over high heat. Bring to a boil, whisking frequently—you'll see that the cream thins out at first—and cook until the sauce thickens slightly, about 2 minutes. You should have about 2½ cups of sauce. Serve each mushroom cap with a scant 3 tablespoons of the sauce.

Jalapeño-Stuffed
Red Potatoes

Serve 3 of these terrific little stuffed potatoes for an unusual appetizer, perhaps 4 or 5 as a side dish, or a few more, accompanied by a salad, as a light lunch or supper. They also make great "pass-arounds" for a stand-up party. When choosing the Stilton cheese, look for a package with lots of blue veins and a brand with good blue cheese flavor and a slightly salty taste up front. Keep it in the refrigerator until you're ready to use it—it crumbles better when it's cold.

12 red potatoes, each about 1½ inches in diameter
8 tablespoons (1 stick) unsalted butter, in all
1 cup chopped onions
½ cup seeded and chopped fresh red jalapeño chile peppers
½ cup seeded and chopped fresh green jalapeño chile peppers
¾ cup heavy cream
3 ounces Stilton cheese, crumbled

Seasoning Mix

2 teaspoons paprika
2 teaspoons salt
1 teaspoon ground cumin
1 teaspoon dried oregano
¾ teaspoon garlic powder
¾ teaspoon dry mustard
½ teaspoon onion powder
½ teaspoon white pepper

1. Combine the seasoning mix ingredients in a small bowl.

2. Cut the potatoes in half, leaving the skins on. To make them sit flat, cut off a very small piece from the side opposite the cut side. Place the potatoes in a large pot of water, bring to a boil, and boil until a fork can be inserted easily about ¼ inch into each potato, about 20 to 25 minutes. Run the potatoes under cold water to stop the cooking, drain, and set them aside.

3. Preheat the oven to 450°F.

continued

9

4. Using a melon baller, carefully hollow out each potato half, leaving a shell about ¼ inch thick, and set the meat from the potatoes aside. Place the potato halves on an ungreased sheet pan with the hollow side facing down.

5. Melt 2 tablespoons of the butter in a small skillet. As soon as the butter melts and begins to sizzle, add 2 teaspoons of the seasoning mix and stir briefly to combine. When the butter begins to foam, immediately remove the skillet from the heat and transfer the butter to a small ramekin or bowl.

6. Brush the outsides of the potato shells with the seasoned butter, then turn them over and brush the insides. Bake the shells until the skins are slightly crisp, about 15 minutes. Remove them from the oven and set them aside.

7. Meanwhile, in a 10-inch skillet over high heat, melt another 2 tablespoons of the butter. When the butter begins to sizzle, about 3 minutes, add the onions, all the jalapeño peppers, and 1 tablespoon plus 2 teaspoons of the seasoning mix. Cook, stirring frequently, until the vegetables are browned, about 7 to 9 minutes. In a 2-quart saucepan over high heat, combine the heavy cream and the remaining 4 tablespoons butter. As soon as the butter melts, add the reserved potato meat, the browned vegetables, and the remaining seasoning mix. Cook, stirring almost constantly, until the mixture is thick and bubbling like a volcano, about 5 to 8 minutes. Refrigerate until cold—spread out on a plate or sheet pan if you're in a hurry. Transfer the mixture to a food processor (do not use a blender, as it will make the texture too soft) and pulse until the mixture is smooth, about 1 to 2 minutes. The mixture should still have a grainy appearance and should look something like very thick Dijon mustard.

8. Notice that the next step calls for a pastry bag—when using one, always turn the widest part of the top opening back over the outside (as though you were preparing to turn it inside-out) to expose the middle of the inside to make it easier to place the filling right into the area near the tip. Just before filling, twist the bag near the tip around 1 full turn and poke some of the body of the empty bag toward and slightly into the twisted part (this sounds confusing, but you'll understand when you're actually doing it) to keep the filling from coming out while you're filling the bag. Use a spatula to fill the bag and wipe it against the inside of the bag to scrape the filling from the spatula. Then, once you have the bag filled, pull the folded-over portion back into a fully extended position and twist the top few inches of the bag shut to keep the filling from coming out of the bag. Press the filling down toward the tip, untwist the section near the tip, and you're ready to fill the potato halves. If you don't have a pastry bag, substitute a heavy-duty plastic zipper bag and cut a small triangle from a bottom corner.

9. Place the mixture in a pastry bag and pipe it into the potato shells, filling them so that the filling is mounded about ½ inch over the top of the shell. Divide the crumbled Stilton cheese among the stuffed potatoes, gently pressing it slightly into the potato filling.

10. Place the sheet pan in the oven and bake until the cheese melts and begins to brown, about 10 to 15 minutes. Serve hot.

Duck Boudin with
Cream Sauce

Makes 8 appetizer servings   *Boudin, made with rice as well as some kind of meat and seasonings, is one of the most familiar Cajun snack foods. It's a tradition for an entire family to go to the grocery store on Saturdays to buy boudin in links. It's pronounced "boo-dan," just barely saying the "n." Boudin is very versatile—you can serve it as an appetizer, as a main course, or made into small patties with eggs for breakfast.*

Boudin Mixture

> **One 4½- to 5-pound duck, cut into quarters**
> **1 pound chicken gizzards**
> **½ pound chicken livers**
> **2 cups chopped green onions or scallions**
> **8 cups cooked long-grain rice**

Cream Sauce

> **2 tablespoons vegetable oil**
> **1 cup chopped green onions**
> **½ cup seeded and chopped green bell peppers**
> **½ cup chopped onions or scallions**
> **½ cup chopped celery**
> **3½ cups heavy cream**
> **4 tablespoons (½ stick) unsalted butter**

Seasoning Mix
2 tablespoons plus ¼ teaspoon salt
1 tablespoon plus 2 teaspoons onion powder
1 tablespoon plus ¾ teaspoon cayenne
1 tablespoon plus ¾ teaspoon garlic powder
2½ teaspoons ground cumin
2½ teaspoons black pepper
2 teaspoons white pepper

1. Combine the seasoning mix ingredients in a small bowl.

2. Place the duck in an 8-quart pot over high heat and add enough water to cover, about 2½ to 3 quarts. Cover the pot and bring to a boil, then reduce the heat to medium and simmer briskly for 30 minutes. Add the chicken gizzards and simmer for another 1 hour and 20 minutes. Remove the duck from the water and set it aside. Add the chicken livers to the water and cook for 10 minutes. Remove the pot from the heat, strain off the liquid (stock), and reserve. You'll need 5½ cups of stock, so if you have less, add as much water as necessary, and if you have more, discard it or save it for another use. Set the gizzards and livers aside to cool.

3. When the duck is cool enough to handle, remove the skin and fat and chop them finely—you should have about ½ cup. Season the chopped skin and fat with 3 tablespoons of the seasoning mix, working it in well with your hands. In a 12-inch nonstick skillet over high heat, cook the chopped skin and fat until they are browned and the fat is completely rendered, about 10 minutes. Set aside.

4. Remove the meat from the duck and chop it—you should have about 3 cups—then place it in a large bowl. Chop the cooked gizzards and livers and add them to the bowl, along with the browned skin and fat, the rendered fat, green onions, rice, 2 tablespoons of the seasoning mix, and 4 cups of the duck stock. Combine thoroughly and reserve 2 cups of this mixture to make the sauce. Refrigerate the remainder until cold.

5. While the boudin mixture is chilling, make the sauce. In a 12-inch skillet over high heat, heat the vegetable oil just until it begins to smoke, about 3 to 4 minutes. Add the green onions, bell peppers, onions, celery, and the remaining seasoning mix. Cook, stirring every 2 minutes, until the vegetables just begin to brown, about 8 minutes. Stir in the remaining duck stock, bring to a boil, and cook for 2 minutes. Whisk in the heavy cream and reserved boudin mixture and bring just to a boil, then reduce the heat to medium and simmer briskly for 4 minutes. Remove from the heat and whisk in the butter until it melts. Keep the sauce warm while you fry the boudin.

6. When the boudin mixture is very cold, shape it into ½-inch-thick patties, using ¾ cup for each. Preheat a large nonstick skillet over high heat and when it is very hot, about 5 or 6 minutes, fry the boudin patties, turning once, until both sides are well browned, about 3 minutes per side. Drain on paper towels. Serve hot. For each serving, put ¾ cup of the sauce on a plate and top with 2 boudin cakes.

Ham Poppers with
Yummy Good Sauce

Makes about 48 pieces; 10 to 12 appetizer servings

Once you taste these great poppers, you're not going to want to wait for a party to serve them again! And I can't think of any time I wouldn't want to eat them—as a snack, as an appetizer, or with other finger food as a light meal. You might want to make the sauce first, so it will be ready as soon as you finish frying the poppers.

3 cups unseasoned dried bread crumbs
½ cup corn flour
½ cup all-purpose flour
2 cups milk
4 large eggs, in all
2 tablespoons lightly packed dark brown sugar
2 tablespoons white balsamic vinegar
2 tablespoons prepared horseradish (not
    horseradish sauce)
2 tablespoons Worcestershire sauce
2 tablespoons Chef Paul Prudhomme's Magic
    Pepper Sauce® or other medium-hot
    pepper sauce
1 teaspoon dark sesame oil
1½ pounds cooked ham, cut into 3 × ½ × ¼-inch
    strips, about 48 pieces
Vegetable oil for frying
Yummy Good Sauce (recipe follows)

Seasoning Mix

2 teaspoons salt

1½ teaspoons dried thyme leaves

1 teaspoon cayenne

1 teaspoon ground coriander

1 teaspoon garlic powder

1 teaspoon onion powder

1 teaspoon paprika

1 teaspoon ground dried Anaheim chile peppers

¾ teaspoon black pepper

¾ teaspoon ground dried chipotle chile peppers

½ teaspoon ground cinnamon

¼ teaspoon white pepper

1. Combine the seasoning mix ingredients in a small bowl.

2. In a flat pan or casserole dish, combine 1 tablespoon plus 1 teaspoon of the seasoning mix with the bread crumbs and mix well. In another flat pan or casserole dish, combine the

corn flour and all-purpose flour and mix well. In a third flat pan or casserole dish, combine the milk and 2 of the eggs and whisk until well combined.

3. Make a paste by combining the brown sugar, vinegar, horseradish, Worcestershire sauce, pepper sauce, sesame oil, the remaining 2 eggs, and the remaining seasoning mix. Place the ham strips in the paste and work the paste in with your hands until the strips are evenly coated.

4. In a large skillet over high heat, pour enough vegetable oil to measure 1 inch deep and heat it to 350°F. An electric skillet works well, or use a regular skillet and a cooking thermometer and adjust the heat as necessary to keep the temperature of the oil as close to 350°F as possible.

5. In this step, it's important to know that although the strips can sit in the egg mixture for a few moments, once you place them in the flour or bread crumbs, you must remove them right away, or the coating will become soggy. When you're ready to fry, place a handful of the strips in the flour mixture and coat them evenly. Immediately transfer the floured strips to the egg mixture and coat them on all sides. Finally, transfer the strips to the bread crumbs, cover them with the bread crumbs, then pick up each strip in your hand and squeeze it briefly to help the coating stick. Immediately place in the hot oil and fry until golden brown, 4 to 5 minutes, remove with a slotted spoon, and drain on paper towels. Repeat the process, working in small batches, until all the strips have been fried. Serve hot with Yummy Good Sauce for dipping.

Yummy Good Sauce

Makes 1¼ cups

1 cup mayonnaise
¼ cup ketchup
2 tablespoons Chef Paul Prudhomme's Magic Pepper Sauce, or
   other medium-hot pepper sauce
3 tablespoons honey

Place all the ingredients in a bowl and stir until completely combined. Serve at room temperature and refrigerate any leftover sauce.

Jambon Glacé

Makes 4 loaves; 16 generous appetizer servings   *Very similar to south Louisiana's famous Daube Glacée, these little loaves may be sliced and served on lettuce leaves as a cool and refreshing appetizer, or cut into smaller squares to serve with crackers as a party hors d'oeuvre. Use a very sharp knife to slice the loaves—you wouldn't believe what a difference in texture and flavor, not to mention appearance, a clean cut makes. I wouldn't have thought the knife would matter, until in the Research and Development Kitchen we tried one loaf sliced with a regular kitchen knife and another sliced with a sharp chef's knife. Amazing.*

Five ¼-ounce envelopes unflavored gelatin
2 cups water
¾ cup clover honey
4 tablespoons (½ stick) unsalted butter
1½ cups chopped red onions
¼ cup peeled and minced fresh ginger
2 cups peeled sweet potatoes cut into ¼-inch cubes
1 tablespoon minced fresh garlic
1 cup seeded and chopped red bell peppers
1 cup seeded and chopped yellow bell peppers
1½ pounds cooked ham, trimmed of fat and cut into ¼-inch cubes

Seasoning Mix

2 teaspoons paprika
1½ teaspoons dry mustard
1 teaspoon garlic powder
1 teaspoon salt
¾ teaspoon onion powder
½ teaspoon ground allspice
½ teaspoon ground cardamom
½ teaspoon ground coriander
½ teaspoon black pepper
½ teaspoon white pepper

1. Combine the seasoning mix ingredients in a small bowl.

2. Combine the gelatin, water, and honey in a bowl and whisk until completely dissolved. Set aside.

3. Melt the butter in a 12-inch nonstick skillet over high heat, then add the onions, ginger, sweet potatoes, garlic, both the bell peppers, and the seasoning mix. Cook, stirring and scraping the bottom of the skillet frequently, for 4 to 5 minutes. *The vegetables will be just beginning to take on a little "brown" flavor from the heat.* Add the ham and stir well, then cover the skillet. Let the mixture cook for 5 minutes, then uncover and stir. Re-cover and cook for 4 minutes. Uncover and stir and scrape the bottom of the skillet—at this point the vegetables will be faded in color, *somewhat sweeter from the browning*, and beginning to stick slightly. Re-cover and cook for an additional 2 minutes, then scrape the bottom of the skillet again and add the gelatin/honey mixture. Scrape the bottom again to loosen all the stuck-on material. Bring the mixture to a full boil, then remove from the heat and set aside to cool.

4. Ladle the mixture evenly into small loaf pans—we used pans 3½ × 5 × 2 inches, although the size is not critical for a dish that jells rather than bakes— stirring as you ladle so that the liquid and solids are evenly distributed. Or you could use individual molds or muffin tins. Refrigerate until the gelatin has completely set, at least 4 hours, preferably overnight. When ready to serve, unmold and, if you used loaf pans, cut into thick slices.

Onion Tarts

Makes 12 tarts; 12 appetizer servings

As do most people who really love to cook, I like to experiment, not only with different ingredients and seasonings but with unusual or nontraditional methods of cooking. This recipe is the result of just such "playing around" in the kitchen. The tarts' bases are not made from pie crust dough, but resemble spicy sponge cake, and the onions are simmered in sugar syrup for a delicate sweetness totally different from the flavor obtained by caramelizing. Because baking pans range so widely in type and quality, you may want to bake 1 tart first, check the bottom to see if it's too brown, and, if so, reduce the oven temperature to 300° or even 275°F and/or shorten the cooking time.

Use any variety or color of onions you want, because raw taste and texture don't matter as long as you cook them until they're sweet.

Seasoning Mix

1½ teaspoons paprika

1½ teaspoons salt

1 teaspoon dry mustard

¾ teaspoon ground anise

¾ teaspoon dried thyme leaves

½ teaspoon cayenne

1½ cups granulated sugar

3 cups water

4 medium-size onions, cut into ¾-inch cubes (about 4 cups)

4 large eggs, separated

6 tablespoons (¾ stick) unsalted butter, softened

1 tablespoon plus 1½ teaspoons confectioners' sugar

¼ cup heavy cream

1½ teaspoons pure vanilla extract

½ cup all-purpose flour, sifted

¼ teaspoon salt

1 teaspoon baking powder

1 tablespoon sesame seeds

1. Combine the seasoning mix ingredients in a small bowl.

2. Make a sugar syrup by combining the sugar and water in a 2-quart pot over high heat. Stir constantly until the sugar is completely dissolved and bring to a boil, then add the onions. Reduce the heat to medium-low and simmer until the sharp onion taste disappears. The time will depend entirely on the sweetness or acidity of your onions. With a slotted spoon, transfer the onions to a bowl and sprinkle them with 1 tablespoon plus 2 teaspoons of the seasoning mix. Toss gently to coat the onions evenly, then set them aside to cool to room temperature. Set the sugar syrup aside to cool to room temperature also.

3. Beat the egg whites with an electric mixer in a medium-size bowl until they reach the soft peak stage, then slowly beat in ¼ cup of the reserved syrup. Preheat the oven to 350°F.

4. Combine the egg yolks, butter, confectioners' sugar, heavy cream, vanilla, 2 tablespoons of the reserved syrup (discard the rest of the syrup), and the remaining seasoning mix in the large bowl of an electric mixer fitted with a whisk attachment. Whip at medium speed until the mixture is creamy and light orange-colored. Add the flour, salt, and baking powder and mix at medium speed until blended. Gently but thoroughly fold in the beaten egg whites and sesame seeds. Divide the batter evenly among 12 muffin crown tins or individual tart pans (roughly 4 to 5 inches in diameter)—about ¼ cup of batter for each tart—and spread it evenly. Divide the onions evenly among the rounds—about ¼ cup loosely packed for each.

5. Bake until the tops are light golden brown, about 20 minutes. Remove the pans from the oven and carefully remove the tarts from the pans by gently slipping a knife around the edges to loosen any stuck places, then lifting the tart out with a small spatula. Serve hot to some very lucky friends or family members.

ALBUQUERQUE ACADEMY
LIBRARY

Salmon-Stuffed Mushroom Caps

Makes 8 appetizer servings

What a pretty appetizer to serve your guests! The salmon atop each mushroom is a gorgeous color, and the many vegetables in the accompanying sauce are multicolored as well as delicious. The Anaheim chile peppers in the seasoning mix have a mild flavor and a great roasted taste, and the New Mexico chile peppers should have a fairly low heat level, say a 3 on a scale of 1 to 10.

9 tablespoons vegetable oil, in all
1½ cups chopped onions
1 cup chopped celery
3 cups chopped mushrooms
4 ounces tasso or smoked ham, cut into
    ¼-inch cubes
1 tablespoon peeled and minced fresh ginger
1 tablespoon minced fresh garlic
3 cups chopped mirliton (chayote)
3 cups chopped butternut squash
3 cups vegetable stock, in all
2 tablespoons plus 1 teaspoon all-purpose
    flour
1 cup seeded and chopped red bell peppers
1 cup seeded and chopped green bell peppers
8 mushroom caps, each about 3 inches in
    diameter
2 cups cooked long-grain rice
1 small salmon fillet (about 3 ounces)

Seasoning Mix

2¼ teaspoons salt

1½ teaspoons ground dried
    Anaheim chile peppers

1¼ teaspoons garlic powder

1 teaspoon cayenne

1 teaspoon ground coriander

1 teaspoon ground cumin

1 teaspoon ground ginger

1 teaspoon onion powder

1 teaspoon paprika

1 teaspoon ground dried
    New Mexico chile peppers

1 teaspoon dried thyme
    leaves

½ teaspoon dry mustard

½ teaspoon black pepper

¼ teaspoon white pepper

1. Combine the seasoning mix ingredients in a small bowl.

2. In a 4-quart pot over high heat, heat 3 tablespoons of the vegetable oil just until it begins to smoke, about 3 to 4 min-

utes. Add the onions, celery, and chopped mushrooms, cover, and cook, uncovering to stir and carefully scrape the bottom every 2 minutes, for 14 minutes. Add the tasso, ginger, garlic, mirliton, and squash and stir well, then add 1 cup of the stock. Stir well again until the ingredients are combined, then stir in the flour until the white is no longer visible. Add the bell peppers and 1 tablespoon plus 2¼ teaspoons of the seasoning mix. Continue to cook—enjoying the great fragrance coming from the pot—stirring and scraping the bottom of the pot every 2 minutes, until the mixture begins to stick hard, about 15 minutes. *The sweet taste of the ginger says "hello" here, or maybe even "aloha," for there is a reminder of pineapple; then the smoky taste of the tasso asserts itself. The mouth feel is a little slippery at this point, and the seasonings are very mild, building slightly through the middle, then fading very rapidly.* Stir in the remaining 2 cups stock and continue to cook, stirring and scraping every 1 or 2 minutes, for 8 minutes. Stir in 1 tablespoon of the seasoning mix and continue to cook for 5 minutes, then remove from the heat and set aside. *Now the sweet ginger is still predominant, with the tasso flavor right behind, but the mouth feel has become rich and round. The seasonings, while still mild, tend to linger a bit more now, with the subtle ginger flavor serving as an undertone throughout the taste.*

3. Sprinkle the mushroom caps, inside and out, with the remaining seasoning mix. Stuff each cap with ¼ cup of the rice, pressing it into the mushroom and mounding it slightly. Cut very thin slices off the salmon fillet, making each slice wider and longer than the mushroom caps. Trim each piece of salmon into a circle slightly larger than the mushroom—easy to do if you place the mushroom on top of the salmon and use it as a cutting guide. Cover the rice in each mushroom cap with a circle of salmon, poking the edges of the salmon down into the sides of the mushroom cap so that the rice is completely covered.

4. Heat the remaining 6 tablespoons vegetable oil in a 10-inch skillet over high heat just until it begins to smoke, about 3 to 4 minutes. Cook the mushroom caps 2 minutes per side, then remove them from the heat. For each portion, place ¾ cup of the sauce on a salad-size plate, and top with 1 mushroom cap.

Shrimp Calas

Rice cakes, or calas, are a traditional Creole breakfast or snack food, and are usually sweet. The word "cala" is derived from an African name for rice, and indeed calas always contain rice combined with a dough. These calas, with their wonderful spices and shrimp, take off in an entirely different direction, and are great as an appetizer, or with a salad and vegetable as a light meal. To make the shrimp stock, you'll want to buy unpeeled shrimp—about ½ pound if the heads are on, a little less if they're headless, to have the ¼ pound called for. Use chicken stock if you can't get unpeeled shrimp.

2 cups shrimp stock, in all
¾ cup uncooked Converted® rice
3 large eggs, in all
1 tablespoon cane vinegar, or your favorite
    vinegar
1 tablespoon balsamic vinegar
1 tablespoon Worcestershire sauce
2 tablespoons lightly packed light brown sugar
1 cup plus 1 tablespoon vegetable oil, plus
    additional for frying, in all
¾ cup chopped onions, in all
½ cup seeded and chopped bell peppers
½ teaspoon minced fresh garlic
¾ cup all-purpose flour
1½ teaspoons baking powder
½ cup milk
¼ pound peeled raw shrimp, chopped

Seasoning Mix

¾ teaspoon salt

½ teaspoon garlic powder

½ teaspoon paprika

½ teaspoon dried basil

½ teaspoon cayenne

½ teaspoon dry mustard

½ teaspoon onion powder

½ teaspoon ground dried
    árbol chile peppers

¼ teaspoon black pepper

¼ teaspoon ground dried
    guajillo chile peppers

¼ teaspoon dried thyme
    leaves

1. Combine the seasoning mix ingredients in a small bowl.

2. Cook the rice: Place 1½ cups of the stock in a 1-quart saucepan with a tight-fitting cover and bring to a boil over high heat. Add the rice and return just to a boil, then reduce the heat to low. Cover and simmer until almost all the liquid is absorbed, about 20 minutes. Remove from the heat and let sit, covered, for 10 minutes. Fluff the rice, then spread it in a thin layer on a sheet pan and allow it to cool to room temperature.

3. Make the mayonnaise: In a food processor or blender, combine 2 of the eggs, the cane vinegar, balsamic vinegar, Worcestershire, brown sugar, and 2 teaspoons of the seasoning mix. Process just until frothy, 15 to 25 seconds. With the appliance running, slowly add 1 cup of the vegetable oil in a thin stream until it is completely incorporated. *This rich and creamy mayonnaise has a sweet-and-sour taste, with a hint of café au lait. The gentle acidic flavor finishes the taste with a subtle note of herbs and spices.* Refrigerate until ready to serve. Makes about 2 cups.

4. Prepare the vegetable mixture: In an 8-inch skillet over high heat, heat the remaining 1 tablespoon of oil just until it begins to smoke, about 3 to 4 minutes. Add the onions and bell peppers and cook, stirring frequently, until the vegetables are bright in color and beginning to soften, about 6 minutes. Add the remaining 1 tablespoon of seasoning mix and stir well. Continue to cook, stirring almost constantly, until the vegetables are dark brown on the edges and caramelized throughout, about 3 minutes. Stir in the remaining ½ cup of stock and continue to cook, stirring constantly, for 1 minute. Add the garlic, stir well, and remove from the heat. *The vegetables are sweet and still a little crunchy. The seasonings are very intense and reminiscent of allspice. The flavor of the salt is very pronounced, along with a deep herb and spice flavor.* Place the mixture on a sheet pan and let cool to room temperature.

5. Make the batter: In a food processor stir the flour and baking powder briefly to combine; add the milk and the remaining egg. Process until it has the consistency of pancake batter (which is what it tastes like at this point), about 1 to 2 minutes. Transfer to a large bowl and stir in the rice, vegetable mixture, and shrimp.

6. To fry and assemble: In a 12-inch skillet over high heat, pour enough vegetable oil to measure 1½ inches deep and heat it to 300°F. An electric skillet works well, or use a regular skillet and a cooking thermometer and adjust the heat to keep the oil as close to 300°F as possible. Scoop up about 2 tablespoons of the batter and carefully drop it into the hot oil; repeat until the skillet is full without crowding. Cook, turning once, until golden brown, about 2 minutes per side. Drain on paper towels and repeat until all the cakes have been cooked.

7. Arrange 2 calas on a small plate with a dollop of mayonnaise on the side.

Shrimp Chowchow
and Mixed Vegetables

Makes about 5½ cups; 10 appetizer servings   *The dressing can be used with just about any fresh vegetables you have on hand—perhaps leftovers from a previous meal—or whatever looks good at the market when you shop. Notice that the shrimp are cooked not with heat but by the acid in the vinegars and citrus juices. A number of Hispanic cultures—most notably in Peru and Mexico—use this method with seafood and call the result ceviche. Be sure to buy the dark, rich-tasting variety of sesame oil—look for a quality Asian label—as it adds an important flavor note to the dressing.*

Seasoning Mix

1½ teaspoons cracked black peppercorns

¾ teaspoon dried basil

½ teaspoon cayenne

½ teaspoon dill weed

½ teaspoon ground ginger

½ teaspoon dry mustard

¼ teaspoon salt

1 pound raw shrimp, 21 to 25 shrimp per pound
½ cup cane vinegar, or your favorite vinegar
½ cup white balsamic vinegar
1 teaspoon dark sesame oil
½ cup plus 1 tablespoon honey
¼ cup freshly squeezed lemon juice
¼ cup freshly squeezed lime juice
¼ cup finely diced onions
¼ cup seeded and finely diced red bell peppers
¼ cup seeded and finely diced yellow bell peppers
1 cup raisins
¼ cup small broccoflower florets
¼ cup chopped celery
¼ cup small cauliflower florets
½ small red bell pepper, cut into julienne strips about 1½ inches long

½ small yellow bell pepper, cut into julienne strips about
    1½ inches long
½ small green bell pepper, cut into julienne strips about
    1½ inches long
¾ cup chopped mirliton (chayote)
¼ cup toasted unsalted peanuts

1. Combine the seasoning mix ingredients in a small bowl.

2. Blanch the shrimp for 1 minute in boiling water. Immediately remove from the pot and cool under cold running water to stop the cooking. Peel and cut them into ¼-inch-thick slices.

3. In a 1-quart container with a tight-fitting lid, combine the cane vinegar, white balsamic vinegar, sesame oil, honey, and citrus juices. Whisk vigorously until well mixed, then whisk in the seasoning mix. Add the onions, finely diced bell peppers, raisins, and shrimp. Cover tightly, shake to mix well, and refrigerate at least overnight.

4. When ready to serve, combine the remaining vegetables and the peanuts in a bowl and pour the dressing over them. Toss gently to distribute all the ingredients and coat the vegetables with the dressing. Serve in cups or small bowls.

Smoked Trout Mousse

Makes about 2 cups; 4 appetizer servings

The wonderful smoked trout flavor and aroma come through all the spices and citrus juices, accomplishing just what an appetizer is supposed to do—get your taste buds in the mood for the great meal that follows! You can pipe the mousse onto toast rounds or crackers, or serve as a dip with sturdy chips. And if you have time to chill it thoroughly before serving, you can mold it in a smooth bowl or dish and turn it out onto a serving platter; just don't try to unmold it from a fancy, convoluted decorative mold, for, as you see, it contains no gelatin, so is fairly tender.

2 tablespoons olive oil
1 cup chopped onions
¼ cup seeded and chopped green bell peppers
¼ cup seeded and chopped red bell peppers
¼ cup seeded and chopped yellow bell
    peppers
2 tablespoons unsalted butter
2 teaspoons peeled and minced fresh ginger
1 teaspoon minced fresh garlic
1 tablespoon freshly squeezed lemon juice
1 tablespoon freshly squeezed lime juice
1 tablespoon lightly packed light brown sugar
½ cup seafood stock
One 8-ounce package cream cheese, softened
8 ounces smoked trout, speckled trout
    preferably, or your favorite smoked fish,
    skin off and broken into pieces

Seasoning Mix

1¼ teaspoons salt

1¼ teaspoons paprika

1 teaspoon ground ginger

1 teaspoon dry mustard

1 teaspoon onion powder

¾ teaspoon ground anise

¾ teaspoon dried basil

¾ teaspoon cayenne

¾ teaspoon garlic powder

¾ teaspoon ground dried
    ancho chile peppers

¾ teaspoon ground dried
    New Mexico chile peppers

½ teaspoon white pepper

1. Combine the seasoning mix ingredients in a small bowl.

2. Heat the olive oil in a heavy 10-inch skillet, preferably nonstick, over high heat just until the oil begins to smoke, about 3 to 4 minutes. Add the onions, all the bell peppers, and 2 tablespoons of the seasoning mix. Stir well and cook, stirring and scraping the bottom of the skillet frequently, until the vegetables begin to brown on the edges, about 4 to 6 minutes. The vegetables should just begin to darken from the heat and seasoning mix and still be slightly crunchy. *An intense toasted seasoning flavor should be developing in the brown bits on the bottom of the pan.* Add the butter, ginger, and garlic and stir until the butter melts. Add the citrus juices and brown sugar and continue to cook, stirring frequently, until the juices are almost evaporated, about 4 to 5 minutes. Stir in the stock, scrape the bottom of the pan to loosen all the brown material on the bottom, then add the remaining seasoning mix. Stir well and continue to cook, stirring frequently, until the mixture thickens a bit, about 3 to 4 minutes. Remove from the heat—you should have about 1 cup of the mixture. Transfer to a sheet pan and refrigerate until cold. *A delicately seasoned taste up front is led by the flavor of anise. The middle taste will be a brown flavor mingled with the herb and spice flavors and moderate heat from the chiles. To understand how flavors change with temperature, taste the mixture both when it is hot and then after it has been chilled. Note how the placement and intensities of the flavors change when the mixture is cold. Notice especially how the citrus and anise flavors intensify and fill your mouth.*

3. In a food processor combine the vegetable mixture with the cream cheese and smoked trout. Process until the mixture is fairly smooth, about 1 minute.

Soup

Wonderful by Itself
or to Enliven the Meal!

I can't imagine growing up without hearty, flavorful soup at least three or four times a week, especially in wintertime. Many of the recipes in this section are pretty close to the kinds my mother cooked for her large family, for a pot of soup was a wonderful way to feed a tableful and was infinitely variable, depending on what was growing in the garden or could be found in nearby waters. We've made some changes, though, to reflect the wider variety of foods available today.

Bronzed Tilapia and
Portobello Soup

The amount of stock you use in this soup is very important, for the liquid should be the consistency of a soup, not at all thick like a stew. We've said 4 to 6 cups—the exact amount will depend on how much evaporation occurs during cooking. Here's one of those times when you should look at what's in the pot and make a decision based on what you see there.

This is a very nourishing soup, and as we Cajuns say, "It's so good it makes you want to slap your mama!" No disrespect intended—it just means we really love it. By the way, use all one color bell pepper if you prefer, instead of the three colors.

Three 6-ounce tilapia fillets
2 tablespoons plus 2 teaspoons vegetable oil, in all
3 tablespoons unsalted butter, in all
1½ cups chopped onions, in all
1½ cups chopped celery, in all
2 cups peeled parsnips cut into ½-inch pieces
3 tablespoons all-purpose flour
4 to 6 cups (see headnote above) rich seafood or shrimp stock
2 cups portobello mushroom caps and stems cut into ¾-inch pieces
½ cup seeded and chopped green bell peppers
½ cup seeded and chopped red bell peppers
½ cup seeded and chopped yellow bell peppers

Seasoning Mix

2½ teaspoons salt
1¼ teaspoons onion powder
1¼ teaspoons paprika
1 teaspoon dried basil
1 teaspoon ground coriander
1 teaspoon garlic powder
1 teaspoon dry mustard
¾ teaspoon cayenne
¾ teaspoon black pepper
¾ teaspoon dried thyme leaves
½ teaspoon dried oregano
½ teaspoon white pepper
¼ teaspoon ground cloves

1. Combine the seasoning mix ingredients in a small bowl.

2. Trim any remaining bits of skin from the tilapia fillets. Rub the fillets lightly on both sides with 2 teaspoons of the vegetable oil and sprinkle one side of the fillets with 2 teaspoons of the seasoning mix.

3. Place a 14-inch nonstick skillet over high heat until the pan is very hot, about 4 minutes. Place the fillets in the pan, seasoned side down. Sprinkle the other sides evenly with 2 teaspoons of the seasoning mix. Cook, turning once, until the fillets are just cooked through, about 2 to 3 minutes per side. The fish is cooked when the flesh flakes away easily. Transfer the fillets to a large plate and, with a fork, gently break the meat into bite-size pieces. Set aside.

4. Place a 5-quart pot over high heat and add the remaining 2 tablespoons vegetable oil and 2 tablespoons of the butter. When the butter melts and sizzles, add 1 cup of the onions, 1 cup of the celery, the parsnips, and the remaining seasoning mix. Cover and cook, uncovering every 2 minutes to stir, for 10 minutes, then uncover and stir in the flour until the white is no longer visible. If the mixture sticks hard on the bottom, add a little of the stock and scrape to loosen it. Add the remaining 1 tablespoon butter and stir until the butter melts and is incorporated. Cover and cook until the vegetables stick hard to the bottom of the pot, about 4 minutes. Stir and scrape the bottom of the pot, then add 4 cups of the stock and scrape until all the brown bits are loosened from the bottom of the pot. Re-cover and cook for 8 minutes. *At this stage, the front flavor is moderately salty, with light flavors from the flour underneath. The middle taste is the bell pepper flavor, sweetness from the parsnips, and the light herb and spice flavors, which linger into the final taste.* Add the mushrooms, all the bell peppers, and the remaining ½ cup onions and ½ cup celery. Stir well and continue to cook until the mixture boils rapidly, about 6 to 8 minutes.

5. Reduce the heat to medium, then stir and re-cover the pot. Continue to cook for 6 more minutes, then add the fish. *When you taste the soup, you'll notice that the sweetness has moved forward to become a front flavor, now salty-sweet, followed immediately by a roux and vegetable flavor and a rapid building and fading of the seasonings. Also note the underlying taste of the seafood or shrimp stock, which binds all the other tastes together.* At this point check the liquid—here's where you add more stock if necessary to obtain a good "soup" consistency. Increase the heat to high, bring the liquid to a full boil, and cook for 1 more minute. Remove from the heat and serve immediately.

Bucktown Soup

Makes about 8 cups; 4 main-course or 8 appetizer servings

This soup is inspired by a neighborhood right next to Lake Pontchartrain called Bucktown, which is famous for its seafood markets and restaurants. If you don't have a smoker, chances are there's a specialty market that operates a smoker for its customers, and if you call a day ahead the staff should be glad to smoke the fillet for you. Also ask them to save the unsmoked fish heads and tails to make your stock; if they receive their fish already filleted, you can use chicken stock instead. Many markets also sell presmoked fish.

2 tablespoons olive oil
2 cups chopped onions, in all
1½ cups chopped celery, in all
2 cups peeled sweet potatoes cut into ¼-inch
   cubes (about 2 large 1-pound potatoes in all)
4½ cups fish stock, preferably, or chicken stock,
   in all
2 teaspoons minced fresh garlic
3 tablespoons all-purpose flour
2 tablespoons freshly squeezed lime juice
   (about 1 medium lime)
2 cups heavy cream
8 ounces good quality smoked fish fillets, such
   as trout, mackerel, or salmon, skin
   removed, cut into 1-inch pieces

Seasoning Mix

1½ teaspoons onion powder

1½ teaspoons salt

1 teaspoon cayenne

1 teaspoon dried oregano

¾ teaspoon dry mustard

¾ teaspoon black pepper

½ teaspoon garlic powder

½ teaspoon white pepper

½ teaspoon dried thyme
   leaves

1. Combine the seasoning mix ingredients in a small bowl.

2. Heat the olive oil in a heavy 3-quart pot over high heat just until it begins to smoke, about 3 to 4 minutes. Add 1 cup of the onions, 1 cup of the celery, 1 cup of the sweet potatoes, and 2 cups of the stock. Stir well, then cover and cook for 5 minutes. Remove the cover, stir well, and cook for 2 minutes. Stir in the garlic and seasoning mix and cook for 2 more minutes. Stir in the remaining 1 cup onions and ½ cup celery, re-cover, and cook for 2 more minutes. Add ½ cup of the stock and the remaining 1 cup sweet potatoes. Stir well, then re-cover and cook for 2 more minutes. Uncover and stir well, then re-cover and cook for 2 more minutes. *An immediate saltiness rises above a very subdued middle taste, led by a sweet, boiled onion flavor. The final taste fades in the mouth.*

3. Uncover and stir in the flour, then stir constantly until the white is no longer visible. Stir in 1 cup of the stock, then re-cover and cook for 4 more minutes. Uncover, stir in the remaining stock and the lime juice, then re-cover and cook for 3 minutes. *Now notice the very unusual taste produced by the combination of lime juice and the natural sweetness of the vegetables. For a brief moment, the flavor suggests a lime dessert, then the taste changes to herbal.* Uncover, add the heavy cream and smoked fish, stir gently but well, then re-cover and cook for 4 more minutes. Bring just to a boil, then reduce the heat to medium-low and simmer for 15 minutes. Serve hot with plenty of dark bread.

Chicken and Oyster Gumbo

Makes about 14 cups; 7 main-course or 14 appetizer servings

This great dish has the look and feel of traditional gumbo, but adding parsnips, which were unheard of in most Acadian kitchens until a few years ago, really makes a big difference. They sweeten the entire dish, help enrich the broth, and provide a good texture contrast for the okra. By the way, you can use all one color bell peppers, but I like the look of the three colors. And if you can't find the chile peppers we list, use the varieties that are fresh and pretty at your market, but do use at least three different types for a "round" flavor. When buying okra, select pods that are no longer than 3 inches, as larger ones can be very fibrous.

One 3- to 4-pound chicken, cut into 8 pieces
6 tablespoons vegetable oil, in all
2 cups chopped onions, in all
½ cup chopped celery
½ cup seeded and chopped green bell peppers, in all
½ cup seeded and chopped red bell peppers, in all
½ cup seeded and chopped yellow bell peppers, in all
5½ cups chicken stock, in all
3 bay leaves
¼ cup all-purpose flour
2 tablespoons seeded and finely chopped fresh banana peppers (also called wax peppers)
2 tablespoons seeded and finely chopped fresh poblano chile peppers
¼ cup seeded and finely chopped fresh jalapeño chile peppers, preferably half red and half green, or all green

Seasoning Mix

2 teaspoons salt
1¾ teaspoons paprika
1½ teaspoons onion powder
1¼ teaspoons dried basil
1 teaspoon cayenne
1 teaspoon garlic powder
¾ teaspoon ground cumin
¾ teaspoon dry mustard
¾ teaspoon black pepper
½ teaspoon white pepper
½ teaspoon dried thyme leaves

1 tablespoon finely chopped fresh garlic

½ pound andouille, cut into ½-inch-thick rounds and each round quartered

3 cups okra cut into ¼-inch-thick rounds (about ¾ pound whole)

1 cup peeled and finely diced parsnips (about 2 medium-size)

1 pint shucked oysters in their liquid (about 1 pound)

3½ cups cooked Converted rice

1. Combine the seasoning mix ingredients in a small bowl.

2. Sprinkle the outside of the chicken evenly with 2 tablespoons of the seasoning mix and rub it in well with your hands. Place 2 tablespoons of the vegetable oil in a 5-quart pot over high heat. When the oil just begins to smoke, about 3 to 4 minutes, add the chicken, large pieces first and skin sides down first. Cook until the skin is lightly browned and the seasoning is a rich mahogany brown, about 3 to 4 minutes per side. Remove each piece to a plate as it browns and add the smaller pieces, until all the chicken is browned.

3. Carefully pour off all but 2 tablespoons of the oil in the pot. Add 1 cup of the onions, the celery, and ¼ cup each of all the bell peppers. Return the pot to high heat and stir well, scraping up the brown bits on the bottom of the pot as you stir. Add ½ cup of the stock and use it to deglaze the pot—scraping the bottom and loosening all the brown bits. Cover and cook until the stock evaporates, about 5 to 10 minutes, depending on the thickness of your pot and the amount of heat your stove produces. Uncover and add the bay leaves, then re-cover, remove from the heat, and set the pot aside.

4. The next step is to make the roux. It's very important to keep stirring at all times and to keep all of the flour moving. If you don't, the flour will burn and the roux will be bitter. If you see little black specks in the roux, it has burned. If this happens, throw it out, clean the pot, and begin again. If your roux seems to be browning too fast, take it off the stove and continue to whisk until it cools slightly, then return it to the heat. Heat the remaining ¼ cup vegetable oil in a 10-inch skillet over high heat until it is smoking hot (500°F), about 5 minutes. Add the flour and whisk constantly, making sure that the oil and flour are thoroughly combined. When the roux is the color of dark chocolate, add the remaining onions, the remaining bell peppers, and all the chile peppers. Remove from the heat and add the garlic and 1 tablespoon of the seasoning mix. Continue to whisk until the mixture cools slightly, 1 to 2 minutes. *The deeply browned flour has a unique taste (almost impossible to describe, but it's a strong, nutty wheat taste) that is essential to many Louisiana dishes. Notice how this flavor enhances the*

sweetness of the vegetables. Remember this rich, dark flavor, for you will want to duplicate it in any recipe that calls for you to make a roux.

5. Return the 5-quart pot with the vegetable mixture to high heat and add the roux. Stir well to combine, then add the andouille and 1 cup of the stock. Stir well until the roux is dissolved, then cover and cook just until the mixture begins to simmer, about 3 minutes. *Now the taste is of a broad gravy flavor, with low heat intensity and vegetable tastes coming in the middle. At the finish, all the flavors drop off, leaving only the tingle of heat from the chiles.* Add the okra, the parsnips, the remaining 4 cups stock, and the remaining seasoning mix. Stir well, then return the chicken pieces to the pot, submerging them in the liquid. Bring to a boil, then reduce the heat to low and cover. Cook at a slow simmer until the chicken is cooked through, 20 to 25 minutes. *The broth is now rich with gumbo flavors. The taste of the roux and the heat from the seasonings are building together, and remain in the mouth for a long time. The rich flavor of the cooked chicken fat creates a delicate final flavor. Note how the taste change with each spoonful, depending on the ingredients that you chew.* Remove from the heat, then uncover and add the oysters and their liquid. Stir gently to distribute the oysters evenly, then re-cover and let sit for 5 minutes—the heat of the gumbo will cook the oysters. They will be plump and meltingly tender. Remove the bay leaves.

6. Serve hot in soup bowls or cups with cooked rice in the center.

Shrimp Mango Bisque

Makes 11 to 12 cups; 5 to 6 main-course or
11 to 12 appetizer servings

Because the flavor of the mango is an integral part of this bisque, use the best quality you can find and be sure that it is very ripe. A ripe mango will be very soft to the touch and delightfully sweet inside. The best mangoes are tree-ripened, but unless you live in Florida, you're probably not going to find them. If your mangoes are still hard and green, don't refrigerate them but instead place them in a brown paper bag and check their ripening progress every day until they are soft and fragrant. Your stock will be especially rich and flavorful if you start it well in advance of beginning the recipe—the shrimp will keep just fine in a bowl for up to 24 hours if covered tightly with plastic wrap and refrigerated until you need them.

Seasoning Mix
2¾ teaspoons salt
2 teaspoons paprika
1½ teaspoons dried basil
1¼ teaspoons onion powder
1 teaspoon cayenne
1 teaspoon ground coriander
1 teaspoon garlic powder
1 teaspoon dry mustard
¾ teaspoon black pepper
½ teaspoon white pepper

1½ cups chopped onions, in all
½ cup seeded and chopped green bell peppers, in all
½ cup seeded and chopped red bell peppers, in all
½ cup seeded and chopped yellow bell peppers, in all
½ cup seeded and chopped banana peppers, (also called wax peppers), in all
½ cup seeded and chopped poblano chile peppers, in all
¼ cup vegetable oil
¾ cup all-purpose flour
2 cups peeled and diced very ripe plantains (about 2 plantains)
7 cups shrimp stock, in all

continued

2 ripe mangoes, peeled, pitted, and puréed
   in a blender
1½ pounds raw shrimp, 21 to 25 shrimp
   per pound
½ cup loosely packed chopped fresh
   parsley leaves

1. Combine the seasoning mix ingredients in small bowl.

2. Combine the onions, bell peppers, and chile peppers, then divide the mixture in half. Place half in a small bowl near the stove so you can add them quickly in the next step.

3. Heat the vegetable oil in a heavy 5-quart pot over high heat until it is smoking hot (500°F), about 5 minutes. Make a roux—add the flour to the hot oil and whisk constantly, making sure that the oil and flour are thoroughly combined, until the roux is a caramel color, about 2 minutes. When making a roux, it is very important to keep stirring at all times and to keep all of the flour moving. If you don't, the flour will burn and the roux will be very bitter—useless. If you see little black specks in the roux, it has burned. If this happens, throw it out, clean the pot, and begin again. If your roux seems to be browning too fast, take it off the stove and continue to whisk until it has cooled slightly, then return it to the heat. As soon as the roux is a caramel color, quickly add the combined onions and peppers at hand and 3 tablespoons of the seasoning mix. Keep whisking constantly for about 15 seconds, then remove the pot from the heat and continue to whisk until the roux has cooled down slightly, about 2 minutes. The roux will continue to darken to a deep brown as you whisk. *A well-made dark roux has a sweet, nutty taste.*

4. Return the pot to high heat, add the plantains, and stir well to mix them with the roux. Cook, stirring frequently, until the plantains take on a slightly darker color, about 4 to 5 minutes. Carefully add 4 cups of the stock—stand back, as it's likely to splatter and steam—and bring to a boil, whisking frequently and well to dissolve the roux. At this point, the liquid will have a yellowish brown color and *a soft seafood taste*. When the mixture boils, scrape the bottom well, then add the remaining onion-and-pepper mixture, the remaining seasoning mix, and the remaining 3 cups stock. Cover and return to a boil, then reduce the heat to medium and simmer, uncovering and stirring every few minutes, until the plantains break into small pieces, about 12 minutes. Whisk in the mango purée,

re-cover, increase the heat to high, and bring to a full boil. *The bisque should now have a subtle, fruity, and well-defined flavor.* Uncover, add the shrimp, re-cover, and bring back to a full boil. Cook just until the shrimp are pink, opaque, and plump, about 1 to 2 minutes. Stir in the parsley, remove from the heat, and serve over rice.

Corn and Andouille Soup

We cook this soup fairly quickly—only about an hour and 15 minutes—rather than on the back of the stove all day as we used to, so you can really taste the separate flavors of the corn and andouille. It still has the traditional, down-home goodness of country cooking, though, thanks to the brown sugar, basil, and peppers.

3 cups chopped onions, in all
3 cups seeded and chopped green bell
    peppers, in all
1 pound andouille or your favorite smoked
    pork sausage, quartered lengthwise,
    then cut into ½-inch pieces
7 cups chicken stock, in all
7 cups fresh corn kernels
    (from about 6 ears)
2 cups peeled and chopped fresh
    tomatoes
6 tablespoons all-purpose flour
1 tablespoon minced fresh garlic

Seasoning Mix

1 tablespoon plus 1½ teaspoons lightly packed dark brown sugar

2¼ teaspoons paprika

1½ teaspoons salt

1¼ teaspoons dried basil

¾ teaspoon garlic powder

¾ teaspoon dry mustard

¾ teaspoon onion powder

½ teaspoon cayenne

½ teaspoon ground cumin

½ teaspoon black pepper

¼ teaspoon white pepper

1. Combine the seasoning mix ingredients in a small bowl.

2. Preheat a heavy 4-quart pot over high heat until very hot, about 3 to 4 minutes. Add 2 cups of the onions, 2 cups of the bell peppers, the andouille, and 2 tablespoons of the seasoning mix. Cook, stirring and scraping the bottom of the pot every 3 to 4 minutes, for 20 minutes. *During this time you can taste an almost overwhelming sweetness with a mere hint of the andouille's richness.* If necessary to prevent burning during this time, add a little of the stock, stir well, and scrape the pot bottom, then continue cooking. At the end of the 20 minutes reduce the heat to low, then add the corn, tomatoes, flour, garlic, the remaining onions, the remaining bell peppers, 4 cups of the stock, and the remaining seasoning mix. *At this point the broth is rich and smooth, with well-balanced seasonings and a distinct rich, smoky flavor.* Cook, stirring and scraping the pot every 8 to 10 minutes, for 40 minutes. Stir in the remaining stock, increase the heat to high, and bring the soup just to a boil. Reduce the heat to low and simmer for 15 minutes. Remove from the heat and serve immediately.

Crab and Sweet Potato Soup

Makes about 8 cups; 4 main-course or 8 appetizer servings

It ought to go without saying, but it's so important I'm going to say it anyway: Use the very best quality lump crabmeat you can find, as fresh as possible, with only a clean, delicate odor. The result will be worth the extra trouble, including talking with the manager of the seafood department of the market where you shop to get top quality and freshness.

2 tablespoons olive oil
1½ cups chopped onions
2 cups lightly packed thinly sliced shiitake
    mushrooms caps, in all
5½ cups crab stock, preferably, or seafood
    stock, in all
2 medium-size sweet potatoes (each about
    10 ounces), in all, baked in a 350°F oven
    until tender and peeled
1 tablespoon plus 2 teaspoons peeled and
    minced fresh ginger
¾ cup peeled daikon cut into ½-inch cubes
¾ cup peeled jicama cut into ½-inch cubes
¾ cup fresh green beans cut into ½-inch lengths
1 tablespoon chopped orange zest
1 tablespoon lightly packed dark brown sugar
1 cup heavy cream
1 pound lump crabmeat, picked over carefully
    to remove any bits of shell and cartilage

Seasoning Mix

2½ teaspoons salt

2 teaspoons paprika

1 teaspoon onion powder

¾ teaspoon cayenne

¾ teaspoon dill weed

¾ teaspoon garlic powder

½ teaspoon white pepper

1. Combine the seasoning mix ingredients in a small bowl.

2. Heat the olive oil in a 5-quart pot over high heat just until it begins to smoke, about 3 to 4 minutes. Add the onions and cook, stirring frequently, until they begin to brown on the edges, about 6 to 7 minutes. Add 1 cup of the mushrooms

and 2 tablespoons of the seasoning mix. Stir well and continue to cook, stirring frequently, until the mushrooms are reduced in size and dark, about 3 minutes. Add 1 cup of the stock and cook until the liquid evaporates and the mixture begins to stick to the bottom of the pot, about 4 minutes. Scrape the bottom well to loosen all the brown bits on the bottom, then remove from the heat. *This process produces a rich, sweet taste in the vegetables. You will notice the sweetness right away, followed quickly by saltiness from the stock, then an intense heat.*

3. Transfer the vegetables to a food processor—don't wash the pot, as you'll use it again in a minute—and add one of the baked sweet potatoes and ½ cup of the stock. Process until smooth, then return the purée to the pot over high heat and add the ginger, the remaining seasoning mix, and 3 cups of the stock. Scrape the sides and bottom of the pot well and stir until all the ingredients are combined. Bring to a boil, reduce the heat to medium, and simmer briskly until the mixture thickens, about 10 to 15 minutes. At this point the liquid will be a brown-orange color *with a blunt taste of seafood that is also rich in herb and spice flavors.*

4. Add the daikon, jicama, and green beans and continue to simmer for 4 more minutes. *At this point, the soup has a well-seasoned taste but does not have a leading flavor.* Add the orange zest and brown sugar and stir well. *This will provide the flavor direction for the soup.* Bring to a boil, then reduce the heat to medium and continue to simmer until the orange flavor permeates the soup, about 4 minutes. Add the heavy cream, the remaining mushrooms, and the remaining 1 cup stock. Stir well, then return to a boil and simmer over medium heat for 5 minutes. Add the crabmeat and stir well. Increase the heat to high, return the mixture to a full rolling boil, then remove from the heat—at this point the crabmeat will be hot and ready to enjoy.

5. Cut the remaining baked sweet potato into 4 pieces. For each serving, place 1 piece of the sweet potato in a large soup bowl and ladle 2 cups of the soup over it. Serve immediately.

French Market Soup

A lot of you who don't live in south Louisiana think it never gets cold down here, but believe me, it does. Why, it even snows every 7 or 8 years! A blustery winter day is when you'll really appreciate this soup, though it's great any time of year. It's a complete meal, too, because it has meat, green vegetables, and tomatoes, with their vitamin C. Serve it with pumpernickel bread or with hot buttered corn bread and no one will leave the table hungry.

3 tablespoons unsalted butter
3 cups chopped onions
1 cup chopped celery
1½ cups seeded and chopped bell peppers
1 pound ground beef
1¼ teaspoons minced fresh garlic
¼ cup all-purpose flour
7 cups beef stock, in all
One 15-ounce can diced tomatoes
7 cups cored green cabbage cut into 1-inch
   pieces (about 1 medium-size head)
One 15-ounce can tomato purée

Seasoning Mix

2 tablespoons sugar

1 tablespoon plus 1 teaspoon salt

2½ teaspoons onion powder

2 teaspoons dried basil

2 teaspoons cayenne

2 teaspoons garlic powder

1½ teaspoons ground coriander

1¼ teaspoons dried oregano

1¼ teaspoons black pepper

1 teaspoon dried thyme leaves

½ teaspoon white pepper

1. Combine the seasoning mix ingredients in a small bowl.

2. In a heavy 5-quart pot over high heat, melt the butter until it sizzles, about 2 to 3 minutes. Add the onions, celery, bell peppers, and 2 tablespoons of the seasoning mix. Cook, stirring every 2 to 3 minutes, until the vegetables begin to brown and lose their color, about 10 to 12 minutes. Push the vegetables to one side—so the meat can brown by being in contact with the pot bottom—then add the ground beef, garlic, and the remaining seasoning mix. Continue to cook, turning the meat and breaking up the clumps, about once a minute, until it is brown, about 5 minutes, then mix the meat with the vegetables. *At this point, the mixture has the taste of a highly seasoned meat loaf, with the leading taste being salt and the last taste being the pepper.*

3. Stir in the flour until the white is no longer visible. The meat will be a little pasty but should absorb all the flour—if not, add a little stock—and the flour will form a crust on the pot bottom. Continue to stir and scrape until the crust sticks hard, almost faster than you can scrape, then add the diced tomatoes, cabbage, and 1 cup of the stock. Scrape the bottom again, loosening all the brown bits. Cook, stirring almost constantly, for 5 minutes, then add the tomato purée. Stir and scrape the pot bottom well, then cover and cook, uncovering to stir every 3 to 4 minutes, for 10 minutes. *Adding no liquid during this cooking time subjects the mixture to a lot of heat and removes the raw taste of the tomatoes. Stir in 5 cups of the stock. Now the taste is much like minestrone, with a brief, lightly acid touch. The heat finishes the taste—but not nearly as much as previously—more of a tingling sensation. Notice how the acid taste from the tomatoes reduces as the soup continues cooking.* Cook for 4 minutes, then stir in the remaining stock. Bring just to a boil, reduce the heat to low, and simmer for 20 minutes. Serve hot.

Old-Fashioned
Chicken Soup

Makes 14 cups; 7 main-course or 14 appetizer servings

All those Jewish mothers were right—it's been scientifically proven that hot chicken soup is good for colds, flu, and the grumps. If you use a fryer instead of the hen we specify, you'll want to reduce the simmering time before adding the vegetables by half an hour, as the frying chicken is leaner and will cook faster.

One 5- to 7-pound hen or roasting chicken,
    cut into 8 pieces
10 cups chicken stock, preferably, or water,
    in all
3 tablespoons vegetable oil
2 cups chopped onions
1½ cups chopped celery, in all
¼ cup chopped fire-roasted garlic
½ cup all-purpose flour
4 cups peeled white potatoes cut into ¾-inch
    pieces
3 cups carrots cut into ½-inch pieces
2 cups chopped fresh tomatoes, peeled

Seasoning Mix

2½ teaspoons salt

1¾ teaspoons paprika

1¼ teaspoons dried basil

1¼ teaspoon garlic powder

1¼ teaspoon onion powder

1¼ teaspoons ground dried
   ancho chile peppers

¾ teaspoon black pepper

½ teaspoon dry mustard

½ teaspoon white pepper

1. Combine the seasoning mix ingredients in a small bowl.

2. Place the chicken on a sheet pan, sprinkle the skin sides evenly with 1 tablespoon plus 1 teaspoon of the seasoning mix, and gently pat it in. Set aside.

3. In an 8-quart pot over high heat, bring 8 cups of the stock to a boil, then reduce the heat to a simmer.

4. While the stock is coming to a boil, heat the vegetable oil in a heavy 14-inch skillet over high heat until the oil just begins to smoke, about 4 minutes. Add some of the chicken pieces, seasoned side down and larger pieces first, without overcrowding the skillet. Cook, turning once, until the skin is nicely browned but not too dark, about 2 to 3 minutes per side. Reduce the heat if the pieces are getting too dark. As the pieces are browned, transfer them to the simmering stock. Repeat with the remaining pieces and add to the skillet any seasoning mix that falls off the chicken onto the sheet pan.

5. When all the chicken has been browned and transferred to the stock, add the onions and ½ cup of the celery to the skillet. Stir well for 2 minutes, scraping the bottom as you stir. Add ½ cup of the stock and scrape the bottom well, loosening the browned bits from the pan: Cook, stirring frequently, until the vegetables are light brown and the liquid evaporates, about 10 minutes. Add the roasted garlic and the remaining seasoning mix. Continue to cook, stirring frequently, until a deep brown crust forms on the bottom of the skillet, about 5 minutes. Add ½ cup of the stock and scrape the bottom well, then add the flour and stir until the white is no longer visible. Continue to cook until a crust forms again, about 4 minutes. Add the remaining 1 cup stock and scrape the bottom completely. Add the contents of the skillet to the pot and stir well. Remove some of the stock from the pot and use it to dissolve any bits of seasoning remaining in the skillet, then transfer all this—stock and seasonings—back to the pot. Cover and simmer for 1 hour, then add the potatoes, carrots, tomatoes, and remaining celery. Stir well, re-cover, and simmer for 1 more hour. Serve hot.

Potato, Leek, and
Tasso Soup

Makes about 9 cups; 4 to 5 main-course or 9 appetizer servings

The taste of the tasso—spicy, rich, and complex—is so important to the overall success of this soup that if you can't find a really top quality product, you'll be better off using a really good cooked ham. Because most cooked hams have water added, that water is going to evaporate when you brown the pieces, which means first that some of the pieces may pop out of the pot (which isn't funny—it could happen, so be prepared—you may want to lower the heat slightly and stand back so the hot pieces don't burn you!) and second that some of the volume will be lost, so you may want to use about 1½ cups of diced ham. Adding avocado may sound a little unusual, so omit it if you prefer, but I think it's great!

2 tablespoons unsalted butter
2 tablespoons vegetable oil
1 cup finely diced tasso, preferably, or any
    premium-quality cooked ham (see headnote
    above)
2½ cups well-washed leeks, white and light
    green parts only, cut into ½-inch pieces,
    in all
7 cups chicken stock, in all
3 cups peeled white potatoes cut into
    ¾-inch pieces
1 cup heavy cream
1 tablespoon firmly packed light brown sugar
2 cups chopped and slightly mashed ripe
    avocados (about 4 medium-size avocados),
    optional

Seasoning Mix

2¾ teaspoons salt

2¼ teaspoons onion powder

2¼ teaspoons paprika

1¼ teaspoons ground dried
    pasilla chile peppers

1 teaspoon cayenne

1 teaspoon garlic powder

1 teaspoon dry mustard

¾ teaspoon white pepper

½ teaspoon black pepper

½ teaspoon ground cumin

1. Combine the seasoning mix ingredients in a small bowl. If you are using tasso, which is highly seasoned, remove 1 teaspoon of this mixture and discard it, or save it for another use. Use all 13¼ teaspoons of this mixture if you are using regular ham, which is not highly seasoned and requires the additional seasoning mix.

2. Place the butter and vegetable oil in a 5-quart pot over high heat. When the butter is melted and sizzling, add the tasso (or ham) and cook, stirring frequently, until the meat begins to darken slightly and shrink, about 3 to 4 minutes. With a slotted spoon, remove the meat from the pot—it will have a nicely browned appearance and rich taste—and set it aside.

3. To the pot add 1 cup of the leeks and 1 tablespoon of the seasoning mix. Continue to cook, stirring occasionally, until the mixture begins to stick to the bottom of the pot, about 4 minutes. At this point, the leeks are shrinking and fading in color, and *you will notice a wonderful "browned" fragrance coming from the pot and a similar sweet "brown" taste in the leeks themselves.* Continue to cook for 2 more minutes, then add 6 cups of the stock. Stir and scrape the bottom of the pot, loosening any of the brown bits and dissolving them into the liquid. Add the remaining 1½ cups of leeks, the potatoes, and the remaining seasoning mix and stir well. Bring to a boil, reduce the heat to medium-low, then cover and cook, uncovering to stir occasionally, for 15 minutes. *The soup will have developed a great smoky taste at this point.* Re-cover and continue to cook until the potatoes are tender, about 20 minutes. Transfer the mixture to a food processor, in batches if necessary, and purée, then return it to the pot and stir in the remaining 1 cup stock. Re-cover and cook for an additional 15 minutes. Stir in the heavy cream, brown sugar, and reserved meat. Raise the heat to medium and cook, stirring occasionally, for 15 minutes, then remove the pot from the heat.

4. To serve, ladle the soup into bowls and divide the avocado among the portions, or pass the avocado separately.

Roasted Sweet
Potato Bisque

Makes 10 cups; 5 main-course or 10 appetizer servings

This rich bisque, brimming with a great variety of colors, textures, and flavors, is sure to be good for whatever ails you! If you use vegetable stock, it's totally vegetarian, yet is still hearty and completely satisfying.

4 sweet potatoes (about 2 pounds), baked in a
    350°F oven until tender and peeled
6 tablespoons (¾ stick) unsalted butter
1 tablespoon finely chopped fire-roasted garlic
6 to 6½ cups chicken or vegetable stock, in all
1 cup onion cut into 1-inch pieces
2 cups cored green cabbage cut into 1-inch
    pieces
2 cups peeled parsnips cut into ½-inch pieces
4 cups Swiss chard leaves (or any leafy green,
    such as collard greens or spinach) torn into
    1-inch pieces
6 tablespoons seeded and finely chopped fresh
    jalapeño peppers

Seasoning Mix

2½ teaspoons salt

1½ teaspoons paprika

1 teaspoon dill weed

1 teaspoon ground dried
    Anaheim chile peppers

¾ teaspoon onion powder

¾ teaspoon black pepper

¾ teaspoon ground or
    rubbed sage

½ teaspoon ground
    cinnamon

½ teaspoon garlic powder

½ teaspoon ground nutmeg

½ teaspoon white pepper

1. Combine the seasoning mix ingredients in a small bowl.

2. Process the sweet potatoes in a food processor until smooth.

3. Place the butter in a heavy 5-quart pot over high heat. As soon as the butter sizzles, about 2 minutes, add the sweet potato purée, roasted garlic, and 2 tablespoons of the seasoning mix. Cook, stirring frequently, for 8 minutes. *The mixture has a very rich sweet potato taste with hints of roasted flavor. As the spices develop, note the pumpkin pie–like flavor that finishes the taste.* Add 4 cups of the stock and continue to cook, stirring frequently and scraping the pot bottom to avoid sticking, until the mixture thickens, about 6 minutes.

Add 2 cups of the stock and continue to cook, stirring and scraping frequently, until the mixture is thick and bubbling like a volcano, about 8 minutes. Add the onion, cabbage, parsnips, chard, and jalapeños. Stir and scrape the bottom well, then reduce the heat to low. Cover and simmer, stirring and scraping every few minutes, until the parsnips are cooked through, about 20 minutes. Add the remaining ½ cup stock if necessary to obtain the consistency of a white chowder. Remove from the heat and serve immediately.

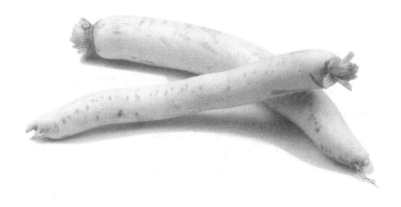

Turkey Poblano Gumbo

Makes about 7 cups; 7 main-course or 14 appetizer servings

Ooooooh, but the poblano peppers add a great taste to this gumbo! They're not nearly as hot as most chile peppers, but they still give that wonderful southwestern U.S.A. flavor to this favorite southwestern Louisiana dish.

1 pound boneless turkey breast, skin removed and cut into ½-inch pieces
½ cup vegetable oil
1 cup all-purpose flour
2 cups chopped onions
1 cup seeded and chopped green bell peppers
1 cup seeded and chopped red bell peppers
1 cup seeded and chopped yellow bell peppers
3 cups seeded fresh poblano chile peppers cut into ½-inch pieces
1 pound andouille, or your favorite smoked pork sausage, quartered lengthwise, then cut into ½-inch pieces
6 cups turkey or chicken stock, in all

Seasoning Mix

1 tablespoon plus ½ teaspoon salt
2 teaspoons dried basil
2 teaspoons paprika
1½ teaspoons dry mustard
1½ teaspoons onion powder
1½ teaspoons ground dried Anaheim chile peppers
1¼ teaspoons garlic powder
1 teaspoon cayenne
1 teaspoon dried chervil
1 teaspoon ground cumin
½ teaspoon black pepper
½ teaspoon white pepper
½ teaspoon dried thyme leaves

1. Combine the seasoning mix ingredients in a small bowl.

2. Sprinkle the turkey evenly with 1 tablespoon plus 2 teaspoons of the seasoning mix and rub it in well. Set aside.

3. The next step is to make a roux, which will give the gumbo its rich, authentic flavor. When making a roux, it is very important to keep all the flour moving constantly. If you don't, the flour will burn and the roux will be bitter. If you see little black specks in the roux, it has burned. If this happens, throw it out, clean the pot, and begin again.

If your roux seems to be browning too fast, take it off the stove and continue to whisk until it cools slightly, then return it to the heat.

4. Heat the vegetable oil in a heavy 4-quart pot over high heat until it is smoking hot (500°), about 5 minutes. Add the flour and whisk constantly, making sure that the oil and flour are thoroughly combined, until the roux is red-brown, about 6 to 8 minutes. Now add the onions, bell peppers, poblanos, andouille, and the remaining seasoning mix. Stir well, reduce the heat to medium, and cover. Cook, uncovering to stir and scrape every 2 to 3 minutes to prevent burning (as there is no liquid in the pot), for 18 minutes. Add the seasoned turkey meat and 3 cups of stock. Stir and scrape the pot completely, return the heat to high, and bring to a boil, then cook, stirring and scraping every 1 to 2 minutes, for 8 minutes. *The first taste is moderately salty, followed quickly by the broad brown and slightly sweet flavor of the roux. As the roux taste fades, it is replaced by a rising spice and herb flavor and a mild heat in the back of the mouth. The overall intensity is high now, but notice that the balance and intensity improve after the remaining stock is added.* Now add the remaining 3 cups stock, bring just to a boil, reduce the heat to low, and simmer until the gumbo is thick and golden, about 10 minutes. Serve over hot rice.

Vegetable Cheese Soup

Makes about 8 cups; 4 main-course or 8 appetizer servings

This is very similar to the kinds of soup I grew up with, but in those days if we had put sweet potatoes in at all, we'd have chopped them up and added them with the rest of the vegetables. We never would have thought of using them to thicken the broth, as we've done here. Gingerroot was unknown in our kitchen then, but I think it adds a wonderful tang, even in very small amounts. Use this recipe as the basis for soups with your favorite fresh vegetables; almost any will work, as long as they have enough substance—in texture and taste—to stand up to the cheeses. And you can use one color of bell peppers instead of all three colors—just be sure the total is 1½ cups.

Seasoning Mix
2½ teaspoons salt
1¾ teaspoons onion powder
1¼ teaspoons garlic powder
1 teaspoon cayenne
½ teaspoon black pepper
½ teaspoon white pepper

2 sweet potatoes (about 10 ounces each)
3 tablespoons unsalted butter
1½ cups chopped onions, in all
1 cup chopped celery
2 cups peeled white potatoes cut into ¾-inch pieces
1 tablespoon finely chopped fresh garlic
1 tablespoon peeled and finely chopped fresh ginger
½ cup seeded and chopped green bell peppers
½ cup seeded and chopped red bell peppers
½ cup seeded and chopped yellow bell peppers
2½ cups vegetable stock, in all
1½ cups heavy cream
1 cup zucchini cut into ½-inch pieces
1 cup yellow squash cut into ½-inch pieces

1 cup small broccoli florets
1 cup freshly grated Gruyère cheese
½ cup freshly grated sharp Cheddar cheese

1. Combine the seasoning mix ingredients in a small bowl.

2. Preheat the oven to 350°F.

3. Bake the sweet potatoes until they are soft, about 1 hour, then peel and mash them. Some sweet potatoes are stringy and if yours are, push them through a strainer. You should have about 1¼ cups. Set aside.

4. Melt the butter in a heavy 4-quart saucepan, preferably nonstick, over high heat. When it sizzles, add 1 cup of the onions, the celery, and the seasoning mix. Stir well, then cover. Cook, uncovering to stir every 2 minutes, until the onions begin to brown on the edges, about 8 minutes. Uncover, *taste the wonderful mounting sweet flavor that cooking over high heat gives the vegetables,* and add the white potatoes, garlic, and ginger. Stir and scrape well, then re-cover the pot and cook until the potatoes are a light gold color, about 3 minutes. Uncover and add all the bell peppers and the remaining ½ cup onions. Stir well and re-cover. Continue to cook until the mixture begins to stick (*at which time the vegetables will be even sweeter than before—they're great when caramelized this way!*), about 2 minutes, then add ½ cup of the stock and scrape the bottom of the pot well, loosening any brown bits, which are full of flavor, stuck to the bottom. Re-cover and bring the mixture to a simmer, about 2 minutes, then uncover and stir in the heavy cream and 1 cup of the stock. Re-cover and bring just to a boil, then reduce the heat to medium-low and simmer for 5 minutes. Uncover and whisk in the mashed sweet potatoes, then re-cover and bring to a boil. Uncover and add the zucchini, yellow squash, broccoli, Gruyère and Cheddar cheeses, and the remaining 1 cup stock. Stir well, then re-cover and simmer until the vegetables are just cooked, about 7 minutes. *The squash and broccoli retain much of their natural bright colors and flavors, and are just tender-crisp, in contrast with the white potatoes and bell peppers, which were changed considerably by their cooking method.* Remove from the heat and serve immediately.

Salads Are Like Sunshine

When there are thirteen children in the family, as there were in mine, plus neighbors and relatives who just happen to drop in, every meal is like a party, and what is more typical of a party than plenty of taste-tempting salad, of one or more varieties, to round out lunch or dinner? Most of the salads in this chapter are so hearty they could easily stand on their own as a meal. If you feel the need, you could always serve them with a little bread, preferably homemade.

Black Bean Salad with
Roasted Parsnip Dressing

Makes about 8 cups; 8 side-dish or appetizer servings

This recipe was developed as a salad, but you can serve it as an appetizer or a side dish, and anyone with a yen for the flavors of the Southwest will enjoy making a meal of it! Try it on a fried corn tortilla, on a bed of shredded lettuce, or as a satisfying dip with plenty of sturdy chips. This recipe doubles easily for lots of company!

½ pound dried black beans
1½ quarts water
1¼ cups chopped onions, in all
¾ cup seeded and chopped red bell peppers, in all
¾ cup seeded and chopped yellow bell peppers, in all
¾ cup seeded and chopped green bell peppers, in all
1 pound parsnips, peeled and cut into pieces about 3 inches long and 1 inch thick
2 tablespoons plus 1½ teaspoons olive oil, in all
¼ cup plus 2 tablespoons rice vinegar
2 tablespoons mirin (sweet rice wine)
¼ cup cane syrup, preferably, or any sweet syrup
1 tablespoon lightly packed dark brown sugar
½ cup chopped celery
1½ cups chopped fresh tomatoes, peeled

Seasoning Mix
2¼ teaspoons salt
1¾ teaspoons ground cumin
1¾ teaspoons paprika
1¼ teaspoons garlic powder
1¼ teaspoons dried oregano
1 teaspoon ground coriander
¾ teaspoon onion powder
¾ teaspoon ground dried ancho chile peppers
¾ teaspoon ground dried New Mexico chile peppers
¾ teaspoon dry mustard
¾ teaspoon black pepper
½ teaspoon ground cinnamon
½ teaspoon white pepper

1. Day 1: Rinse the beans, picking out any foreign matter. Place in a large bowl, add enough water so that they are covered by about 3 inches, and soak overnight.

2. Day 2: Combine the seasoning mix and set aside.

3. Drain the beans and place them in a 4-quart pot with the 1½ quarts water, 2 tablespoons plus ¾ teaspoon of the seasoning mix, 1 cup of the onions, and ½ cup each of the red, yellow, and green bell peppers. Stir well, cover, and bring to a boil over high heat. Reduce the heat to medium and cook, uncovering to stir and scrape the bottom of the pot occasionally, until the liquid is reduced so that it just covers the beans, and the beans are tender, about 1½ to 2 hours.

4. While the beans are cooking, start the dressing. Preheat the oven to 425°F. Place the parsnips on a sheet pan and brush all their surfaces with 1½ teaspoons of the olive oil. Roast in the oven, turning once or twice so they will brown evenly, until they are a medium golden brown, about 8 to 10 minutes. Set aside.

5. When the beans are cooked, transfer 1½ cups of them to a blender and add the parsnips, the remaining 2 tablespoons olive oil, the rice vinegar, mirin, cane syrup, brown sugar, and the remaining 2 tablespoons plus 1¼ teaspoons seasoning mix. Process until smooth, about 30 to 40 seconds. (Makes about 3¼ cups of dressing.)

6. Place the remaining beans in a 2-quart mixing bowl and add the remaining ¼ cup each red, yellow, and green bell peppers, the celery, and the tomatoes. Toss to mix, then pour the dressing over the salad and toss gently until all the vegetables are coated with the dressing.

Bronzed Black Drum Salad with Creamy Vinaigrette

Makes 4 servings *Good-looking presentation here! You can use any firm vegetable instead of the fennel and carrot if you like.*

1 pound drum (or other firm-fleshed fish)
  fillets
½ teaspoon olive oil
1 large egg
½ cup plus 2 tablespoons vegetable oil
2 tablespoons white balsamic vinegar
3 tablespoons mirin (sweet rice wine)
2 tablespoons white wine vinegar
1 tablespoon Chef Paul Prudhomme's
  Magic Pepper Sauce, or any other
  medium-hot pepper sauce
1 fennel bulb, cut into julienne strips
  (about 1½ cups)
1 medium-size carrot, cut into julienne strips
  (about ¾ cup)
1 large onion, cut into julienne strips
  (about 2 cups)
8 cups mixed salad greens
24 pitted Kalamata or any good quality
  black olives
1½ cups sliced unpeeled cucumber
3 ripe Roma tomatoes, preferably, or
  1 medium-size ripe tomato, sliced
  (about 1½ cups)

Seasoning Mix

2 teaspoons salt
1 teaspoon onion powder
¾ teaspoon garlic powder
¾ teaspoon dry mustard
¾ teaspoon ground dried
  New Mexico chile peppers
¾ teaspoon paprika
½ teaspoon black pepper
½ teaspoon white pepper

1. Combine the seasoning mix ingredients in a small bowl.

2. Sprinkle the fish fillets with 1 tablespoon of the seasoning mix, coating all sides of the fillets evenly. Drizzle the olive oil over one side of the fillets.

3. Place a 12-inch skillet over high heat until it is very hot, about 4 minutes. Place the fillets in the skillet, oiled side down. Cook the fillets, turning twice, until they are golden brown on both sides and just cooked through, about 5 to 6 minutes in all. Remove the fish from the skillet and let cool to room temperature. With a fork, flake the fish into bite-size pieces.

4. Place the egg in a blender and process briefly; then, with the blender running, slowly add the vegetable oil in a thin stream until the mixture thickens to a thin mayonnaise consistency. Adding each ingredient one at a time and processing briefly between each addition, add the white balsamic vinegar, mirin, and white wine vinegar. Stir in the pepper sauce and the remaining seasoning mix and process briefly. Set aside or refrigerate if you are not using immediately. (Makes about 1½ cups dressing.)

5. Blanch the fennel by placing it in boiling water just until it begins to soften, about 1 to 2 minutes, and rinse under cold running water to stop the cooking process. Blanch the carrot and onions (or other vegetables) in the same manner.

6. On 4 large salad plates, assemble each salad in layers in the following order (bottom to top), dividing the ingredients evenly among the 4 servings: the salad greens, onions, carrots, fennel, 1 cup of the dressing (¼ cup for each salad), the bronzed fish, and the remaining ½ cup of the dressing (2 tablespoons for each salad). Arrange one quarter of the olives, cucumbers, and tomatoes around each salad.

Clam and Pasta Salad

Shellfish and pasta—what a wonderful combination! The combination of balsamic vinegars and olives whispers a Mediterranean influence, and we've also used puréed mirliton and acorn squash in the dressing. Serve with a length of authoritative bread, perhaps brushed with flavored olive oil, and something cold to drink, and you have a great lunch or light supper.

2 cups water

48 fresh littleneck clams in their shells, scrubbed

1½ cups peeled acorn squash chopped into ½-inch pieces

1 medium-size mirliton (chayote), peeled, seeded, and chopped into ¼-inch pieces (about 1 cup)

2 tablespoons unsalted butter

½ cup chopped onions

1 tablespoon minced fresh garlic

2 tablespoons balsamic vinegar

2 tablespoons white balsamic vinegar

2 tablespoons cane syrup, preferably, or any sweet syrup

2 tablespoons lightly packed dark brown sugar

6 ounces egg noodles, cooked according to package directions and drained (about 4 cups cooked)

¼ cup seeded and minced red bell peppers

¼ cup seeded and minced yellow bell peppers

½ cup chopped celery

2 tablespoons pitted and minced green olives

2 tablespoons pitted and minced black olives

¼ cup sunflower seeds, roasted

Seasoning Mix

2 teaspoons sugar

1½ teaspoons dry mustard

1½ teaspoons salt

1 teaspoon ground cumin

1 teaspoon onion powder

1 teaspoon paprika

1 teaspoon ground dried New Mexico chile peppers

1 teaspoon dried thyme leaves

¾ teaspoon ground dried guajillo chile peppers

½ teaspoon ground dried ancho chile peppers

½ teaspoon cayenne

½ teaspoon white pepper

¼ teaspoon black pepper

1. Combine the seasoning mix ingredients in a small bowl.

2. In a 2-quart pot over high heat, place the water and clams. Cover and bring to a boil, then reduce the heat to medium and steam the clams until they open, about 8 to 10 minutes. Remove the pot from the heat, uncover, and allow the clams to cool in the cooking water. When the clams are cool enough to handle, strain the liquid from the pot and reserve it, about 1 cup. Remove the meat from the clams and reserve. Discard the shells and discard any clams whose shells don't open.

3. Place the acorn squash in a small saucepan and add enough water to cover. Bring to a boil, reduce the heat to medium-low, and simmer for 15 minutes. Drain and set aside.

4. Place the mirliton in a small saucepan and add enough water to cover. Bring to a boil, reduce the heat to medium-low, and simmer until the mirliton is tender, about 10 minutes. Drain and set aside.

5. In an 8-inch skillet over high heat, melt the butter, and, when it begins to sizzle, add the onions. Cook, stirring constantly, until the onions just begin to turn translucent but not brown, about 3 minutes. Reduce the heat to medium and cook, stirring frequently, for 2 more minutes. Add the garlic and continue to cook, stirring about once a minute, for 6 minutes. Add the seasoning mix and cook, stirring almost constantly and watching carefully to prevent burning, for 4 more minutes. If you see smoke that is bluish or if the mixture smells as though it's about to burn, remove the skillet from the heat immediately. *Now the onions should be brown and sweet and will have picked up the complex flavors of the spices in the seasoning mix. The heat from the dried chile peppers will be almost overwhelming at this point but will subside as this mixture is combined with the other ingredients.*

6. Transfer the mixture from the skillet to a blender and add the squash, reserved clam cooking liquid, both varieties of balsamic vinegar, cane syrup, and brown sugar. Process at medium speed until the mixture is smooth, about 1 minute.

7. In a bowl combine the cooked noodles, clams, both colors of bell peppers, the celery, mirliton, both kinds of olives, the sunflower seeds, and the purée. Toss gently until well combined. Serve immediately or let it cool to room temperature before serving.

Fruit Salad with
Poppy Seed Dressing

Makes 7 cups; 3 to 4 main-course or 7 salad servings

The flavors of the fruit really make this dish, so choose the best and ripest varieties available in your market. I use Gala or Fuji apples and locally grown oranges. Use mandarins, tangerines, or satsumas if they are available. Taste your fruit first—if it is sweet and good to eat, it will be good in this salad. There are many varieties of honey on the market today, so you can choose one with an interesting flavor. I like eucalyptus honey or a good local wildflower honey.

Dressing

½ cup sour cream

1 cup mayonnaise

4 ounces cream cheese, softened

¼ cup honey

2 tablespoons freshly squeezed lemon juice

2 tablespoons freshly squeezed lime juice

Fruit Salad

2 cups peeled and cored apple cut into ¾-inch
    pieces (about 1 large apple)

2 cups peeled and seeded ripe papaya cut into
    ¾-inch pieces (about 1 large papaya)

1 ripe banana, peeled, cut into 4 pieces
    lengthwise, and each length cut into ¾-inch
    pieces

1 cup red seedless grapes, each grape cut in half

1 cup cored pear cut into ¾-inch pieces

1 ripe mango, peeled, seeded, and cut into
    ¾-inch pieces (about ¾ cup)

Seasoning Mix

1 tablespoon plus 1 teaspoon lightly packed dark brown sugar

2¼ teaspoons poppy seeds

1 teaspoon ground cinnamon

¾ teaspoon dill seeds

¾ teaspoon ground ginger

½ teaspoon ground coriander

½ teaspoon salt

½ teaspoon ground savory

1 cup orange segments
1 cup pink grapefruit segments

1. Combine the seasoning mix ingredients in a small bowl.

2. Make the dressing by processing the sour cream, mayonnaise, cream cheese, honey, and citrus juices in a food processor until smooth, about 1 to 2 minutes. Turn off the processor and add the seasoning mix. Process briefly, just until the seasoning is combined, being careful not to overprocess, or you'll grind up the poppy seeds.

3. In a large mixing bowl, combine the fruit and dressing. Toss gently until the fruit and dressing are combined. Refrigerate at least 4 hours, preferably overnight before serving.

Golden Egg and
Potato Salad

Makes 7 cups; 7 side-dish or salad servings *The beautiful golden dressing for this salad packs a wonderful punch, but the seasonings are so carefully balanced that the real potato flavor comes right through. If there's someone in your crowd who doesn't care much for hot peppers, simply reduce the amount of each kind—cayenne, ancho chile, black, and white—not the number, and you'll still have a great salad. Remember, with any food that contains raw eggs, as this mayonnaise does, if you're taking it on a picnic or to a covered-dish supper, keep it refrigerated until ready to serve.*

7 large eggs, in all
3 cups chicken stock
One 13.5-ounce can unsweetened coconut milk
2 pounds baby white potatoes, washed but not
    peeled
½ cup plus 2 tablespoons olive oil, in all
1½ cups chopped onions
½ cup seeded and chopped red bell peppers
½ cup seeded and chopped yellow bell peppers
½ cup seeded and chopped green bell peppers
¾ cup chopped celery
3 tablespoons white balsamic vinegar
2 teaspoons sugar

Seasoning Mix

1 tablespoon plus
    ¾ teaspoon salt

2 teaspoons ground
    coriander

2 teaspoons onion powder

1¾ teaspoons dried basil

1¾ teaspoons garlic powder

1½ teaspoons dry mustard

1½ teaspoons ground
    turmeric

1¼ teaspoons cayenne

1 teaspoon ground dried
    ancho chile peppers

1 teaspoon black pepper

½ teaspoon white pepper

1. Combine the seasoning mix ingredients in a small bowl.

2. Place 6 of the eggs (the seventh egg is for the dressing) in a 1-quart saucepan and add enough room-temperature water to cover. Slowly bring to a boil over medium heat and boil

until the eggs are hard-cooked, about 20 minutes. Immediately drain off the hot water and place the pan of eggs under cool running water—this will make them easier to shell. When the eggs reach room temperature, shell them and cut into ½-inch pieces. Place in a large bowl and set aside.

3. Combine the stock, coconut milk, and 3 tablespoons plus 1 teaspoon of the seasoning mix in a 5-quart pot. Stir well, breaking up any clumps of seasoning mix, cover, and place over high heat. Bring to a boil, then add the potatoes. Re-cover the pot and cook until the potatoes are tender, about 30 minutes. Remove the potatoes and set them aside to cool. Measure the liquid remaining in the pot—you need 1 cup, so if you have more, discard the excess, and if less than 1 cup remains, add water to make 1 cup. As soon as the potatoes are cool enough to handle, cut them into ½-inch pieces and add them to the bowl with the eggs.

4. Heat 2 tablespoons of the olive oil in a 10-inch skillet, preferably nonstick, over high heat just until the oil begins to smoke, about 3 to 4 minutes. Add the onions, all the bell peppers, the celery, and the remaining seasoning mix. Reduce the heat to medium and cook, stirring frequently with a wooden spoon and scraping the bottom of the skillet, until the vegetables are only slightly crunchy, fading in color, and with a sweet flavor from cooking in the olive oil, about 10 to 12 minutes. Remove from the heat, transfer the vegetables to a plate, and let cool in the refrigerator to room temperature.

5. In a blender, process the remaining egg until it is light-colored, about 15 seconds. Add the remaining ½ cup olive oil in a slow, thin stream until it is absorbed. Add the reserved potato cooking liquid, the vinegar, and sugar and continue to process, scraping down the sides of the blender, until the ingredients are combined into a mayonnaise, about 1½ to 2 minutes.

6. Add the cooled vegetable mixture to the bowl of potatoes and eggs. Add the mayonnaise and stir gently but thoroughly until the ingredients are evenly distributed and coated with the mayonnaise. Serve immediately at room temperature or refrigerate until cold. This should be eaten the day it is made.

Olive Salad
Pasta Salad

Makes about 8 cups; 4 main-course or 8 side-dish servings

The name of this recipe is not a mistake! That's because olive salad is a big favorite with the Italian-American population in New Orleans. It's an essential ingredient in our famous muf-fuletta sandwiches, and is often combined with other salad ingredients or, as we've done here, with pasta. You can buy it bottled, but our from-scratch version works better for this recipe.

½ cup olive oil
3 small gherkin pickles, chopped
2 tablespoons seeded and finely chopped fresh banana peppers (also called wax peppers)
2 tablespoons seeded and finely chopped red bell peppers
2 tablespoons finely chopped celery
2 tablespoons finely chopped pitted black olives
2 tablespoons seeded and finely chopped fresh Anaheim chile peppers
2 peperoncini (small pickled peppers sold in jars), chopped
1½ tablespoons drained and chopped capers
¾ teaspoon minced fresh garlic
¾ cup chopped pimiento-stuffed green olives
½ cup small cauliflower florets
¼ cup finely chopped fresh parsley leaves
¼ cup chopped onions
¼ cup finely chopped carrots
¼ cup white balsamic vinegar

Seasoning Mix

1 tablespoon dried basil
1 tablespoon dried oregano
1½ teaspoons salt
1 teaspoon garlic powder
1 teaspoon onion powder
¾ teaspoon black pepper
¾ teaspoon cayenne
½ teaspoon white pepper

1 pound penne (or your favorite) pasta, cooked
    according to the package directions, rinsed with
    cold water, drained, sprinkled with ¼ teaspoon
    olive oil, and well but gently mixed, at room
    temperature
1 medium-size ripe tomato, peeled, seeded, and
    finely chopped

1. Combine the seasoning mix ingredients in a small bowl.

2. Heat the olive oil in a 12-inch skillet over high heat just until it begins to smoke, about 3 to 4 minutes. Add everything (including the seasoning mix) except the penne and tomato. Cook, stirring frequently, for 4 minutes and remove from the heat. Combine with the pasta and tomato in a large serving bowl and toss well. Serve at room temperature.

Paul's Potato Salad

Makes about 5 cups; 5 to 6 servings

The first time we made this salad in the Research and Development Kitchen, we had enough to feed at least a battalion, if not an entire army, so we cut all the quantities in half. But if you have a battalion at your house, it's easy to double! The definite smoky flavor of the andouille may remind you of German potato salad, but the cane syrup and cane vinegar are pure Louisiana!

1½ pounds small new potatoes (about 10), skins on, cut into ¾-inch pieces

4 large hard-cooked eggs, shelled

6 ounces andouille, or other top quality smoked pork sausage, cut into ¼-inch pieces

¼ cup chopped shallots

1 tablespoon peeled and finely chopped fresh ginger

¼ cup seeded and finely chopped yellow bell peppers

¼ cup seeded and finely chopped green bell peppers

¼ cup white vinegar

1½ teaspoons Chef Paul Prudhomme's Magic Pepper Sauce, or other medium-hot pepper sauce

½ cup water

¼ cup mayonnaise

2 tablespoons cane syrup

2 tablespoons cane vinegar or other sweet vinegar

¼ cup chopped green onions or scallions, green parts only

Seasoning Mix

1 tablespoon cracked black peppercorns

1 tablespoon firmly packed light brown sugar

1 teaspoon dill weed

½ teaspoon dry mustard

¼ teaspoon salt

1. Combine the seasoning mix ingredients in a small bowl.

2. Boil the potatoes in enough water to cover just until they are fork-tender, about 20 minutes. Drain and set aside.

3. Separate the hard-cooked eggs; chop the whites and set them and the yolks aside.

4. Preheat a heavy 10-inch skillet, preferably nonstick, over high heat, until it is very hot, about 3 to 4 minutes. Add the andouille and cook, stirring a few times, until the edges begin to brown, about 3 minutes. Add the shallots, ginger, and bell peppers and stir well to combine; then cook, stirring once or twice, until the peppers first brighten, then brown on the edges, about 3 to 4 minutes. Add the seasoning mix, white vinegar, pepper sauce, and water. Stir well and cook until the vegetables are tender and the liquid reduces somewhat, about 4 to 5 minutes. Remove from the heat. *At this point, the prominent taste is the strong flavor of the brown sugar and the acid combining with the smoky taste of andouille, because the seasoning intensity masks the other flavors.*

5. Make the dressing: Strain the liquid from the skillet and transfer it to a blender, then transfer the vegetable mixture to a 2-quart mixing bowl. To the blender, add the hard-boiled yolks and process just until blended, about 15 to 20 seconds. Add the mayonnaise and process until blended, about 20 to 25 seconds, then add the cane syrup and cane vinegar. Process for 15 seconds and, with the machine running, add ½ cup of the potato pieces and process until smooth—you'll notice bits of potato skin, but that's okay. There should be about 1½ to 1¾ cups dressing. *The highlight of the dressing is its very rich molasses taste from the cane syrup, somewhat balanced by the tartness of the vinegar. The tiny amount of potato adds textural richness rather than flavor.*

6. Add the remaining potatoes to the vegetable mixture in the bowl, then add the chopped hard-cooked egg whites and green onions. Pour the dressing over the salad and toss gently to distribute the ingredients evenly. Serve warm, at room temperature, or cold. And it will be even more delicious the next day!

Red Hot Rice Salad

Makes 8 cups; 4 main-course or 8 side-dish servings

We've listed specific chile peppers that were fresh and appealing-looking at our local supermarket, but we understand that you might find different varieties, so choose the kinds that are available and freshest when you're ready to prepare this salad. It's going to be very important to taste them, though, because you don't want the result to be too hot. Test a pepper's heat by cutting off the top and touching it to the tip of your tongue. If it tastes too hot, then it'll be too hot for you in the dish, so if you prefer a mild flavor, by all means use mild chiles, or at least mostly mild chiles, but be sure to use at least 2 or 3 varieties. And if you can't find mild varieties, just use less.

Seasoning Mix

2 tablespoons lightly packed dark brown sugar

2 teaspoons garlic powder

2 teaspoons onion powder

2 teaspoons salt

1¼ teaspoons dried basil

1¼ teaspoons cayenne

1¼ teaspoons dill weed

¾ teaspoon white pepper

¼ cup olive oil
1 cup finely chopped shallots
½ cup seeded and finely chopped fresh
    Anaheim chile peppers
¼ cup seeded and finely chopped fresh
    poblano chile peppers
¼ cup seeded and finely chopped fresh mild
    red chile peppers
¼ cup seeded and finely chopped fresh banana
    peppers (also called wax peppers)
½ cup freshly squeezed orange juice
¼ cup freshly squeezed grapefruit juice
¼ cup cane vinegar or other sweet vinegar
¼ cup rice vinegar
¼ cup white balsamic vinegar
1 tablespoon Chef Paul Prudhomme's
    Magic Pepper Sauce, or other
    medium-hot pepper sauce

¼ cup finely chopped fresh cilantro leaves
7 cups cooked Converted rice

1. Combine the seasoning mix ingredients in a small bowl.

2. In a large skillet, heat the olive oil over high heat just until it begins to smoke, about 3 to 4 minutes. Add the shallots, all the peppers, and the seasoning mix. Cook, stirring frequently, until the peppers have darkened slightly, but still retain their color and crunch, about 4 minutes. Add the liquid ingredients and stir well. Remove from the heat and transfer to a large bowl. Add the cilantro and cooked rice and toss well. Refrigerate for at least 4 hours, preferably overnight, before serving.

Rice Salad with Attitude!

Makes about 9 cups; 4 to 5 main-course or
8 to 10 side-dish servings

This great-tasting vegetarian dish can be used as a salad, side dish, appetizer, or main course—it's that versatile!

2 cups uncooked brown rice

5 cups water

3 tablespoons olive oil, in all

1 cup chopped onions

½ cup seeded and chopped red bell peppers

½ cup seeded and chopped yellow bell peppers

½ cup seeded and chopped green bell peppers

1 tablespoon minced fresh garlic

1 tablespoon peeled and minced fresh ginger

1 ripe Roma tomato, peeled and chopped

½ cup chopped carrots

3 tablespoons unsalted butter

1 cup vegetable stock, in all

1 cup sugar snap peas, ends trimmed and cut into 1-inch pieces

1 cup chopped yellow squash

1 cup chopped zucchini

¼ cup lightly packed chopped fresh cilantro leaves

1 tablespoon plus 2 teaspoons firmly packed light brown sugar

Topping

1 cup vegetable oil

1 cup chopped cashews

¼ cup sliced almonds

¼ cup pine nuts

½ cup raisins

Seasoning Mix

2 teaspoons paprika

2 teaspoons salt

1½ teaspoons onion powder

1 teaspoon ground cardamom

1 teaspoon ground cinnamon

1 teaspoon ground coriander

1 teaspoon ground cumin

1 teaspoon ground ginger

¾ teaspoon black pepper

½ teaspoon cayenne

½ teaspoon garlic powder

½ teaspoon dry mustard

½ teaspoon ground nutmeg

½ teaspoon white pepper

½ teaspoon ground dried ancho chile peppers

1. Combine the seasoning mix ingredients in a small bowl.

2. Place the rice and water in a large pot over high heat. Cover and bring to a boil, then reduce the heat to low and simmer, covered, until the water is absorbed and the rice is tender, 45 minutes to an hour. Uncover, fluff with a fork, and set aside to cool.

3. Place 2 tablespoons of the olive oil in a 10-inch skillet over high heat until it is very hot, about 3 to 4 minutes. Add the onions, all the bell peppers, the garlic, ginger, tomato, carrots, butter, and 4 tablespoons of the seasoning mix. Stir well to coat the vegetables with the oil and seasonings, and cook, stirring occasionally, until the vegetables begin to brown (if they seem to be browning too quickly, reduce the heat), about 10 to 12 minutes. *During this period you can see the rich golden brown color and taste the slight sweetness of the onions, taste a slight bitterness from the herbs—a good, strong taste, well balanced with nothing leading, and a hint of curry. Also be sure to taste the delicious sweetness in the brown bits that form on the bottom of the skillet.* Stir in the remaining 1 tablespoon olive oil, the remaining seasoning mix, and ½ cup of the stock. Cook for 2 minutes, then add the sugar snap peas, the yellow squash, the zucchini, the cilantro, the remaining ½ cup stock, and the brown sugar. *At this point, a strong seasoning taste will dominate the sauce, with the chile peppers up front, which will recede when the mixture is added to the rice.* Stir well, cook until most of the liquid evaporates, about 8 to 10 minutes longer, then remove from the heat and set aside to cool.

4. Make the topping: Heat the vegetable oil in a small skillet over high heat to about 325°F, about 2½ to 3 minutes. Add the cashews and cook, turning constantly, for 40 seconds. Add the almonds and pine nuts, and continue to cook and stir until they are lightly browned, only about 1 to 2 minutes. Remove from the heat, stir in the raisins, and drain off the oil.

5. When the vegetable mixture is cool, add it to the rice, tossing gently but thoroughly to distribute all the ingredients evenly. Divide the nut-and-raisin topping among the portions and serve.

Spinach Salad

Makes 8 to 10 cups;

4 to 5 main-course or 8 to 10 side-dish servings

A good spinach salad should be in every cook's repertoire, and while this one has many traditional elements, the tasso and cane vinegar give it a decided Louisiana accent.

¼ cup olive oil
9 ounces tasso, or any premium-quality cooked ham,
    cut into ¼-inch cubes
1 medium-size onion, cut into julienne strips
1 small red bell pepper, seeded and cut into
    julienne strips
1 small yellow bell pepper, seeded and cut into
    julienne strips
1 tablespoon minced fresh garlic
¼ cup freshly squeezed lime juice
¼ cup freshly squeezed lemon juice
1 teaspoon granulated sugar
¼ cup firmly packed light brown sugar
¼ cup dried currants
¼ cup raisins
¼ cup cane vinegar or any sweet vinegar
1 grapefruit, peeled and sectioned
Two 10-ounce packages fresh spinach

1. Preheat a heavy 10-inch skillet over high heat for 3 to 4 minutes. Add the olive oil, tilting the pan so the oil spreads over the entire bottom, then add the tasso, spreading it evenly. Cook, stirring and scraping the bottom occasionally, until the tasso is lightly browned, about 4 to 5 minutes. *During this time notice that the seasonings from the tasso—and if it's good quality it will have lots of seasoning— mingle with the oil. You might even say they make that olive oil sing!*

2. Add the onion, stir well and scrape up any brown bits that may stick to the bottom of the skillet, and cook, stirring occasionally, until the onion is brown around the edges *(as its sugar caramelizes, it'll lose its acid taste as well)*, about 4 to 5 minutes, then stir in the bell peppers, garlic, and citrus juices (what a great fragrance!) and cook, stirring and scraping occasionally, until the colors of the peppers becomes very bright, almost glowing, then darken as they are lightly browned from the heat, about 6 to 8 minutes. *Now there is an intense citrus taste in the front of the mouth, with flavors from the tasso coming behind. The vegetables still taste raw. As the peppers cook, their sweetness counters the acidity of the lemon and lime. The sour taste begins to spread in the mouth as it develops, and the caramelized flavor of the tasso deepens.*

3. Stir in the granulated sugar, brown sugar, currants, raisins, vinegar, and grapefruit. Cover, remove from the heat, and let cool to room temperature, during which time the currants and raisins will plump and *absorb the other flavors.*

4. When the dressing is cool, remove the stems and any bruised leaves from the spinach and wash well. Shake or spin the spinach dry, place it in a large serving bowl, and pour the dressing over it. Toss lightly to coat all the spinach leaves and distribute the ingredients evenly. Serve at once.

Chartres Street
Crabmeat Salad

Don't be put off by the apparent length of this recipe—there's nothing complicated about it, and when you're finished you'll have a dish that will dazzle your family or guests. It's gorgeous to look at and heaven in your mouth!

8 ripe avocados, preferably Calavos
Juice of 1 lemon

Vegetable Mixture

2 tablespoons olive oil
1 cup chopped onions
¼ cup seeded and chopped green bell peppers
¼ cup seeded and chopped red bell peppers
¼ cup seeded and chopped minced fresh jalapeño chile peppers
1 tablespoon minced fresh garlic

Mayonnaise and Sauce

2 teaspoons Chef Paul Prudhomme's Magic Pepper Sauce, or other medium-hot pepper sauce
1 large egg
1½ cups vegetable oil

Crab Salad

¼ cup thinly sliced green onions, white and light green part only
1 pound lump crabmeat, picked over to remove the shells and cartilage

Seasoning Mix

2 teaspoons salt
1½ teaspoons onion powder
1 teaspoon garlic powder
1 teaspoon dry mustard
1 teaspoon paprika
¾ teaspoon dried basil
¾ teaspoon black pepper
½ teaspoon cayenne
½ teaspoon dill weed
½ teaspoon white pepper

Pasta

>3 quarts water
>
>8 ounces uncooked pasta (radiatore, gemelli, or
>fusilli work well, or use tricolor pasta for an
>eye-catching presentation)
>
>1 teaspoon salt
>
>1 tablespoon olive oil
>
>1 medium-size carrot (or you can use sweet potato or
>jicama), cut into julienne strips
>
>1 medium-size cucumber, peeled, seeded, and cut
>into julienne strips

1. Combine the seasoning mix ingredients in a small bowl.

2. Cut the avocados in half lengthwise and remove the pits. Carefully remove the peel, leaving the halves in 1 piece. Coarsely dice 2 of the avocados (4 halves) and sprinkle the remaining halves with a little lemon juice to prevent discoloration. Set aside.

3. Make the vegetable mixture. In a 12-inch skillet, heat the olive oil over high heat just until it begins to smoke, about 3 to 4 minutes. Add the onions, all the bell peppers, the jalapeño peppers, garlic, and 2 tablespoons of the seasoning mix. Cook, stirring frequently, until the vegetables' color is similar to that of autumn leaves—the onions light golden and the bell peppers with rich but sub-dued colors—about 4 minutes. *At this point there is an up-front seasoning taste, followed by the sweetness of caramelized onions and bell peppers, and finishing with heat in the back of the mouth.* Continue to cook until the vegetables are mushy, the bell pepper colors are faded, and the onions are dark brown, about 4 more minutes. *Now the caramelization brings out the natural sweetness of the onions and takes away their pungency. Note how the deep brown sweetness compares with the earlier less brown flavor.* Remove from the heat and set aside.

4. Make the mayonnaise and sauce: Combine the pepper sauce and egg in a food processor. Process briefly to combine, then add the cooled vegetable mixture. Process until the mixture is puréed, then add the vegetable oil in a slow, steady stream until the mayonnaise is thick and the oil is absorbed. Remove 1¼ cups of this mayonnaise and refrigerate it for later use. The mayonnaise will have lots of small specks from the cooked vegetables and seasonings. *The primary taste is a rich creaminess with a slightly roasted middle flavor. The back taste gives a light bite from the black pepper. The overall effect is light and well balanced, which will*

allow the flavor of the crab to come through. To the mayonnaise remaining in the food processor add the reserved chopped avocado and the remaining seasoning mix and process until smooth. Refrigerate this sauce until ready to use.

5. Make the crab salad: Combine the green onions, crabmeat, and reserved mayonnaise. Fold gently till well mixed, but do not overmix. Refrigerate until ready to use. (Makes about 3 cups.)

6. Cook the pasta: In a 5-quart pot, bring the water to a boil. Add the pasta, salt, and olive oil, return to a boil, and cook until the pasta is about three quarters done, about 8 minutes. Add the carrot and continue to cook until the pasta reaches the *al dente* stage, about 4 minutes longer. Drain the pasta and rinse immediately under cold water until the pasta is cool. Drain thoroughly, place in a large bowl, and add the cucumber strips and sauce. Toss gently until evenly coated.

7. To serve, place 1 to 1½ cups of pasta on a plate, place an avocado half on the pasta, and mound ½ cup of the crab salad on top of the avocado.

A Little of This,
a Little of That

Condiments, Dressings,
Dips, and So Forth

Here in New Orleans we talk about *lagniappe,* which means a little something extra. These recipes are a little something extra, for they add an extra touch to a dish or a meal—a flavor enhancement to go along with a main course, a sauce for dipping, or a dressing to turn fruit or vegetables into a salad. Rural Louisiana cooks were adept at using local herbs in sauces and dressings, and you can detect that influence here.

Basil Yogurt
Dressing

I developed this dressing recipe using my own pepper sauce, so if you use a different sauce, you'll need to adjust the amount to taste. Pepper sauces vary considerably in heat, and some have a very bitter taste. The amount of pepper sauce is small, which means this dressing is not particularly hot—tasty, but not burning. By the way, you'd be correct if you guessed that yogurt wasn't in wide use in south Louisiana years ago—we discovered it fairly recently, just as the rest of the country did. But we've been using buttermilk and homemade mayonnaise as the bases for salad dressings for generations and, as I've mentioned elsewhere, we're quick to recognize any good flavor and add it to the ingredients we use often.

One 16-ounce container plain yogurt
2 tablespoon white balsamic vinegar
1 tablespoon tamari
3 ounces smoked Cheddar cheese, freshly grated
½ cup lightly packed chopped fresh basil leaves
1 tablespoon freshly squeezed lime juice
2 tablespoons cane syrup or any sweet syrup
2 tablespoons Chef Paul Prudhomme's
    Magic Pepper Sauce, or other
    medium-hot pepper sauce

Process all the ingredients in a blender until the mixture is smooth, about 20 seconds. Refrigerate until ready to serve.

Caraway Mango
Mayonnaise

Fresh fruit salad, vegetable salad, green salad, dipping sauce—you could run out of food before you run out of ways to use this mayonnaise!

2 large eggs
1½ cups vegetable oil
1 tablespoon rice vinegar
1 tablespoon cane vinegar, or your favorite
   vinegar
¼ cup white balsamic vinegar
1 tablespoon lightly packed dark brown sugar
1½ cups peeled, seeded, and chopped ripe
   mangoes (about 2 small)
1 tablespoon caraway seeds, roasted

Seasoning Mix

1¼ teaspoons salt

1 teaspoon garlic powder

1 teaspoon onion powder

¾ teaspoon ground
   coriander

½ teaspoon ground cumin

½ teaspoon paprika

½ teaspoon dried thyme
   leaves

¼ teaspoon black pepper

¼ teaspoon white pepper

1. Combine the seasoning mix ingredients in a small bowl.

2. In a blender, process the eggs until they are frothy, about 20 seconds. With the blender running, slowly add the vegetable oil in a thin stream until the mixture has the consistency of mayonnaise. Add the 3 vinegars, the brown sugar, mangoes, and the seasoning mix and process until the dressing is smooth. Stir in the caraway seeds until well distributed. Refrigerate until ready to use.

Dried Shrimp Dip

Makes almost 6 cups

Dried shrimp are available in small packages at Asian stores and some supermarkets, often near the checkout register. Maybe you've seen them before, and wondered what in the world to do with them—now you have one suggestion! The shrimp should be small, crescent-shaped fellows, less than the diameter of a dime. If your dried shrimp are larger, chop them into ¼-inch pieces before measuring. The best way to "powder" them is to grind them in an electric coffee grinder, gently shaking and turning the grinder while it's working.

This dip is a perfect complement to boiled shrimp, and I think it's great with raw vegetables, especially those with a sharp taste, like turnips, or those reminiscent of Asian cooking, such as bok choy.

Seasoning Mix

1 tablespoon ground dried Anaheim chile peppers

1 tablespoon ground dried New Mexico chile peppers

1½ teaspoons dried oregano

1 teaspoon dried basil

1 teaspoon ground dried pasilla chile peppers

¾ teaspoon ground cumin

¾ teaspoon dried thyme leaves

½ teaspoon cayenne

½ teaspoon dillweed

3 tablespoons unsalted butter
1 cup chopped onions
½ cup seeded and chopped green
    bell peppers
½ cup seeded and chopped yellow
    bell peppers
3 tablespoon seeded and minced
    fresh serrano chile peppers
¼ cup seeded and minced fresh
    jalapeño chile peppers
1 tablespoon peeled and minced fresh
    ginger
½ cup dried shrimp, powdered
    (see headnote above)
One 13.5-ounce can unsweetened coconut milk
2 tablespoons lightly packed dark brown sugar
¼ cup freshly squeezed lime juice

2 large eggs

2 cups vegetable oil

¼ cup cane syrup, or your favorite syrup, such as fruit or pure
   maple syrup (but not pancake syrup)

1 tablespoon brown mustard seeds, roasted

1. Combine the seasoning mix ingredients in a small bowl.

2. In a 10-inch skillet over high heat, melt the butter. As soon as it begins to sizzle, add the onions, bell peppers, and chile peppers. Cook, stirring every 2 to 3
minutes, until the vegetables wilt and *have a sweet rich aroma and taste* and the
edges just begin to brown, about 8 to 10 minutes. Stir in the seasoning mix, the
ginger, dried shrimp powder, and coconut milk. Bring just to a boil, reduce the
heat to low, and simmer for 8 minutes, then add the brown sugar. *Taste the mixture just before and after adding the brown sugar, and see what a tremendous difference even the 2 tablespoons can make! The sweetness takes the edge off the chile
peppers in the seasoning mix and boosts the dimensions of the sauce.* Cook, stirring
constantly, for 2 minutes, then remove from the heat and stir in the lime juice—
you'll taste just a hint of pleasant tartness now. Set aside to cool.

3. In a blender process the eggs until they are light and frothy, about 30 seconds.
With the blender running, add the vegetable oil in a thin stream until it is absorbed
and the mixture reaches the consistency of thick mayonnaise, about 30 seconds
longer. Stir in the vegetable mixture, cane syrup, and mustard seeds and process
until the ingredients are blended, about 20 seconds. Refrigerate until ready to
serve.

Four Pack
Chile Dip

Makes about 3½ cups *This is great as a dip for fresh vegetables or chips, and it's equally wonderful drizzled over sliced hard-boiled eggs and tomatoes. Or be creative and come up with your own ways to use it, and feel free to make any changes you want—then it will be truly your own recipe!*

2 large eggs
½ cup chopped onions
1 tablespoon minced fresh garlic
½ teaspoon salt
1 tablespoon ground dried Anaheim chile peppers
1 tablespoon ground dried New Mexico chile peppers
1 teaspoon ground dried árbol chile peppers
1 teaspoon ground dried guajillo chile peppers
1 tablespoon lightly packed dark brown sugar
2 tablespoons freshly squeezed lemon juice
5 tablespoons balsamic vinegar
1 tablespoon tamari
½ cup seeded and chopped green bell peppers
½ cup seeded and chopped yellow bell peppers
2 cups vegetable oil

1. In a blender, process all the ingredients together except the vegetable oil until the mixture is smooth, about 20 seconds.

2. With the blender running, slowly add the oil in a thin stream until the mixture has the consistency of a thin mayonnaise. Refrigerate until ready to serve.

Green Cheese
Vinegar Dressing

Makes 3 cups *The cheese will crumble easily if it's cold, so don't remove it from the refrigerator until you're ready to add it to the blender. This is a quick and easy recipe, and with its tangy taste it's sure to become one of your favorites—it might even inspire you to eat more fresh vegetable salads, which will make you healthy and good-looking!*

½ cup chopped onions
1 cup chopped green onions or scallions
½ cup rice vinegar
½ cup cane vinegar, or your favorite vinegar
½ cup white balsamic vinegar
¾ cup light corn syrup
½ teaspoon salt
½ cup loosely packed chopped fresh oregano leaves
2 tablespoons seeded and minced fresh jalapeño chile peppers
1 tablespoon seeded and minced fresh serrano chile peppers
4 ounces Danish blue cheese or other good quality blue cheese, crumbled

Process all the ingredients together in a blender until the mixture is smooth, about 30 seconds. Refrigerate until ready to use.

Glazed Mirlitons and Other Good Vegetables!

Makes about 2 quarts

This relish adds a zing to any full-flavored meat or poultry and keeps for several weeks if refrigerated in a tightly closed container. If you can't find mirlitons, feel free to substitute—the recipe works well with many different vegetables, especially squashes.

3 cups water

1½ cups sugar

4 cups peeled mirlitons (chayote) cut into
    ½-inch pieces

1 cup seeded and chopped red
    bell peppers

1 cup seeded and chopped yellow
    bell peppers

2 cups chopped red onions

1½ cups peeled parsnips cut into
    ¼-inch pieces

½ cup chopped celery

¼ cup seeded and chopped fresh
    poblano chile peppers

¼ cup finely chopped fire-roasted
    fresh garlic

¾ cup chopped carrots

1 cup acorn squash cut into ½-inch pieces

½ cup white balsamic vinegar

¼ cup white wine vinegar

¼ cup apple cider vinegar

1 lemon, peeled and sectioned

1 lime, peeled and sectioned

Seasoning Mix

1 teaspoon cayenne

1 teaspoon dry mustard

1 teaspoon salt

½ teaspoon ground cloves

½ teaspoon ground
    coriander

½ teaspoon garlic powder

½ teaspoon onion powder

1. Combine the seasoning mix ingredients in a small bowl.

2. In a 3-quart saucepan over high heat, bring the water, sugar, and seasoning mix to a boil, stirring constantly until the sugar is dissolved. Add the mirlitons and cook for 4 minutes, then add the bell peppers and onions. Cook for 1 minute, then add the parsnips, celery, poblano chile peppers, and roasted garlic. Cook for 2 minutes, then add the carrots and acorn squash. Cook for 4 minutes and remove from the heat. Remove the vegetables from the pot and set them aside to cool.

3. Measure the liquid remaining in the saucepan and add enough water to make 3 cups total. Return this liquid to the pan and add the remaining ingredients. Bring just to a boil, then remove from the heat and let cool. When all the vegetables are cold, combine them in a large mixing bowl, then add the liquid. Stir well but gently until combined, then refrigerate until cold before serving.

Green Tomato
Chowchow

Makes 2 quarts *This will perk up any meat, poultry, or fish, adding color and taste to your meal. Because it's so pretty, it makes a great gift. If you can't find green tomatoes at your market, ask the produce manager to order them.*

4 cups water

2 cups sugar

½ cup white wine vinegar

¼ cup white balsamic vinegar

1 tablespoon tamari

1 teaspoon dark sesame oil

1 cup seeded and chopped fresh Anaheim chile peppers

1 cup seeded and chopped fresh poblano chile peppers

1 cup seeded and chopped fresh banana peppers (also called wax peppers)

1 cup seeded and finely chopped fresh jalapeño chile peppers

2 cups chopped onions

2 cups peeled sweet potatoes cut into ½-inch cubes

4 cups green tomatoes cut into ¾-inch pieces

Seasoning Mix

2 teaspoons paprika

1½ teaspoons salt

1 teaspoon dillweed

1 teaspoon garlic powder

1 teaspoon dry mustard

¾ teaspoon dried basil

¾ teaspoon cayenne

¾ teaspoon onion powder

½ teaspoon dried oregano

½ teaspoon white pepper

1. Combine the seasoning mix in a small bowl.

2. In a 4-quart pot, combine the water, sugar, vinegars, tamari, sesame oil, and seasoning mix. Bring to a boil, stirring constantly until the sugar is dissolved. Add all the vegetables and cook until the peppers appear translucent, the sweet potatoes are cooked, and the onions are soft and translucent, about 9 minutes. Pour off the cooking liquid and measure it—you should have about 3½ cups. If you have less, add enough water to make 3½ cups; if you have more, simmer the liquid until it is reduced to 3½ cups. Return the liquid to the vegetables and refrigerate until ready to serve.

Guajillo Mayonnaise

Makes about 2 cups   *Chile peppers vary tremendously in heat, depending on many conditions, including where they were grown, the weather that year, and the season of the year. For this reason, we suggest that you make the mayonnaise with half of the guajillo, taste the mixture, then add more or not, depending on how hot it is and your own taste buds. Although we put a designated heat level on the packages of single chile peppers we market, for the time being your own taste is your best guide.*

1 large egg
1 large egg yolk
¼ teaspoon white pepper
½ teaspoon salt
1 tablespoon prepared brown mustard
1 tablespoon prepared yellow mustard
¼ cup freshly squeezed orange juice
2 tablespoons pure maple syrup (not pancake syrup)
1 tablespoon cane vinegar, or your favorite vinegar
1 to 2 tablespoons ground dried guajillo chile peppers,
    in all, to your taste
1½ cups vegetable oil

In a blender, process all the ingredients except the vegetable oil and 1 tablespoon of the guajillo chile peppers, until the mixture is smooth, about 10 to 20 seconds. With the blender running, slowly add the oil in a thin stream until the oil is completely blended and the mixture reaches the consistency of mayonnaise. Taste, then add as much of the remaining guajillo chile pepper as you wish to reach the desired heat and flavor, and process just until it's blended in. Refrigerate until ready to serve.

Mango Chowchow

Makes 2¾ cups   *What a terrific way to spice up broiled chicken, beef, or pork! You'll think you're in the tropics! You can also serve this colorful, tangy relish with chips as an appetizer. Condiments similar to this one have long been favorites in south Louisiana—always made with vinegar and sugar and whatever was fresh and good, such as corn, onions, and even figs.*

2 medium-size ripe mangoes (about 1 pound total),
    peeled, seeded, and chopped (about 1½ cups)
½ cup shallots cut into ¼-inch pieces
¼ cup seeded fresh Anaheim peppers cut into
    ¼-inch pieces
¼ cup seeded fresh jalapeño chile peppers (red
    preferably, or green) cut into ¼-inch pieces
2 tablespoons Chef Paul Prudhomme's
    Magic Pepper Sauce, or other
    medium-hot pepper sauce
3 tablespoons rice vinegar
¼ cup cane vinegar, or your favorite vinegar
½ cup loosely packed finely chopped fresh
    cilantro leaves
½ cup seeded red bell peppers cut into
    ¼-inch pieces
¼ cup seeded green bell peppers cut into
    ¼-inch pieces
½ teaspoon salt
3 tablespoons white balsamic vinegar
¼ cup cane syrup, or your favorite syrup, such
    as fruit or pure maple syrup (but not pancake
    syrup)

Combine all the ingredients in a large bowl and stir until well blended. Refrigerate for at least 4 hours, preferably overnight, before serving, and refrigerate any leftover relish.

Nutty Papaya Sauce

Makes about 5 cups *This is another recipe that was developed using my own pepper sauce, so you'll have to adjust the amount to taste if you use a different brand. Pepper sauces, just like fresh peppers, come in a wide variety of heat units (even the same species of fresh pepper can vary according to season of the year or location where it's grown), and some sauces have a very harsh flavor. The great flavor of the toasted seeds really stands out in this tangy sauce. It is spicy, but not too hot for the capsicum-challenged. Serve this sauce with any meat, poultry, or fish.*

> 2 large eggs
> 2 cups vegetable oil, in all
> 1 cup green pumpkin seeds, roasted
> 1 ripe papaya (about 1 pound), peeled, seeded, and
>   chopped (about 2 cups)
> 2 tablespoons Chef Paul Prudhomme's Magic
>   Pepper Sauce, or other medium-hot pepper
>   sauce
> 1 teaspoon salt
> 1 teaspoon ground dried árbol chile peppers
> 1 teaspoon ground dried guajillo chile peppers
> 2 tablespoons balsamic vinegar

In a blender, process the eggs until light and frothy, about 30 seconds. With the blender running, add 1 cup of the vegetable oil in a thin stream until it is incorporated and the mixture starts to look like mayonnaise. Turn off the machine and add the pumpkin seeds. Process until the mixture has a pasty consistency and the seeds are finely ground. With the blender running, add the remaining oil in a thin stream, then process until the ingredients are thoroughly combined and the mixture is smooth. Stir in the remaining ingredients and process just until combined, about 20 seconds. Refrigerate until ready to serve.

Okra and Pearl
Onion Vinaigrette

Use this okra and onion combination just as you would any relish or chutney, with any kind of meat, fish, or poultry, or add to a platter of pickled vegetables. It's terrific on a picnic or with a holiday meal and, as you can see, is quick and easy to prepare.

3 quarts water
3 cups peeled red pearl onions
3 pounds okra, ends trimmed

Vinaigrette

6 tablespoons white balsamic vinegar
6 tablespoons rice vinegar
¼ cup Chef Paul Prudhomme's Magic Pepper
  Sauce, or other medium-hot pepper sauce
¼ cup apple cider vinegar
4 teaspoons cane vinegar, or your favorite
  vinegar
1 tablespoon medium-dry sherry

Seasoning Mix

1 tablespoon salt
1 tablespoon sugar
2 teaspoons dried basil
2 teaspoons ground
  coriander
2 teaspoons garlic powder
2 teaspoons onion powder
1½ teaspoons ground ginger
1¼ teaspoons cayenne
1 teaspoon ground dried
  árbol chile peppers
¾ teaspoon black pepper

1. Combine the seasoning mix ingredients in a small bowl. In a 6-quart pot, bring the water to a boil. Add the onions and the seasoning mix. Cook, stirring frequently, for 3 minutes, then add the okra. Cover and cook for 5 minutes. Remove from the heat, drain the vegetables, and let cool.

2. Combine the vinaigrette ingredients, then stir to blend thoroughly. Combine the vegetables with the vinaigrette. Refrigerate for at least 4 hours, preferably overnight, before serving, and refrigerate any leftovers.

Sean's Coconut
Dipping Sauce

Makes about 3½ cups *Okay, I have to admit this recipe is not really based on anything traditional to south Louisiana, except the technique for making mayonnaise, which we can't claim as ours alone. But egg rolls, spring rolls, and other fried wrapped foods are just as popular here as they are anywhere in the country, so we developed this piquant sauce to serve with them.*

1 cup plus 2 tablespoons vegetable oil, in all
½ cup minced onions
1 teaspoon peeled and minced fresh ginger
One 13.5-ounce can coconut milk, in all
2 teaspoons sugar
2 teaspoons freshly squeezed lime juice
1 large egg
½ cup sweetened shredded coconut

Seasoning Mix

1 teaspoon ground cardamom

1 teaspoon salt

1 teaspoon turmeric

½ teaspoon ground allspice

½ teaspoon cayenne

½ teaspoon ground cinnamon

½ teaspoon black pepper

¼ teaspoon ground coriander

1. Combine the seasoning mix ingredients in a small bowl.

2. In a 10-inch skillet over high heat, heat 2 tablespoons of the vegetable oil just until it is hot but not smoking, about 2½ to 3 minutes. Whisk in the seasoning mix, then add the onions and ginger. Cook, stirring constantly, for 3 minutes, then stir in 1 cup of the coconut milk, the sugar, and the lime juice. Bring just to a boil, reduce the heat to medium, and simmer briskly for 7 minutes. Remove from the heat and set aside to cool to room temperature.

3. In a blender, process the egg until light and frothy, about 30 seconds. With the blender running, add the remaining 1 cup vegetable oil in a thin stream and process just until it is absorbed and the mixture reaches the consistency of mayonnaise. Add the onion mixture and the remaining coconut milk and process for 15 seconds to combine. Stir in the shredded coconut until it is evenly distributed. Transfer to a bowl and refrigerate until ready to serve.

Sour Cream and
Pepper Jack Dressing

It's a little peppery, Jack, but it's great!

3 tablespoons Chef Paul Prudhomme's Magic Pepper Sauce, or other
    medium-hot pepper sauce
One 8-ounce container sour cream
¼ cup cane vinegar, or other semi-sweet vinegar
2 tablespoons red wine vinegar
2 tablespoons freshly squeezed lemon juice
3 ounces Pepper Jack cheese, freshly grated
½ cup seeded and chopped red bell peppers
2 tablespoons seeded and minced fresh jalapeño chile peppers
3 tablespoons orange blossom honey, or your favorite honey
½ teaspoon salt
1 teaspoon ground dried pasilla chile peppers

Process all the ingredients in a blender until the mixture is smooth, about
30 seconds. Refrigerate until ready to serve.

Spinach Sauce for Seafood

Makes 4 cups   *Tangy and piquant, this sauce is great with all types of seafood, especially raw shellfish, such as oysters and clams.*

2 tablespoons olive oil

2 tablespoons fresh fennel leaves (stems removed), chopped

½ cup finely chopped shallots

1 ripe papaya, peeled, seeded, and chopped (about 2 cups)

One 10-ounce package fresh spinach, stemmed and torn into pieces

2 tablespoons honey

2 tablespoons cane vinegar, or your favorite vinegar

2 tablespoons cider vinegar

Seasoning Mix

1½ teaspoons salt

1 teaspoon dried basil

1 teaspoon dry mustard

1 teaspoon onion powder

1 teaspoon paprika

1 teaspoon ground dried Anaheim chile peppers

1 teaspoon ground dried chipotle chile peppers

½ teaspoon ground fennel seeds

½ teaspoon dried oregano

1. Combine the seasoning mix ingredients in a small bowl.

2. In a 10-inch skillet over high heat, heat the olive oil just until it begins to smoke, about 3 to 4 minutes. Add the fennel and immediately remove the skillet from the heat. Add the shallots and the seasoning mix and stir constantly until the mixture darkens, about 2 minutes.

3. Transfer the mixture from the skillet to a food processor, add the papaya, and process until smooth. Add the spinach, a handful at a time, and process just until combined. Don't worry if the spinach won't mix in at first. Just turn off the appliance, push the spinach down into the mixture with a spatula, pulse at low speed for a few seconds, push some more spinach down, and so forth, until it's all combined. Add the honey and vinegars and process until smooth. Refrigerate until ready to serve.

Sweet and Sour
Barbecue Sauce

Makes 2 cups   *We developed this great barbecue sauce specifically for the Slow-Roasted Baby Back Pork Ribs (page 166), but it's a traditional, delicious recipe that will enhance just about anything you put it on, including your fingers! It has all the usual good stuff you expect in a barbecue sauce—tomato, brown sugar, vinegar, and smoke flavoring—plus the added zip of ancho chile peppers and my own Magic Pepper Sauce.*

One 15-ounce can tomato sauce
1 cup chicken stock
½ cup lightly packed dark brown sugar
¼ cup cane vinegar, or your favorite vinegar
¼ cup balsamic vinegar
1 tablespoon Chef Paul Prudhomme's
    Magic Pepper Sauce, or other
    medium-hot pepper sauce
1 tablespoon Worcestershire sauce
2 teaspoons bottled liquid smoke flavoring

Seasoning Mix

1¼ teaspoons onion powder

1¼ teaspoons ground dried ancho chile peppers

1¼ teaspoons salt

¾ teaspoon garlic powder

¾ teaspoon dry mustard

¾ teaspoon dried thyme leaves

¼ teaspoon black pepper

¼ teaspoon white pepper

1. Combine the seasoning mix ingredients in a small bowl.

2. In a 12-inch nonstick skillet over high heat, combine the seasoning mix and the remaining ingredients. Bring just to a boil, whisking constantly, then reduce the heat to medium and simmer briskly, whisking every 1 to 2 minutes, until the sauce thickens and resembles a thin ketchup, about 20 to 25 minutes. Remove from the heat and serve with our Slow-Roasted Baby Back Ribs or with your favorite barbecued meat or poultry, or just eat it with a spoon! Refrigerate any leftover (ha ha!) sauce.

Beef, Lamb, Pork, and Veal

Because I grew up on a farm, we always had meat, though it might not have been of the very highest quality—that was usually sold to pay for the other things we needed. But my mother could turn the least piece of meat into something great by her cooking methods and her innovative use of seasonings. And you know what? Even a top-quality cut of meat can be improved by proper cooking and creative seasoning. Many of the ingredients that weren't available when I was a youngster but are readily available now, such as portobello mushrooms and a wide variety of chile peppers, add an incredible amount of flavor to meat.

Beef in a Four-by-Four Chile Cream

Makes about 8 cups; 4 servings

We had plenty of eggplants in our garden when I was growing up, but we never heard of fennel or kohlrabi. Once introduced to these vegetables, though, it didn't take us long to figure out a few dozen different ways to enjoy them. The rich, creamy sauce enhanced with all the chile peppers—both dried and fresh— definitely makes you sit up and take notice!

One 18-ounce boneless sirloin steak,
    ¾ to 1 inch thick
3 tablespoons plus 1 teaspoon olive oil, in all
½ cup heavy cream
½ cup sour cream
½ cup plain yogurt
4 ounces cream cheese, cut into cubes and
    softened
1½ cups chopped onions, in all
1 cup chopped fennel bulb
3 tablespoons unsalted butter
¼ cup seeded and finely chopped fresh
    Anaheim chile peppers
¼ cup seeded and finely chopped fresh banana
    peppers (also called wax peppers)
¼ cup seeded and finely chopped fresh
    poblano chile peppers
¼ cup seeded and finely chopped fresh
    jalapeño chile peppers
2 cups peeled kohlrabi cut into ½-inch pieces
1 teaspoon ground dried chipotle chile peppers
1 tablespoon ground dried New Mexico chile
    peppers
2 cups beef stock
3 cups peeled eggplant cut into ½-inch pieces

Seasoning Mix

2 teaspoons salt
1¾ teaspoons paprika
1½ teaspoons onion powder
1 teaspoon dried basil
1 teaspoon cayenne
1 teaspoon garlic powder
1 teaspoon dry mustard
¾ teaspoon ground cumin
¾ teaspoon white pepper
¾ teaspoon dried thyme
    leaves
½ teaspoon black pepper

1. Combine the seasoning mix ingredients in a small bowl.

2. Brush the steak lightly on each side with ½ teaspoon of the olive oil. Sprinkle each side of the steak evenly with ¾ teaspoon of the seasoning mix and gently pat it in.

3. Heat a heavy 10-inch skillet, preferably nonstick, over high heat until it is very hot, about 5 to 6 minutes. Put the steak in the hot skillet. Cook, turning once, until the steak is browned on the outside but still very rare in the center, about 3 to 4 minutes per side. Remember that stoves differ tremendously in the amount of heat they produce, so watch the meat, not the clock! Transfer the steak to a cutting board and, as soon as it's cool enough to handle comfortably, cut it into medallions and set aside.

4. In a blender, process the heavy cream, sour cream, yogurt, and cream cheese just until smooth, about 30 seconds to 1 minute. Set aside.

5. Place the remaining 3 tablespoons olive oil in a 5-quart saucepan over high heat until the oil just begins to smoke, about 3 to 4 minutes. Add the onions and fennel and stir well. Cover and cook, uncovering to stir after 3 minutes, just until the onions begin to brown at the edges, *when they'll have a slightly sweet taste,* about 5 to 6 minutes. Uncover and add the butter and 2 tablespoons of the seasoning mix. Stir well, re-cover, and cook for 4 minutes, then uncover and add the fresh chile peppers, kohlrabi, ground chile peppers, and the remaining seasoning mix. Re-cover and cook, stirring occasionally, until the mixture begins to stick lightly to the bottom of the pot, about 4 to 6 minutes. Uncover, *taste the rich "brown" sweetness of the vegetables,* and add the stock. Scrape the bottom of the pan well. Re-cover and cook for 7 more minutes, *when the onions will be well caramelized and very sweet,* then uncover and whisk in the eggplant and the cheese-and-cream mixture. Cook uncovered, whisking frequently, for 6 more minutes. *Notice that the eggplant is crisp and slightly sharp-tasting at first, reminiscent of a melon that's not quite ripe, then softens and becomes more mellow-tasting as it cooks.*

6. Stir in the beef medallions and any accumulated juices. Bring to a full boil and cook until the meat is cooked through and the kohlrabi is tender and cooked all the way through. To determine if the kohlrabi is thoroughly cooked, remove a piece and cut it in half—it should be semi-transparent all the way through. This last step will take about 5 to 7 minutes longer. Serve with rice or pasta.

Bronzed Steak with
Mashed Sweet Potatoes

Makes 4 servings *Bronzing is similar to blackening and has the advantage of being doable indoors. For best results, have the meat at room temperature. If you have a big black cast-iron skillet, by all means use it, but you can bronze food in any sturdy pan that's big enough to hold the food. Chances are your steaks aren't going to fit in 1 skillet at the same time, so you'll want to either cook 2 and keep them warm during the short time it takes to cook the second pair, or have 2 skillets going at the same time. By the way, the taste of the vinegar tends to become more noticeable if the potatoes are reheated, so I encourage your guests to clean their plates!*

5 large sweet potatoes (about 10 ounces each)
¼ cup plus 1 tablespoon olive oil, in all
1 cup chopped onions
1 cup chopped fennel bulb
¼ cup rice vinegar
4 tablespoons (½ stick) unsalted butter
Four 14-ounce boneless sirloin steaks,
　½ to ¾ inch thick, or use your favorite
　cut of steak

Seasoning Mix

1 tablespoon salt
2 teaspoons paprika
1½ teaspoons garlic powder
1½ teaspoons onion powder
1½ teaspoons cayenne
1½ teaspoons ground cumin
1½ teaspoons dry mustard
1 teaspoon dill seeds
¾ teaspoon black pepper
½ teaspoon white pepper

1. Combine the seasoning mix ingredients in a small bowl.

2. Preheat the oven to 350°F.

3. Prick each potato with a fork, then bake until they are cooked through and soft, about 1 hour.

4. While the potatoes are baking, prepare the vegetables. In a heavy 10-inch skillet, preferably nonstick, heat ¼ cup of the olive oil over high heat just until it begins to smoke, about

3 to 4 minutes. Add the onions, fennel, and 2 tablespoons plus 2¾ teaspoons of the seasoning mix. Cook, stirring frequently, until the vegetables are a rich coppery brown, about 8 to 12 minutes. Add the vinegar and scrape the bottom of the skillet thoroughly, loosening all the brown bits sticking to the bottom of the skillet. *You can taste the dark sweetness of the caramelized onions and a little bit of bitterness from the vinegar, as well as saltiness from the seasoning mix.* Add the butter and continue to cook, stirring constantly, until the butter is melted and incorporated, about 3 minutes. Remove from the heat and set aside.

5. As soon as the potatoes are cooked, peel them and transfer to a food processor. Add the reserved vegetables and process until the potatoes are smooth and the vegetables are puréed, about 2 minutes. *The potatoes finish with a pleasant onion flavor* and a beautiful butterscotch color. Keep them warm while you bronze the steaks.

6. Brush the steaks lightly with the remaining 1 tablespoon olive oil. Sprinkle each steak evenly with ¾ teaspoon of the seasoning mix per side.

7. Heat a large heavy skillet until it is very hot, about 5 to 6 minutes. Put the steaks into the hot skillet and cook, turning once, until they are brown on the outside but still rare in the center, about 4 to 5 minutes per side (or cook as you prefer). Serve immediately, dividing the sweet potatoes among the plates.

Bronzed Steak Enchiladas with New Mexico Pepper Sauce

Makes 12 enchiladas; 4 servings

The name of this dish— starting off as it does with Bronzed Steak—gives you a hint that these are not going to be your average fast-food enchiladas! You will recognize the flavors, from the cumin in the seasoning mix to the roasted garlic, as being authentic Southwest, yet the method of preparation is straight out of south Louisiana. As lagniappe, the wonderful sour cream mixture makes a great dip for crackers or chips! And because nothing in it depends upon the main recipe, you can make it independently, whenever you want to serve something a little different and special to your guests.

Seasoning Mix

2½ teaspoons salt

2 teaspoons ground dried New Mexico chile peppers

1¼ teaspoons ground cumin

1 teaspoon dried oregano

1 teaspoon ground coriander

1 teaspoon garlic powder

¾ teaspoon onion powder

½ teaspoon cayenne

½ teaspoon white pepper

½ teaspoon black pepper

Flank Steak

1 pound flank steak
1 tablespoon olive oil

New Mexico Pepper Sauce

2 cup chopped onions
1 cup seeded and chopped green bell peppers
1 cup seeded and chopped yellow bell peppers
4 cups beef stock, in all
2 tablespoons minced fire-roasted garlic
¼ cup seeded and chopped fresh Anaheim
    chile peppers, or any mild chiles, such as
    poblanos or banana (also called wax) peppers
¼ cup seeded and chopped fresh red
    (preferably, or green) jalapeño chile peppers
2 tablespoons tomato paste
One 8-ounce can tomato sauce

Sour Cream Mixture

> One 16-ounce container sour cream
> 1 cup freshly grated Monterey Jack cheese
> Juice of 1 lime (about 2 tablespoons)
> ½ cup seeded chopped fresh red (preferably, or green) jalapeño chile peppers
> 2 tablespoons loosely packed minced fresh basil leaves
> 1 tablespoon loosely packed minced fresh thyme leaves

Assembly

> ¼ cup vegetable oil
> Twelve 5½-inch-diameter corn tortillas
> 6 ounces freshly grated Cheddar cheese

1. Combine the seasoning mix ingredients in a small bowl.

2. Place the piece of flank steak on a large plate or sheet pan and season the meat evenly on both sides with 1 tablespoon plus 1 teaspoon of the seasoning mix. Press the sides and edges of the meat into the seasoning that is left on the plate so that all parts of the meat are evenly covered.

3. Heat the olive oil in a 10-inch skillet over high heat just until the oil is about to smoke, about 3 to 4 minutes. Place the seasoned flank steak in the skillet and cook until the meat is bronzed on both sides, about 2 to 3 minutes per side. If you see blue smoke during this time, lower the heat immediately. Transfer the steak from the skillet to a plate or sheet pan set and set it aside to cool.

4. Make the sauce: To the hot skillet add the onions, both colors of bell peppers, and 2 tablespoons of the seasoning mix. Stir well, then add ½ cup of the stock and scrape up all the brown bits on the bottom of the skillet. Cook, stirring frequently, until the vegetables fade in color, about 8 to 9 minutes. Add 1 cup of the stock, the roasted garlic, and the Anaheim and jalapeño peppers. *At this point, the first taste is salt and pepper, followed by a brown gravy flavor combined with garlic and cumin. The finishing taste is a rising heat from the chiles, centered in the front of the mouth and on the lips.*

5. Continue to cook, stirring frequently, until the moisture is almost evaporated, about 9 minutes—you will know that you have reached this point when you scrape the bottom and do not see liquid. Stir in the tomato paste until it is absorbed, checking the bottom of the skillet frequently to keep the mixture from

burning. Continue to cook, stirring constantly, for 2 minutes, then add 1 cup of the stock and scrape the sides and bottom of the pan. Add the tomato sauce and continue to cook, stirring frequently, until the liquid in the mixture barely covers the vegetables and bubbles briskly, making little volcanoes. Remove the mixture from the heat and purée in a food processor. You should have about 3½ cups.

6. Return the purée to the skillet over high heat and whisk in the remaining ½ cup stock. Bring the sauce just to a simmer, then reduce the heat to medium and cook, whisking the sauce every time the bubbles begin to splatter, until the bubbling is constant, about 5 minutes. Remove from the heat.

7. When the meat is cool enough to handle, cut into scallops.

8. Make the sour cream mixture: Combine the sour cream, Monterey Jack cheese, lime juice, jalapeños, basil, thyme, and the remaining seasoning mix in a large bowl, folding the ingredients together with a spatula until evenly blended.

9. Prepare the tortillas: In a small skillet over high heat, heat the vegetable oil to 300°F (use a frying/candy thermometer and adjust the heat as necessary to keep the oil at the correct temperature), about 3 minutes. Place each tortilla in the oil, turning it quickly, so it is just warmed and softened, without becoming crisp—this should take about 8 to 10 seconds for each tortilla. Drain the tortillas on paper towels.

10. Preheat the oven to 350°F.

11. Spread 1 tablespoon of sauce evenly over each tortilla. Divide the meat among the tortillas, placing the scallops down the middle of each tortilla, then place 2 tablespoons of the sour cream mixture on top of the meat. Roll up the tortilla. Repeat this process until all the tortillas are filled.

12. Place 3 tortilla rolls on each of 4 ovenproof plates. Pour ¾ cup of the sauce over each group of tortillas and sprinkle the Cheddar cheese evenly over the portions. Place the plates in the oven and bake until the cheese is melted and bubbly, about 20 minutes. You can also turn this recipe into a casserole if you prefer—just place all the filled tortilla rolls in a 9 × 13-inch baking pan, add the sauce and cheese, and bake. Serve immediately.

Bayou Teche

Potato Pirogues

Pirogues are the boats, each carved or burned from a single tree trunk in a technique learned from the Native Americans, used by the Cajuns of south Louisiana for almost 250 years. They were an important part of life on the bayous and swamps, vital for fishing, and, later, as men had leisure, for racing. Now we sometimes use the word to describe a carved-out vegetable shell that holds individual portions of a dish. Any leftover stew will keep very well, but it will thicken somewhat after refrigeration, so you'll want to add a little stock before reheating it.

3 large baking potatoes (about 10 ounces each)
¼ cup olive oil, plus an additional 2
    tablespoons if you're going to bake the
    potato pirogues, in all
Vegetable oil for frying if you're going to fry
    the skins
1 pound beef stew meat, trimmed of fat and
    cut into ¾-inch pieces
1 medium-size onion, cut into 1-inch pieces
    (about 2 cups), in all
2 cups celery cut into ½-inch pieces, in all
6 tablespoons seeded and finely chopped fresh
    poblano chile peppers, in all
6 tablespoons seeded and finely chopped
    fresh Anaheim chile peppers (or your
    favorite mild chile peppers), in all
3 cups beef stock, in all
¾ cup carrots cut into ½-inch pieces
1½ cups mushrooms cut into ½-inch pieces

Seasoning Mix

1 tablespoon salt

1¾ teaspoons paprika

1¼ teaspoons onion powder

1 teaspoon dried thyme
    leaves

¾ teaspoon dried basil

¾ teaspoon ground
    coriander

¾ teaspoon garlic powder

¾ teaspoon dry mustard

¾ teaspoon black pepper

½ teaspoon cayenne

½ teaspoon ground cumin

½ teaspoon white pepper

¼ teaspoon ground
    cinnamon

continued

1. Combine the seasoning mix ingredients in a small bowl.

2. Preheat the oven to 350°F.

3. Prick each potato with a fork, then bake until the potatoes are almost tender, about 45 minutes. When they are cool enough to handle, cut each in half lengthwise. Scoop the meat out of each half shell, leaving enough potato meat adhering to the shell so that the potato "pirogues" are about ¼ inch thick. Chop the potato meat for use in the stew; you should have about 3 cups.

4. Now decide if you want to bake or fry the potato skins to prepare them to hold the stew. If you're going to bake them, combine 2 tablespoons of the olive oil and 2½ teaspoons of the seasoning mix in a small bowl and mix well. Brush the insides of the potato pirogues with the seasoned oil, place them on a baking sheet, and bake, turning them over after 20 minutes, until the shells are crisp, about 40 minutes in all. To fry the pirogues, omit the olive oil. Pour enough vegetable oil into a deep fryer to measure 4 inches deep and heat it to 350°F. If necessary, use a cooking thermometer and adjust the heat to keep the oil as close to 350°F as possible. An electric skillet also works great. Carefully lower the skins into the hot oil, in batches if necessary to avoid crowding. Fry until the skins are tinged with a rich brown, about 4 to 5 minutes. During the frying process, push the skins down into the hot oil with tongs, as they have a tendency to float. When done, remove with tongs, drain on paper towels, and sprinkle them evenly with the 2½ teaspoons of the seasoning mix. Set the skins aside. While the skins are baking, or after frying them, prepare the stew.

5. Sprinkle the meat evenly with 1 tablespoon of the seasoning mix and work it in with your hands. In a 5-quart pot, heat the remaining ¼ cup olive oil over high heat just until it begins to smoke, about 3 to 4 minutes. Add the meat and spread it evenly across the bottom of the pot. Let it cook for 2 minutes without stirring, which allows the meat to release some of its fat and helps prevent sticking. Now stir the meat well, turning it over, then cook just until it loses its raw look, about 2 more minutes. Transfer the meat to a bowl with a slotted spoon, pressing it against the side of the pot as you remove it in order to leave as much juice as possible in the pot. Set it aside.

6. To the same pot add 1 cup of the onion, 1½ cups of the celery, 3 tablespoons each of the 2 chile peppers, and 2 tablespoons of the seasoning mix. Stir well and cook, stirring frequently, until the vegetables are dark brown with a rich aroma and the bottom of the pot is covered with dark brown particles. During this process, the vegetables will become shiny *with a deep flavor from the seasoning.* As the liquid from the vegetables evaporates, check the bottom frequently and

scrape it well as the particles on the bottom darken. *The secret to this recipe is to let these particles become very dark brown, but not burned, with an intense flavor. You will need to watch this process closely and scrape frequently because you have to get close to the burning stage to get the best flavor. If any juices accumulate from the meat in the bowl, add them to the pot and let them reduce as well—they will add even more flavor to the stew.* As soon as this stage is reached, about 5 to 7 minutes—but watch the pot, not the clock—add 1 cup of the reserved potato meat and immediately mash it down. The starch from the potatoes will begin to brown on the bottom of the pot almost immediately. Scrape the bottom until anything that sticks is loosened. Notice that it comes off layer by layer as you scrape. Turn the pot as you scrape to ensure that you scrape evenly, and be sure to scrape up any rough areas completely, or they will surely burn. Stir until the mixture is well combined. Continue to scrape and stir, deglazing with ½ cup of the stock if necessary to prevent burning, until the potatoes are sticking heavily and the glaze on the bottom of the pot is a rich brown as you scrape it up, about 6 to 8 minutes.

7. Add 1½ cups of stock and scrape the bottom of the pot until all the material sticking to the bottom is dissolved. The mixture should have a rich brown color. Add 1½ cups of the reserved potato meat, the remaining stock, the reserved meat, and the remaining 1 teaspoon seasoning mix. Cover and bring just to a boil, then reduce the heat to medium, uncover and simmer for 10 minutes. Add the remaining onions, the carrots, the remaining ½ cup celery, the remaining 3 tablespoons of each chile pepper, and the mushrooms and simmer until the meat is tender, about 10 to 15 minutes longer. *At this stage, the mixture will have an intense "brown" flavor, slightly salty, with a subtle finishing taste of cinnamon. As the stew finishes cooking, taste again and enjoy the flavors of the mushrooms and potatoes as they blend into the liquid.* Whisk in the remaining ½ cup potato meat and remove from the heat.

8. Fill each pirogue with 1¼ cups of the stew, letting it overflow onto the plate, and serve immediately.

Calf's Liver with
Fire-Roasted Pepper Sauce

Makes 4 servings   *Even people who usually don't care for liver are going to love this! The liver itself should be a beautiful golden brown color, and the sauce is punctuated with colorful and delicious fire-roasted bell peppers. You can use all one color of bell pepper, but I think the combination of the three looks great.*

Four 6- to 8-ounce slices fresh calf's liver,
   about ¼ inch thick
1¼ cups all-purpose flour, in all
4 tablespoons vegetable oil, in all
2 cups beef stock
1 medium-size onion, fire-roasted and
   chopped
½ red bell pepper, roasted and chopped
½ yellow bell pepper, roasted and chopped
½ green bell pepper, roasted and chopped
1 head garlic, fire-roasted and finely
   chopped

Seasoning Mix
2½ teaspoons salt
2 teaspoons paprika
1 teaspoon garlic powder
1 teaspoon onion powder
1 teaspoon dry mustard
1 teaspoon ground dried Anaheim chile peppers
1 teaspoon ground dried New Mexico chile peppers
¾ teaspoon cayenne
½ teaspoon black pepper
¼ teaspoon white pepper

1. Combine the seasoning mix ingredients in a small bowl.

2. Trim off any fatty pieces and tubular-shaped ducts from the liver. Sprinkle the meat evenly with 1 tablespoon plus 2 teaspoons of the seasoning mix and gently pat it in.

3. Combine 1 cup of the flour with 1 tablespoon plus 1 teaspoon of the seasoning mix and place in a shallow pan.

4. In a 12-inch cast-iron skillet, heat 2 tablespoons of the vegetable oil until very hot, about 4 minutes. Dredge the meat, 1 or 2 slices at a time, in the seasoned flour, gently shake off any excess, and transfer to the frying pan. Fry the liver, turning once, until it is a rich golden or light nut-brown, about 3 minutes in all. Remove the liver slices from the skillet as they're cooked and keep warm while you fry the remaining slices.

5. After all the liver is cooked, add the remaining 2 tablespoons vegetable oil and the remaining ¼ cup flour to the same skillet and cook, whisking constantly, until the roux is a rich red-brown, about 8 minutes. Stir in the stock, the remaining seasoning mix, and the roasted vegetables. Bring just to a boil, whisking constantly, then reduce the heat to medium and simmer briskly, whisking every 4 to 5 minutes, until the sauce is thick and smooth, about 15 minutes.

6. To serve, drizzle each slice of liver with some of the sauce and pass the remainder separately.

Roasted Oxtails
with Vegetables

Makes 4 servings

Oxtails may not be available all the time where you shop, but your butcher will probably be happy to order them for you. Ask him to find some nice meaty ones, and when you see them, choose the ones with the greatest amount of meat on them.

8 oxtails (about 6 pounds)
4 cups beef stock, in all
2 medium-size carrots, cut diagonally
    into 1-inch pieces
1 medium-size fennel bulb, cut into
    1-inch pieces
½ medium-size head cabbage, cored and
    cut into 4 wedges
4 parsnips, peeled and cut into
    1-inch pieces
2 large leeks (tough green leaves removed),
    washed well and cut into 1-inch pieces
2 medium-size white potatoes, peeled
    and cut into 1-inch pieces
6 cloves fresh garlic, peeled

Seasoning Mix

1 tablespoon plus
    2 teaspoons salt

2½ teaspoons onion powder

2½ teaspoons paprika

1¾ teaspoons garlic powder

1¼ teaspoons ground
    coriander

1¼ teaspoons ground cumin

1¼ teaspoons black pepper

1 teaspoon dry mustard

1 teaspoon white pepper

1. Combine the seasoning mix ingredients in a small bowl.

2. Preheat the oven to 250°F.

3. Place the oxtails in a baking pan large enough to hold the oxtails and the vegetables. Sprinkle all surfaces of the oxtails evenly but not thickly with 3 tablespoons of the seasoning mix—depending on the size of the tails, you may need a little more or a little less of the seasoning mix. With a spatula or your hands, press the seasoning mix in lightly.

4. Place the pan in the oven and allow the oxtails to cook for 1 hour, then add 2 cups of the stock to the pan and cook for 30 minutes longer. Add 2 cups of the stock and the remaining seasoning mix to the pan. Scrape the bottom of the pan, loosening any brown bits. Cover (aluminum foil works well if your roasting pan doesn't have its own cover) and return to the oven. Cook until the oxtails are tender and the meat easily pulls away from the bones, which may take from 2 to 2½ hours, depending on the size of the oxtails. When the meat is done, remove it from the pan and set aside. Spread the vegetables in the bottom of the pan, stirring gently to make sure they are coated with the pan juices. Increase the oven temperature to 350°F, re-cover the pan, and cook until the vegetables are done, about 1 to 1¼ hours. (After 1 hour return the meat to the pan.)

5. Serve 2 oxtails per person with a portion of the vegetables and pass the pan juice separately.

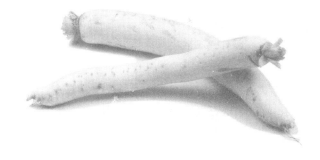

Slow-Seared Rib Eye
with Hot Granny Sauce

Makes 4 servings   *It's important to have the steaks at room temperature, for otherwise the surface will burn long before the interior is cooked. If you're like me, you prefer your meat rare, but raw is something else. Whatever degree of doneness you like, the crust should be very dark brown, varying from a dark tan at the edges to an almost black crust in spots. We talk about the color of the smoke coming from the skillet because to the practiced eye, the color is a great indicator of how steaks are cooking. Blue smoke means burning, which is why we say to turn the steaks as soon as the smoke is blue-gray. This is an excellent method for cooking thick steaks that are usually reserved for the barbecue.*

Four 1-inch-thick rib-eye steak (about 1 pound each), at room temperature
¼ cup olive oil

Hot Granny Sauce

8 tablespoons (1 stick) unsalted butter
1 cup chopped onions
½ cup seeded and finely chopped fresh jalapeño chile peppers
2 cups sliced mushrooms
¼ cup finely chopped green onions or scallions
1 tablespoon Worcestershire sauce
¼ cup beef stock

Seasoning Mix

2¾ teaspoons salt

2½ teaspoons paprika

1¾ teaspoons garlic powder

1¾ teaspoons onion powder

1¼ teaspoons dry mustard

1¼ teaspoons black pepper

1¼ teaspoons ground dried
   New Mexico chile peppers

1 teaspoon white pepper

½ teaspoon ground ginger

1. Combine the seasoning mix ingredients in a small bowl.

2. Make the sauce: Melt the butter in a 12-inch nonstick skillet over high heat. As soon as the butter melts and begins to sizzle, add the onions, jalapeños, and 2 teaspoons of the seasoning mix. Stir well and cook, stirring frequently, until the onions are slightly translucent, about 6 to 8 minutes. Add the mushrooms and green onions and stir well, then add the Worcestershire and stock. Bring to a full boil, stirring constantly, and cook for 1 minute. Remove from the heat and keep warm while you prepare the steaks.

3. Preheat the oven to 250°F. Place an ovenproof serving platter in the oven to warm.

4. Brush each side of each steak with ½ teaspoon of the olive oil (4 teaspoons total). Sprinkle each steak evenly on one side only with 1½ teaspoons of the seasoning mix.

5. Heat the remaining olive oil in a 12-inch nonstick skillet (don't use an iron skillet for this recipe) over high heat. As soon as the oil begins to smoke, add 2 of the steaks, seasoned side down. Sprinkle the top side of each steak with 1½ teaspoons of the seasoning mix. At 2 minutes you'll notice that the smoke coming from the pan will be darker and bluish gray in color. Reduce the heat to medium and cook until the cooked line on the side of the steak is about ¼ inch high, about 2 minutes. Turn the steaks and cook for 5 minutes, then turn and cook until the steaks are cooked to your preference, from 2 to 6 minutes longer.

6. Place the cooked steaks on the platter in the oven and repeat the process for the remaining 2 steaks. Divide the sauce among the portions and serve to some very lucky people.

Short Ribs and Vegetables
with an Asian Touch

Makes 8 servings

There are 3 parts to this dish, but when you have them completed, you have a complete meal for 8—meat, vegetables, and starch. Some of my assistants say they would like to have the Parsnip Pancakes for breakfast or a light lunch all by themselves.

8 beef short ribs (about 6 pounds), each about
    5 × 2½ × 1½ inches
4 to 5 cups beef stock, in all
1 daikon, about 12 inches long, peeled and
    cut diagonally into 1-inch pieces
5 stalks celery, cut diagonally into
    1-inch pieces
5 medium-size carrots, cut diagonally into
    1-inch pieces
1 medium-sized rutabaga, peeled and cut
    into 1-inch pieces
2 medium-size onions, cut into
    1-inch pieces
12 cloves fresh garlic, peeled
6 cups Swiss chard leaves (or spinach or
    other flavorful greens) stems removed and
    torn into 1-inch pieces

Parsnip Pancakes

½ cup chopped onions
½ cup plus 2 tablespoons beef, chicken, or
    vegetable stock
4 tablespoons medium-dry sherry, in all
2 tablespoons rice vinegar
2 tablespoons unsalted butter
½ cup corn flour

Seasoning Mix

1 tablespoon plus
    2 teaspoons sugar

1 tablespoon plus 1 teaspoon
    salt

2½ teaspoons ground
    fenugreek

2 teaspoons ground turmeric

1½ teaspoons ground anise

1½ teaspoons ground
    coriander

1½ teaspoons onion powder

1½ teaspoons ground dried
    chipotle chile peppers

1 teaspoon ground
    cinnamon

1 teaspoon dillweed

1 teaspoon dry mustard

1 teaspoon ground nutmeg

1 teaspoon ground dried
    New Mexico chile peppers

*Chef Paul Prudhomme's
    Louisiana Tastes*

½ cup all-purpose flour

2½ teaspoons baking powder

1 tablespoon plus 1 teaspoon lightly packed
    dark brown sugar

1 cup peeled parsnips cut into ¼-inch cubes

Vegetable oil spray (optional)

1. Combine the seasoning mix ingredients in a small bowl. Reserve 2½ teaspoons of the mix for the parsnip pancakes.

2. Preheat the oven to 250°F.

3. Place the ribs in a baking pan large enough to hold the ribs and the vegetables. Sprinkle all the surfaces of the ribs evenly but not thickly with a total of 4 table-spoons of the seasoning mix—depending on the size of the ribs, you may need a little more or a little less seasoning. With a spatula or your hands, lightly press the seasoning mix into the meat. Turn the ribs so that the bone side is down, then place the pan in the oven. The ribs will cook very slowly until they are tender, which should take about 3 hours. Allow the ribs to cook for 1 hour, then add 2 cups of the stock to the pan and cook for 30 minutes longer.

4. Remove the pan from the oven, remove the ribs from the roasting pan, and set them on a plate or baking sheet. Add 2 cups of the stock and 2 tablespoons of the seasoning mix to the roasting pan. Scrape the bottom of the pan, loosening any brown bits. Add the vegetables to the roasting pan, spreading them evenly and turning them so that they are coated with the seasoned liquid. Place the ribs on top of the vegetables, cover (aluminum foil works well if your roasting pan doesn't have a cover), and return to the oven. Cook for 1 hour, then increase the oven temperature to 350°F and continue to roast until the ribs are tender and the vegetables are cooked through, about 30 minutes longer. Check the pan during the cooking process and add up to 1 cup more stock if too much evaporates—you should have about 2½ cups of liquid in the pan.

5. Make the Parsnip Pancakes: In a 10-inch skillet over high heat, combine the onions, ½ cup of the stock, and 1½ teaspoons of the seasoning mix. Stir well and bring to a simmer. Cook until the onions are translucent, about 3 minutes. *The onions still have some of their raw, acidic flavor. The liquid is salty, with a strong hit of curry in the middle taste and a mildly peppery finish.* Add 2 tablespoons of the sherry and the rice vinegar. Return to a full simmer, then add the butter. As soon as the butter melts completely, stir well and remove from the heat.

6. Combine the corn flour, all-purpose flour, baking powder, and brown sugar in a food processor. Process briefly until the dry ingredients are combined. Add the

onion mixture, the remaining 2 tablespoons sherry, 1 teaspoon of the seasoning mix, and the remaining 2 tablespoons stock. Process until the batter is smooth, about 30 seconds. Add the parsnips and pulse briefly 2 or 3 times, until the parsnips are just mixed in but still whole.

7. Heat a 12-inch nonstick skillet over high heat until it is hot, about 3 minutes. Drop 1 tablespoon of batter into the pan to make a small pancake. Cook, turning several times, until the pancakes are brown on both sides, about 4 to 5 minutes, removing them to a plate; keep warm. If the pancakes darken too quickly, reduce the heat. Spray the pan with a little vegetable oil if the pancakes stick.

8. Serve 1 rib per person with a portion of the vegetables and the parsnip pancakes. Pass the pan juice separately, if desired.

Grilled Flank Steak

Makes 6 to 8 generous servings

Everybody knows how to grill a steak, right? Sure, but this dry rub, which really permeates the meat overnight in the refrigerator, makes the result something very special—perfect for a holiday or a really important day. And cutting the meat into scallops makes every bite tender and delicious, different from anything I tasted growing up. In the unlikely event you have leftovers, this makes fabulous sandwiches.

One 2-pound flank steak

1. Combine the seasoning mix ingredients in a small bowl.

2. Sprinkle the steak evenly with 2½ teaspoons of the seasoning mix for each pound of meat, then rub it in well. Discard any leftover seasoning mix or save it for another use. Wrap the steak in plastic wrap and refrigerate it overnight.

3. Preheat a charcoal or gas grill until the coals are very hot. The grilling surface should be about 5 inches from the coals.

4. Cook the steak on the grill, turning once, until the meat is seared on the outside but still rare (125°F on an instant-read meat thermometer) inside, about 6 minutes per side. If, after the 12 minutes are up, the meat has not reached at least 125°F, continue cooking, checking the temperature often and turning the steak one more time, until the steak is cooked. If one end of the steak is a bit thinner than the rest, place that portion away from the hottest coals so it doesn't overcook. To serve, slice into thin scallops, then get out of the way!

Seasoning Mix

1 tablespoon plus 1 teaspoon salt

1½ teaspoons paprika

1¼ teaspoons dry mustard

1 teaspoon onion powder

1 teaspoon ground dried guajillo chile peppers

¾ teaspoon cayenne

¾ teaspoon garlic powder

½ teaspoon ground cardamom

½ teaspoon ground cloves

Stuffed Sirloin
Tip Roast

Makes 8 servings

It's very important to use a meat thermometer with this roast, because if you let it cook too long, it will be tough, and you surely don't want to ruin a wonderful piece of meat. The carefully balanced seasonings permeate the meat and give it a unique flavor that will make you want to prepare this again and again. The reason we call for brown rice flour in the sauce is that it adds a great taste, in addition to the thickening that any flour will accomplish.

2 tablespoons vegetable oil
1½ cups chopped onions
¾ cup seeded and chopped green bell peppers
¾ cup seeded and chopped red bell peppers
¾ cup seeded and chopped yellow bell peppers
¼ cup peeled and very thinly sliced fresh ginger
½ cup loosely packed fresh fennel leaves (use only the tiny leaves that resemble dill)
1½ cups beef stock, in all
2 teaspoons lightly packed dark brown sugar
1 sirloin tip roast (3 to 3½ pounds)
¼ cup brown rice flour, preferably, or all-purpose flour

Seasoning Mix
2 teaspoons salt
1¼ teaspoons ground dried New Mexico chile peppers
1 teaspoon ground coriander
1 teaspoon garlic powder
1 teaspoon paprika
¾ teaspoon cayenne
¾ teaspoon dried chervil
¾ teaspoon ground cumin
¾ teaspoon onion powder
¾ teaspoon ground dried árbol chile peppers
½ teaspoon ground ginger
½ teaspoon ground mace
½ teaspoon black pepper
¼ teaspoon ground allspice
¼ teaspoon white pepper

1. Combine the seasoning mix ingredients in a small bowl.

2. Preheat a heavy 12-inch skillet over high heat until very hot, about 3 to 4 minutes. Add the vegetable oil, onions, and all the bell peppers. Cook, stirring every 3 to 4 minutes, until the vegetables wilt and begin to brown, about 8 minutes. Stir in the seasoning mix, fresh ginger, and fennel leaves. Cook, stirring and scraping almost constantly, until the mixture sticks hard, about 3 minutes, then add ½ cup of the stock. Continue to stir and scrape until the liquid almost evaporates and the mixture is pasty, about 5 minutes. Remove from the heat and stir in the brown sugar. *The first taste is the seasoning and brown flavors; the seasoning level is very high, especially the ginger and salt, but that's okay because it will be dispersed into the meat. Next comes the sweetness of caramelized vegetables, then a powerful building of the fresh ginger, and the finish is a lingering heat in the front of the mouth.*

3. Preheat the oven to 200°F.

4. With a boning knife, make a series of pockets in the top of the meat, about ¾ inch apart. To make the pockets, insert the knife until it is about three fourths of the way through the roast; then, without enlarging the opening, move the knife back and forth to create pockets. Spoon as much of the stuffing as possible into the pockets. If you have stuffing left over, spread ¼ cup on the top of the roast, and put any additional stuffing underneath the roast in the pan.

5. Roast for 30 minutes, then add the remaining 1 cup stock to the pan. Roast until rare, or until the internal temperature reaches 125°F, about 2 to 3 hours, depending upon the weight of the roast. Remove from the oven and let rest while you make the sauce.

6. Make the sauce: Transfer the pan drippings and all the brown bits from the bottom of the roasting pan to a 10-inch skillet over high heat. Whisk in the flour and bring the mixture just to a boil, whisking constantly. As soon as the mixture thickens, remove it from the heat.

7. To serve, slice the roast into 8 portions, drizzle some of the sauce over it, and pass the remaining sauce separately.

Steak Shawn with
a Granger Gravy

This is the kind of steak and gravy Grandma always made when she could find really good beef!

½ cup all-purpose flour, in all
Four 4-ounce filet mignon steaks
¼ cup vegetable oil
1 large onion, halved lengthwise, then sliced
    into very thin half rounds
2 cups beef stock
1 tablespoon lightly packed dark brown
    sugar
4 tablespoons (½ stick) unsalted butter,
    melted

Seasoning Mix

2¼ teaspoons salt

1¾ teaspoons paprika

1¼ teaspoons onion powder

1 teaspoon ground dried
    Anaheim chile peppers

1 teaspoon black pepper

1 teaspoon garlic powder

¾ teaspoon ground dried
    árbol chile peppers

¾ teaspoon ground cumin

¾ teaspoon white pepper

½ teaspoon dry mustard

1. Combine the seasoning mix ingredients in a small bowl.

2. In another small bowl, combine ¼ cup of the flour with 1 tablespoon plus 2 teaspoons of the seasoning mix and mix well.

3. Sprinkle each side of each steak evenly with 1½ teaspoons of the seasoned flour and pound the steaks with a meat mallet until they are ¼ inch thick. Turn the filets several times as you pound so that the seasoned flour is worked into both sides. You can do the pounding between sheets of waxed paper or in a heavy-duty plastic bag. Set the filets aside.

4. Heat the vegetable oil in a 12-inch skillet over high heat until the oil begins to smoke, about 4 to 5 minutes. Add the remaining ¼ cup flour and whisk constantly until the roux is the color of *café au lait*, about 2 to 3 minutes. Watch the roux closely to be sure it doesn't burn; if that happens, it would be bitter and you'd have to throw it out and start all over. Add the onion and about half the remaining seasoning mix. Continue to whisk constantly until the onion is wilted

down and the roux is a dark caramel brown, about 4 to 8 minutes. Whisk in the stock and brown sugar. Bring to a boil, whisking constantly, and cook until the gravy thickens to the desired consistency, about 4 to 5 minutes. Taste and, if desired, add some or all of the remaining seasoning mix, to taste. Remove from the heat and keep warm while cooking the steaks. Makes about 2 cups gravy.

5. Preheat the oven to 250°F and place an ovenproof serving platter in it.

6. Place a large skillet, nonstick if possible, over high heat until very hot, about 3 to 4 minutes. Cook the steaks 1 or 2 at a time, allowing 1 tablespoon of melted butter per steak. Place the butter in the hot skillet, then the steak(s). Cook until both sides of the filets are golden brown, about 1½ to 2 minutes per side. Place the cooked steaks on the hot platter in the oven. Repeat the process until all the steaks are cooked. Serve 1 steak per person with ½ cup of the gravy.

Lamb Chops in a Black Iron Skillet
with Jalapeño Mint Jelly

Makes 4 servings   *Lamb and mint jelly—nothing new here, you may say. Oh, but there is! Our seasoning mix is unlike the usual combination used on lamb chops or roast, and our jalapeño mint jelly is something to write home about. If you have any jelly left over, you'll find it a wonderful accompaniment for roast or grilled chicken, pork, or other meat, and a dollop melted over cooked carrots makes them mighty tempting!*

Jalapeño Mint Jelly (Makes about 2½ cups)

> 1½ cups water
> 1½ cups sugar
> One ¼-ounce package unflavored gelatin
> ¼ cup seeded and finely chopped fresh
>   jalapeño peppers
> 1 teaspoon pure vanilla extract
> ½ cup finely chopped fresh mint leaves

* * * * *

> 8 lamb loin chops, ½ to ¾ inch thick (about
>   2 pounds total)

1. Make the jelly first: Place the water, sugar, and gelatin in a small saucepan, stir to combine, and bring to a boil over high heat, whisking frequently to dissolve the sugar and gelatin. Reduce the heat to low and add the jalapeños. Simmer for 5 minutes, remove from the heat, and stir in the vanilla and mint leaves. Transfer to a small container and refrigerate until set.

2. Combine the seasoning mix ingredients in a small bowl.

3. Sprinkle the lamb chops evenly with 2 tablespoons plus 2 teaspoons of the seasoning mix and rub it in well. Preheat

Seasoning Mix
2 teaspoons salt
1 teaspoon dried basil
1 teaspoon ground ginger
1 teaspoon paprika
¾ teaspoon ground cumin
¾ teaspoon garlic powder
¾ teaspoon onion powder
½ teaspoon cayenne
½ teaspoon dried oregano
¼ teaspoon black pepper
¼ teaspoon white pepper

Chef Paul Prudhomme's
Louisiana Tastes

a large cast-iron skillet over high heat until it is extremely hot, about 8 to 10 minutes. Cook the lamb chops, turning once, until they are seared on both sides, but still rare inside, about 3 to 4 minutes per side. Serve at once, each portion accompanied by 2 tablespoons of the jalapeño mint jelly. Refrigerate any leftover jelly.

Lamb Jambalaya

Makes 5 main-dish or 10 appetizer servings   *Jambalaya is supposed to assertive, so we want the peppers in the seasoning mix to make a strong statement. Because of all the rice, though, the dish is not too spicy for all but the faintest of heart! My assistants tell me it's a great alternative to seafood and chicken jambalaya. Add a crisp green salad and some hot bread and you have a wonderful, healthful dinner.*

2 tablespoons vegetable oil
2 cups chopped onions
1 cup chopped celery
¾ cup seeded and chopped green bell peppers
¾ cup seeded and chopped red bell peppers
¾ cup seeded and chopped yellow bell peppers
½ pound andouille or your favorite smoked pork sausages, quartered lengthwise, then cut into ½-inch pieces
1 pound lamb sirloin, cut into ½-inch cubes
1 tablespoon seeded and minced fresh jalapeño chile peppers
1 tablespoon minced fresh garlic
1 tablespoon peeled and minced fresh ginger
2 cups uncooked Converted rice
4 cups beef stock, preferably, or chicken stock

Seasoning Mix

2 teaspoons salt
1 teaspoon ground cumin
1 teaspoon dillweed
1 teaspoon garlic powder
1 teaspoon onion powder
1 teaspoon paprika
¾ teaspoon dry mustard
¾ teaspoon ground dried ancho chile peppers
¾ teaspoon dried thyme leaves
½ teaspoon cayenne
½ teaspoon ground dried pasilla chile peppers
¼ teaspoon black pepper
¼ teaspoon white pepper

1. Combine the seasoning mix ingredients in a small bowl.

2. In a 4-quart pot, heat the vegetable oil over high heat just until it begins to smoke, about 3 to 4 minutes. Add the

onions, celery, and all the bell peppers and cook, stirring every 1 or 2 minutes, for 10 minutes. Now the vegetables are shiny; the bell peppers are bright, and the onions are a light tan with a few brown spots. Add the andouille and 1 tablespoon plus 2 teaspoons of the seasoning mix. Cook, stirring and scraping up the brown bits on the bottom of the pot every 2 minutes, until the andouille is well browned, about 10 minutes. If necessary to prevent scorching, reduce the heat a little or add a little stock and deglaze the pot. Now the bell peppers are faded and slightly dark and the onions are a rich oak brown. *The bell peppers' taste rises in the middle, then fades to salt in the finish, while the onions are gently sweet.*

3. Push the vegetables and sausage to one side and add the lamb. Stir the lamb and let it brown slightly, about 4 minutes, then mix it in with the vegetables and sausage and add the remaining seasoning mix. Continue to stir and scrape the pot for 4 more minutes—the mixture will be dark and begin to stick—then add the jalapeños, garlic, ginger, and rice. Stir thorougly to combine, then add all the stock. Scrape the bottom of the pot until all the browned bits are dissolved, and if you reduced the heat earlier, return it to high. Cover and bring just to a boil, reduce the heat to low, stir once, then re-cover and simmer without stirring until the rice is tender and the liquid is absorbed, about 25 minutes. Remove from the heat and let sit, covered, for 10 minutes before serving.

Lamb Stew
with Greens

Makes 6 servings   *In many ways, this beautiful stew is a traditional recipe; goodness knows similar dishes have been prepared for centuries in Louisiana and other sheep-raising areas of the world. While the onions, greens, and celery may be familiar stew ingredients, we also use yucca, introduced by our Hispanic friends, which adds a unique taste and texture. Yucca is strong-flavored, but so is lamb, and I think they work great together. The cayenne and chipotle really punch up the seasoning mix, and the brown sugar, added close to the end, brings just a touch of sweetness, barely perceptible, to the dish. Ummmmm!*

2 pounds boneless (or 3 pounds bone-in) lamb
   stew meat, cut into bite-size pieces
4 cups green onions or scallions cut into
   2-inch lengths
4 cups beef stock, in all
3 large bunches mustard greens, washed well,
   stemmed, and torn into 1-inch pieces
   (about 5 quarts)
2 cups carrots cut into ½-inch pieces
2 cups peeled yucca root cut into
   ½-inch pieces
2 cups chopped celery
2 tablespoons lightly packed light
   brown sugar

Seasoning Mix

2¼ teaspoons salt

1¾ teaspoons ground
   coriander

1¼ teaspoons onion powder

1¼ teaspoons garlic powder

1¼ teaspoons dried tarragon

1 teaspoon dried thyme
   leaves

1 teaspoon cayenne

¾ teaspoon dry mustard

¾ teaspoon ground cumin

¾ teaspoon ground allspice

½ teaspoon ground dried
   chipotle chile peppers

1. Combine the seasoning mix ingredients in a small bowl.

2. Sprinkle the lamb evenly with 2 tablespoons of the seasoning mix and rub it in well.

3. Preheat a heavy 4-quart nonstick pot over high heat until very hot, about 4 minutes. Cook the lamb in a single layer without crowding, in 2 batches if necessary, turning with tongs, until the meat is browned on all sides. Remove the meat from the pot and set it aside.

4. To the same pot add the green onions, ½ cup of the stock, and the mustard greens. Cover and cook, stirring every 2 or 3 minutes, until the greens have wilted, about 10 minutes. During this stage, if it's necessary to prevent scorching, reduce the heat a little or add a little more stock. Add the carrots, yucca root, celery, 2 cups of the stock, and 1 tablespoon seasoning mix. Re-cover and cook, uncovering to stir every 4 or 5 minutes, for 10 minutes. *At this point the broth is very salty, but this high level of salt is necessary to balance the large amount of greens in the recipe. The other seasonings are more apparent in the later part of the taste but are fairly mild because of the overwhelming taste of the salt. Most outstanding of the herbs is the tarragon, infusing the broth, greens, and yucca with its anise flavor.* Reduce the heat to medium, then uncover and add the lamb and the accumulated juices, the brown sugar, the remaining stock, and the remaining seasoning mix. Simmer, uncovered, stirring and scraping every 5 or 6 minutes, until the lamb is cooked through and tender and the liquid is thickened, about 30 minutes. Serve about 1½ cups of the stew per person, over hot rice.

Marinated
Lamb Chops

Makes 2 servings   *Unless you like to wield a long knife, ask your butcher to cut the rack into chops for you—just be sure you get the fat cap. These chops are great cooked in a big skillet, and they're fantastic cooked on a grill! By the way, there is enough seasoning mix to cook these chops twice, so prepare enough lamb for 4 people, or save the leftover seasoning mix for another time.*

When you marinate, you exchange the moisture in the meat with the liquid of the marinade. Some foods need to be tenderized, so you marinate them longer, allowing the acid to break down the fibers. If you're simply adding flavor, then a shorter marinating time is better.

One 8-rib rack of lamb, cut into French-cut
  chops, fat cap reserved
1 cup chopped onions
½ cup chopped celery
½ cup cane vinegar, or your favorite vinegar
½ cup mirin (sweet rice wine)
1 teaspoon dark sesame oil
2 tablespoons Chef Paul Prudhomme's
  Magic Pepper Sauce, or other
  medium-hot pepper sauce
2 tablespoons vegetable oil

Seasoning Mix

1 teaspoon salt
¾ teaspoon ground
  coriander
¾ teaspoon dry mustard
¾ teaspoon paprika
½ teaspoon ground
  cardamom
½ teaspoon ground cumin
½ teaspoon garlic powder
½ teaspoon onion powder
½ teaspoon ground dried
  chipotle chile peppers
¼ teaspoon cayenne
¼ teaspoon ground
  cinnamon
¼ teaspoon ground nutmeg
¼ teaspoon black pepper
¼ teaspoon ground star
  anise
¼ teaspoon white pepper

1. Combine the seasoning mix ingredients in a small bowl.

2. Place the lamb chops in a casserole dish just large enough to hold them in a single layer

3. Finely dice 6 ounces of the fat cap and place in a 12-inch nonstick skillet over high heat. Cook the diced fat, stirring frequently, until the bits are browned and have rendered their fat, about 6 minutes. I call these little brown bits "lamb yummies," and although they are definitely not health food, they are indeed delicious. I cannot think of a more perfect example of the essential flavor of lamb. Add the onion and celery and cook, stirring every 2 minutes, *until the vegetables develop a sweet brown fragrance and taste*, about 10 minutes. Remove the skillet from the heat and stir in the cane vinegar, rice wine, sesame oil, and pepper sauce. Stir and scrape thoroughly, let sit for 5 minutes, then strain the liquid over the lamb chops. Set aside and allow to marinate for 2 hours at room temperature, turning the chops several times. The acid in the vinegar will protect the meat during this short time. *If you taste this marinade, you'll notice an intense vinegar and sweetness, as well as the complex and rather Asian flavors that appear once your tongue becomes accustomed to the acid in the vinegar. When the chops are cooked, the acid flavor will diminish, leaving a rich bouquet of flavors and fragrance.* Remove the chops from the marinade and sprinkle them evenly with 2 tablespoons of the seasoning mix.

4. In a 12-inch nonstick skillet, heat the vegetable oil over high heat just until it begins to smoke, about 3 to 4 minutes. Cook the chops, turning once, until they are a dark crusty brown on the outside, but still rare in the middle, about 2 to 3 minutes per side. Serve immediately.

Roasted Lamb with
Fire-Roasted Pepper Sauce

Makes 6 servings *Our official cookbook tasters deemed this lamb roast "absolutely divine," so I hope it takes you to heavenly heights of flavor ecstasy! The rosemary leaves are essential to the seasoning, but if it's too difficult for you to crush them, you can chop them in a small coffee grinder for just a couple of seconds—the result will be very much the same.*

You can find many kinds of roasted vegetables in jars at the supermarket, though probably not fennel, which you'll probably have to roast yourself.

1¼ cups chopped roasted onions, in all
½ cup plus 1 tablespoon chopped roasted green
    bell peppers, in all
¼ cup plus 1 tablespoon chopped roasted red
    bell peppers, in all
¼ cup plus 1 tablespoon chopped roasted
    yellow bell peppers, in all
1 cup plus 2 tablespoons chopped roasted
    fennel bulb, in all
3 tablespoons minced roasted garlic, in all
2 tablespoons lightly packed light brown sugar
One 4- to 5-pound leg of lamb
¼ cup cane syrup, or your favorite syrup (fruit
    or pure maple syrup)
¼ cup seeded and minced fresh jalapeño
    chile peppers
½ teaspoon salt
1 tablespoon cornstarch dissolved in
    ¼ cup water
2 cups beef or chicken stock

Seasoning Mix

2 tablespoons dried rosemary
    leaves, crushed before
    measuring

2 teaspoons salt

1½ teaspoons paprika

1 teaspoon dried basil

1 teaspoon cayenne

1 teaspoon ground
    cinnamon

1 teaspoon garlic powder

1 teaspoon dried mint

1 teaspoon dry mustard

¾ teaspoon onion powder

½ teaspoon black pepper

¼ teaspoon white pepper

1. Combine the seasoning mix ingredients in a small bowl.

2. Preheat the oven to 250°F.

3. To make the stuffing, combine ¼ cup of the roasted onions, 1 tablespoon of each color roasted bell peppers, ¼ cup plus 2 tablespoons of the roasted fennel, the roasted garlic, brown sugar, and 2 tablespoons of the seasoning mix in a small bowl and set aside.

4. Cut a series of pockets, about ¾ inch long at the opening, 2 inches deep, and ¾ of an inch apart on the skin side of the leg of lamb. Sprinkle the lamb with the remaining seasoning mix, coating all the sides evenly and working some of the seasoning into the pockets. Fill the pockets with as much stuffing as possible and spread the remaining stuffing evenly over the top of the lamb.

5. Insert a meat thermometer into the thickest part of the lamb and place the lamb in a roasting pan—no rack is necessary—and cook, checking the temperature after 2 hours, then again after 3 hours, until the internal temperature of the meat reaches 160°F, about 4 hours. The lamb will be medium rare at the center. Remove the lamb from the pan and let it sit while you make the sauce.

6. To make the sauce, scrape all the brown bits and juices from the roasting pan into a heavy 2-quart saucepan over high heat. Add the remaining roasted onions, bell peppers, and fennel, plus the cane syrup, jalapeño peppers, salt, dissolved cornstarch, and stock to the pan and, whisking constantly, bring just to a boil. Reduce the heat to low and simmer just until the sauce thickens. Remove from the heat.

7. Slice the roast, drizzle some of the sauce over each serving, and pass the remaining sauce separately.

Stellar Lamb
Pouches

Makes 8 servings

Notice that the first ingredient, after the herbs and spices, is lamb bones and fat trimmings. If you buy a large piece of meat, you can trim these off yourself, but if you buy stew meat, already packaged, ask the butcher for extra bones and the trimmings for the stock, which is really important for the final rich taste of the filling. If you plan to serve these pouches with our delicious relish and dipping sauce, you might want to make them ahead so they'll be ready.

Wonton wrappers come in both circles and squares, so when you fold them after filling, you'll form either semi-circles or triangles.

½ pound, or more, lamb bones and fat
    trimmings
3 quarts water
¾ pound boneless lamb stew meat
½ cup peeled white potatoes cut into
    ¼-inch cubes
½ cup peeled parsnips cut into ½-inch pieces
1 cup chopped onions
¾ cup peeled mirliton (chayote) cut into
    ½-inch pieces
¼ pound fresh spinach, washed well and
    stemmed (about 8 cups)
Vegetable oil for frying
48 wonton wrappers

Seasoning Mix

1 teaspoon salt

¾ teaspoon ground dried
    Anaheim chile peppers

¾ teaspoon dried cilantro

½ teaspoon ground cumin

½ teaspoon onion powder

½ teaspoon dried oregano

¼ teaspoon dried basil

¼ teaspoon garlic powder

¼ teaspoon ground dried
    ancho chile peppers

¼ teaspoon ground dried
    árbol chile peppers

¼ teaspoon ground dried
    New Mexico chile peppers

¼ teaspoon ground
    cinnamon

¼ teaspoon cayenne

¼ teaspoon ground nutmeg

1. Combine the seasoning mix ingredients in a small bowl.

2. Make a rich lamb stock: Place the lamb bones and trimmings and water a 6-quart pot over high heat. Bring to a

boil, reduce the heat to low, and simmer until the liquid is reduced to 6 cups, about 2 hours. Strain the stock and place it in a large pot. Set aside.

3. Sprinkle the lamb meat evenly with 1 tablespoon plus 1 teaspoon of the seasoning mix and rub it in.

4. Preheat a heavy 10- or 12-inch skillet over high heat until very hot, about 4 minutes. Add the lamb and cook, turning once, until it is a rich medium brown with patches of darker brown, about 8 minutes. Remove the meat from the skillet and set it aside.

5. To the pot of stock, add the browned lamb, potatoes, parsnips, onions, mirliton, and spinach and place it over high heat. Cover and bring to a full boil—when you see little wisps of steam escaping from under the lid, you know the liquid is boiling—then reduce the heat to medium-high. Cook, uncovering to stir every 15 minutes, until the liquid thickens and the mixture just begins to stick to the bottom of the pot, about 2 hours. Reduce the heat to low, remove the cover, and cook, scraping the bottom of the pot every 10 minutes, until the meat is very tender and pulls apart easily, about 30 minutes. Remove from the heat.

6. When cool enough to handle, remove the lamb from the pot and shred it. Transfer the vegetables to a mixing bowl and thoroughly mash them with a potato masher, then combine them with the shredded lamb and the remaining seasoning mix. Stir until well blended.

7. In a 10- or 12-inch electric skillet, pour enough vegetable oil to measure 2 inches deep and heat it to 350°F, or use a cooking thermometer with a regular skillet and adjust the heat so that the oil stays as close to 350°F as possible.

8. Wonton wrappers can dry out if left uncovered, so keep a slightly moistened cloth towel handy to cover them when you're not working with them. On a hard surface, peel off several wonton wrappers from the package stack and spread them out before you. Place 1 tablespoon of the vegetable-lamb filling in the center of each wrapper. Fold the wrapper over the filling and seal the edges by pressing them together with your fingers. Repeat for the remaining wontons.

9. Fry the wonton pouches in the hot oil until they are golden and crispy and the edges are just beginning to brown, about 3 minutes. Remove with a slotted spoon and drain on paper towels. Serve with Mango Chowchow (page 92) and Green Cheese Vinegar Dressing (page 87).

Lamb Cakes with Roasted Fennel and Olive Sauce

Makes 32 patties; 4 main-course or 8 appetizer servings

These tender patties, with their dramatic sauce, can open a meal with a flourish or make a solid contribution when served as a main course. Most of the time I like to make a sauce with some of the signature ingredients used with the meat. This time, though, I explored a new direction for the sauce, combining fire-roasted fennel bulb and pan-roasted fennel seeds with olives and other good things.

When you roast the fennel bulb, be sure that you roast it long enough so that it is fully cooked on the inside. If, when you start to chop the bulb, you find that it's not fully cooked, roast the pieces again until they're really cooked, not just browned on the surface.

4 cups peeled white potatoes cut into
    1-inch cubes
6 tablespoons (⅜ cup) heavy cream
1 cup plus 3 tablespoons lamb stock, preferably,
    or beef or chicken stock, in all
3 tablespoons unsalted butter
8 cloves garlic, fire-roasted and peeled
2 tablespoons olive oil
2 cups chopped onions
1 cup chopped celery
¼ cup seeded and minced fresh poblano chile
    peppers
¼ cup seeded and minced fresh banana
    peppers (also called wax peppers)
1 tablespoon seeded and minced fresh serrano
    chile peppers

Seasoning Mix

1 tablespoon salt

2¼ teaspoons ground cinnamon

2¼ teaspoons ground nutmeg

2¼ teaspoons onion powder

1½ teaspoons garlic powder

1½ teaspoons paprika

1½ teaspoons ground dried Anaheim chile peppers

1 teaspoon cayenne

1 teaspoon ground dried guajillo chile peppers

1 teaspoon ground star anise

¾ teaspoon ground cloves

¾ teaspoon black pepper

¼ teaspoon white pepper

2 tablespoons peeled and minced fresh ginger
2 teaspoons minced fresh garlic
2 cups peeled and minced parsnips
2 pounds freshly ground lamb
2 tablespoons vegetable oil
Roasted Fennel and Olive Sauce (recipe follows)

1. Combine the seasoning mix ingredients in a small bowl.

2. Place the cubed potatoes in a 2-quart saucepan and add enough water to cover them. Cover, bring to a boil, reduce the heat to medium, and simmer briskly until the potatoes are just tender, about 10 minutes. Drain and discard the cooking water and place the potatoes in a large bowl. Add the heavy cream, 3 tablespoons of the stock, the butter, the roasted garlic, and 2 tablespoons of the seasoning mix. Mash thoroughly with a potato masher and set aside.

3. In a heavy 10-inch nonstick skillet, heat the olive oil over high heat just until it begins to smoke, about 3 to 4 minutes. Add the onions, celery, all the peppers, the ginger, minced garlic, and parsnips. Cook, stirring every minute or so, until the vegetables begin to brown, about 8 minutes. Stir in the remaining seasoning mix and the remaining 1 cup stock. Cook, stirring and scraping the bottom of the skillet frequently, until the mixture begins to stick hard and turns dark brown, about 5 minutes, then remove from the heat. *The vegetables are seasoned to an extreme degree, overwhelming all the other tastes. The anise flavor of the fennel rises in the middle taste, then fades rapidly, leaving a strong aromatic heat from the peppers.*

4. Combine the lamb, the vegetable mixture, and the potato mixture in a large bowl and mix well. Shape the mixture into patties, using about ¼ cup per patty, and refrigerate until very cold. These are very tender patties (there's no binder such as egg) and chilling helps keep them together while they're cooking. In fact, you may wish to slip them into the freezer for a few minutes just before frying.

5. In a heavy 10-inch skillet over high heat, heat the vegetable oil just until it begins to smoke, about 3 to 4 minutes. Fry the patties in batches, carefully turning once, until browned on both sides, about 4 minutes per side. Serve 8 patties with a generous ¾ cup of Roasted Fennel and Olive Sauce as a main course, or halve those amounts for appetizer servings.

continued

Roasted Fennel
and Olive Sauce

Makes 4 cups

2 tablespoons olive oil
1 cup chopped fire-roasted fennel bulb
½ cup chopped shallots
¼ cup seeded and chopped green bell peppers
¼ cup chopped celery
2 tablespoons ground dried Anaheim chile peppers
2 tablespoons seeded and minced fresh jalapeño chile peppers
1 tablespoon minced fire-roasted garlic
3 tablespoons all-purpose flour
3½ cups lamb stock, preferably, or beef or chicken stock
2 tablespoons honey
1 tablespoon fennel seeds, roasted
¼ cup minced pitted green olives
¼ cup minced pitted black olives

1. In a heavy 10-inch nonstick skillet, heat the olive oil over high heat just until it begins to smoke, about 3 to 4 minutes. Add the roasted fennel, shallots, bell peppers, celery, chile peppers, and roasted garlic. Cook, stirring every minute or so, until the vegetables begin to brown, about 10 minutes.

2. Stir in the flour until the white is no longer visible, then stir in ½ cup of the stock. Cook, stirring and scraping constantly, just until the mixture begins to stick, about 2 minutes, then stir in the remaining 3 cups stock. Bring to a boil, reduce the heat to low, and simmer, stirring every 2 minutes, for 8 minutes. Transfer the mixture to a food processor or blender and purée. Return the puréed mixture to the skillet and bring just to a simmer over medium-low heat, then stir in the honey, roasted fennel seeds, and all the olives. Remove from the heat and serve with the lamb patties.

Andouille Shepherd's Pie

Makes 8 generous servings *Who doesn't like shepherd's pie? If you find people who say, "I don't," let 'em taste just a few bites of this version, and they'll probably beg for more! You can use a food processor with a julienne disk—if it's very sharp—to save time when preparing the vegetables. Buy 1 large red bell pepper and 1 large yellow bell pepper, and use half of each for the julienne strips and the other half for the chopped peppers.*

6 cups peeled white potatoes cut into
   ½-inch cubes (about 6 pounds)
2 quarts water
1 cup heavy cream
10 tablespoons (1¼ sticks) unsalted butter,
   in all
1 teaspoon salt
½ pound andouille, or your favorite smoked
   sausage
½ cup onions cut into julienne strips
½ cup carrots cut into julienne strips
½ cup seeded red bell peppers cut into julienne
   strips
½ cup seeded yellow bell peppers cut into
   julienne strips
½ cup seeded and chopped red bell peppers
½ cup seeded and chopped yellow bell peppers
½ cup seeded and chopped green bell peppers
1 cup chopped onions
¾ cup chopped celery
1 tablespoon finely chopped fresh garlic
2 tablespoons Chef Paul Prudhomme's
   Magic Pepper Sauce, or other
   medium-hot pepper sauce
One 12-ounce can evaporated milk
2 large eggs, lightly beaten
1½ pounds ground beef
1 cup unseasoned dried bread crumbs

Seasoning Mix

1 tablespoon plus
   ¾ teaspoon salt
2¾ teaspoons paprika
2 teaspoons garlic powder
1¾ teaspoons cayenne
1¾ teaspoons ground ginger
1¾ teaspoons dry mustard
1½ teaspoons black pepper
1 teaspoon onion powder
1 teaspoon white pepper

139

continued

1. Combine the seasoning mix ingredients in a small bowl. Bring the potatoes to a boil with the water and boil until tender, about 30 minutes. In a large bowl, mash the potatoes with the heavy cream, 6 tablespoons of the butter, 2¼ teaspoons of the seasoning mix, and the salt. Cover the mashed potatoes and set them aside. Resist the temptation to eat the potatoes right now! *They're rich and tasty, with a light gold color and a pleasant light seasoning level.*

2. Coarsely grind the andouille in a food processor or meat grinder and set it aside.

3. Combine all the julienne strips of onions, carrots, and red and yellow bell peppers, and season them with 1 tablespoon of the seasoning mix. Set aside.

4. In a 10-inch skillet, melt the remaining 4 tablespoons butter over high heat. When the butter begins to sizzle, add all the chopped vegetables—the three colors of bell peppers, the onions, celery, and garlic—and 2 tablespoons of the seasoning mix. Cook, almost constantly stirring and scraping the bottom of the skillet to loosen the brown bits, until the vegetables begin to brown, about 6 to 7 minutes. Stir in the pepper sauce and continue to cook and stir for 2 more minutes. *Wow! The flavor now is hot but sweet.* The vegetables are just barely crunchy and losing their brightness. Add the evaporated milk and eggs and stir rapidly until they are fully combined.

5. Continue to cook, stirring frequently, until the mixture thickens, bubbles constantly, and is a beautiful yellow-gold color, about 4 to 5 minutes. *Now the sweetness comes forward; the heat follows and lingers briefly. This mixture's dominant taste is that of a well-seasoned omelet, with a richly seasoned vegetable "filling."* Refrigerate until cold.

6. Combine the ground andouille, ground beef, bread crumbs, and 2 tablespoons of the seasoning mix in a large bowl. Mix with a sturdy spatula, using a downward, chopping stroke to help distribute the meat and bread crumbs without overmixing the meat (which would release too much of the protein in the meat and make it mushy after cooking). When the ingredients appear to be fairly evenly mixed, fold in the chilled vegetable mixture, again being careful not to overmix.

7. Preheat the oven to 325°F.

8. Spread the mixture in the bottom of a 13 × 10 × 2-inch-deep casserole. Spread the julienne vegetable strips evenly over the meat, then, using a large tip on a pastry bag, pipe the mashed potatoes over all. If you don't have a pastry bag, use

Left:

Crab Claws Vinaigrette with
Fire-Roasted Mayonnaise
(page 2)

Below:

Crabmeat au Gratin (page 4)

Opposite, top to bottom:
Crawfish-Stuffed Mushrooms (page 6), *Onion Tarts* (page 18), and *Duck Boudin with Cream Sauce* (page 12)

Left:
Jambon Glacé (page 16)

Below:
Shrimp Chowchow and Mixed Vegetables (page 24)

Opposite:

*Bronzed Black Drum Salad
with Creamy Vinaigrette*
(page 60)

Right, clockwise from top:
Turkey Poblano Gumbo
(page 52), *Shrimp Mango
Bisque* (page 37), and
Potato, Leek, and Tasso Soup
(page 48)

Below:
Spinach Salad (page 76) and
Corn and Andouille Soup
(page 40)

Right:
Fruit Salad with Poppy Seed Dressing (page 64)

Below:
Cheesy Jalapeño Skillet Corn Bread (page 282) and *Crab and Sweet Potato Soup* (page 42)

Left:

Olive Salad Pasta Salad

(page 68)

Below:

Bayou Teche Potato Pirogues

(page 107)

Opposite, clockwise from bottom:
Okra and Pearl Onion Vinaigrette
(page 94), *Mango Chowchow*
(page 92), and *Green Tomato*
Chowchow (page 90)

Above:
Bronzed Steak Enchiladas
with New Mexico Pepper
Sauce (page 104) and
Four Pack Chile Dip
(page 86)

Left:
Banana Corn Fritters
(page 278) and *Calf's Liver*
with Fire-Roasted Pepper
Sauce (page 110)

Right:
*Slow-Seared Rib Eye with
Hot Granny Sauce* (page 114)

Below:
Roasted Oxtails with Vegetables
(page 112)

Left:

Lamb Stew with Greens (page 128)

Below:

*Lamb Chops in a Black Iron Skillet
with Jalapeño Mint Jelly* (page 124)
and *Fluffy Fried Vegetables* (page 288)

Opposite:
Yam-n-Ham! (page 164)

Right:
Pork Roast with Bay Leaves
(page 158) and
Golden Egg and Potato Salad
(page 66)

Below, from left:
Best Country Chicken Pie
(page 178) and
Andouille Shepherd's Pie
(page 139)

Right:
Veal Cutlets with Enoki Mushroom Sauce
(page 174) and
Stuffed Acorn Squash
(page 264)

Below:
Chicken with a Green and White Taste (page 186) and
Green Tomatoes with Stilton Cheese (page 290)

Left:

Chicken Roulades with a Vegetable Stuffing (page 181)

Below:

Chicken Smothered in Black Beans (page 190) and *Stuffed Anaheim Chiles* (page 162)

Opposite:

Vegetables and Chicken Olé! (page 206)

Left:

Bronzed Redfish with a Gingersnap Gravy (page 212) and *Dirty Rice Fritters* (page 284)

Below, clockwise from left:

Spinach Sauce for Seafood (page 97), *Cane Syrup–Creole Mustard Relish* (page 214), *Caraway Mango Mayonnaise* (page 83), *Buckwheat Batter–Fried Shrimp* (page 214), and *Sesame-Crusted Catfish sauce* with *Sesame-Crusted Catfish* (page 242)

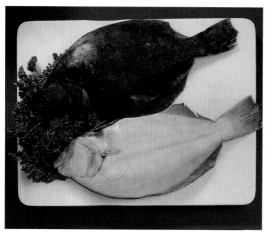

Both sides of the flounder

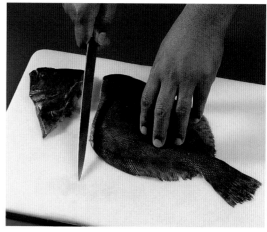

Cut the head off the flounder with a sharp knife

Use a pair of scissors to remove the bones

Stuff the flounder

Opposite:
Stuffed Flounder (page 217)

Opposite:

Pan-Roasted Soft-Shell Crabs (page 228) and *Rice Salad with Attitude!* (page 74)

Left:

Portobello Tuna (page 232)

Below:

St. Joseph's Vegetables (page 258)

Opposite:

Cilantro Salmon with Roasted Onions and Garlic (page 224)

and *Yucca Casserole* (page 272)

Left:

Islands in the Sunset (page 308)

Below:

Chocolate Chocolate Bars (page 302)

Overleaf,

clockwise from bottom:

Apple Pie with Chiles and Cheese (page 298), *Cupcakes with Papaya Sauce* (page 304), and *Sweetie Magic Bread Pudding* (page 316)

a heavy-duty plastic zipper bag with a ½-inch opening cut from a bottom corner. Or simply spread the potatoes evenly with a knife, making decorative swirls if you wish. Be creative—have fun!

9. Bake until the top is tinged with golden brown, about 50 minutes. Remove from the oven and let sit for 10 minutes before serving to allow the juices to be reabsorbed into the food.

Blackened Stuffed Ham with Honey Mango Sauce

This is a different kind of blackening—this time we do it in the oven instead of in a big black skillet on top of the fire outside. But the goal is the same, which is to give the meat a wonderful sweet dark flavor. Makes me happy just to think about it!

One 7-pound cured ham for baking (half hams are readily available at supermarkets and well suited for this recipe)

¼ cup olive oil

2½ cups chopped onions, in all

½ cup seeded and chopped green bell peppers

½ cup seeded and chopped red bell peppers

½ cup seeded and chopped yellow bell peppers

¾ cup seeded and chopped fresh jalapeño chile peppers, in all

1 cup peeled sweet potatoes or carrots cut into ½-inch cubes

1 cup honey, in all

2 tablespoons poppy seeds

½ teaspoon vegetable oil (if necessary)

1 teaspoon salt

1 medium-size ripe papaya, peeled, seeded, and cut into ¾-inch pieces

1 medium-size ripe mango, peeled, seeded, and cut in ¾-inch pieces

¾ cup heavy cream

Seasoning Mix

1½ teaspoons dry mustard

1½ teaspoons paprika

1 teaspoon garlic powder

1 teaspoon onion powder

1 teaspoon ground dried chipotle chile peppers

½ teaspoon ground anise

½ teaspoon ground cinnamon

½ teaspoon ground nutmeg

1. Combine the seasoning mix ingredients in a small bowl.

2. Make a series of 10 pockets in the ham for the stuffing: Insert a knife through the top of the ham, then push the knife down several inches and, without enlarging the opening, move the knife back and forth to form a pocket. Repeat this process, making evenly spaced rows of pockets. Set aside.

3. Place the olive oil in a 12-inch nonstick skillet over high heat just until the oil begins to smoke, about 4 minutes. Add 1½ cups of the onions, all the bell peppers, and ½ cup of the jalapeños. Stir well, then cover and cook until the onions are translucent and the bell peppers bright and candy-colored, about 4 minutes. Add 2 tablespoons plus 2 teaspoons of the seasoning mix, stir well, then re-cover and cook for 6 to 8 minutes. *Because of the absence of salt in the seasoning, the flavor of the vegetables will be surprisingly bland. The vegetable flavors come through very clearly and the finish is a light taste of anise and olive oil. Watch for the rising sweetness of the vegetables and the strengthening of the herbs and spices during the cooking process.*

4. Stir well, re-cover, reduce the heat to medium, and cook for another 4 minutes. Add the remaining onions and the sweet potatoes or carrots. Stir well and re-cover. Continue to cook, stirring and scraping the pan bottom occasionally, until the sweet potatoes or carrots are cooked, about 10 to 15 minutes. Set the skillet and the mixture aside.

5. Preheat the oven to 250°F.

6. Place 1 cup of the vegetable mixture in a small bowl, add ¼ cup of the honey, and mix well. Stuff this mixture into the ham pockets, dividing it evenly among them.

7. Place the ham in the oven and cook for 1½ hours. Increase the oven temperature to 350°F and begin preparing the sauce (see below). With a meat thermometer, check the temperature of the ham regularly while making the sauce. When the temperature in the thickest part of the ham reaches 140°F, about another 30 minutes, remove the ham from the oven. Reserve the liquid in the pan for use in the sauce—if there is not at least 1 cup of liquid, add 1 cup of water and swish it around, but don't scrape up any of the black bits in the bottom of the pan. I frequently tell you to scrape up the brown bits because they're sweet from the caramelizing process, but black bits would give a bitter taste to the sauce.

8. Make the sauce: Return the skillet with the remaining cooked vegetables to the stove over high heat and add the remaining jalapeños. Stir well, then push the mixture to one side and add the poppy seeds to the other side of the skillet.

continued

Tip the pan to allow the juices from the mixture to flow into the poppy seeds. If the poppy seeds are still very dry, add the vegetable oil. Cook until the poppy seeds begin to brown, about 4 minutes. Add the salt, papaya, and mango and stir well until the ingredients are well mixed. Remove from the heat and process until smooth in a food processor. Return the purée to the skillet and add the remaining ¾ cup honey, 1 cup of liquid from the ham, and the remaining seasoning mix. Bring to a boil, whisking constantly. When the mixture bubbles like little volcanoes, add the heavy cream and whisk constantly until the mixture bubbles continuously. *The addition of the cream really turns the flavor around in this sauce, from an unfocused sweetness to a rich, deep flavor that is almost like cane syrup.* This makes 4 cups. If you keep the sauce for serving on the second day, you may need to thin it with a bit of liquid. Slice the ham thinly and don't forget to pass the sauce!

Boudin

Makes about 28 sausages *If your butcher doesn't carry sausage casings, check with local meat packers or sausage makers. If you do obtain your casings from a commercial supplier, buy the smallest quantity possible—explain the small number of sausages you plan to make, and that you're not going into competition with the supplier! The casings should be white, packed in salt to preserve them, and fresh-smelling. Actually making the sausages is much easier if you have someone to help you—one person fills the hopper of the sausage stuffer while the other guides the casing and twists it when necessary to make links. By the way, I usually specify Converted rice in my recipes, because it's fluffier and less sticky than regular rice, but this time we want it to be a little sticky.*

Seasoning Mix
2 tablespoons plus 1 teaspoon salt
1 tablespoon plus 1 teaspoon paprika
1 tablespoon cayenne
1 tablespoon dry mustard
2 teaspoons black pepper
2 teaspoons white pepper

2 pounds pigs' feet, split in half lengthwise and cut into 2-inch pieces (have the butcher do this for you)

1 gallon water

2 pounds boneless Boston butt or pork shoulder

3 large onions, cut into quarters

1 head garlic, split in half parallel to the bottom

4 bay leaves

5 cups cooked white rice

2 cups finely chopped green onions or scallions

About 15 feet sausage casing

1. Combine the seasoning mix ingredients in a small bowl and set aside.

continued

2. Tie the split pigs' feet securely in a double thickness of cheesecloth—the feet have a lot of little bones, and the cheesecloth will keep the bones from getting into the stock. Place the feet in a stockpot with the water, pork, onions, garlic, and bay leaves. Stir in the seasoning mix and bring to a boil. Cook for 30 minutes, then reduce the heat to medium and simmer, stirring and scraping the bottom of the pot occasionally, until the stock is reduced to about 6 cups of liquid, about 4 hours. Strain through cheesecloth or a fine-mesh strainer and set aside the stock, reserving the meat and vegetables.

3. While the stock is simmering, prepare the rice. When it is done, fluff it with a fork and set it aside.

4. When the meat—the pigs' feet and the pork—is cool enough to handle, pull it apart carefully, discarding all the bones and gristle. This will be a little easier if, when you untie the cheesecloth, you keep the feet with their bones separate from the rest of the meat. Squeeze out the soft pulp of the garlic and discard the skins. Combine the meat, garlic pulp, and the reserved onions and grind in a meat grinder using the coarse setting. You should have about 5 cups.

5. Place the ground meat mixture in a large bowl, add 1 cup of the stock, and let it sit for a few minutes. It should look slightly "spongy" from the onions, garlic, and liquid. If not, add a little more stock, ¼ cup at a time, until it does look spongy. If any stock is not absorbed into the mixture, pour it off and refrigerate it along with the rest of the stock. Add the cooked rice and green onions to the mixture, combine gently but thoroughly, then refrigerate for at least 4 hours, preferably overnight.

6. Rinse off the casings under cold running water. Select a length of casing— about 3 feet—and blow into one end gently so that it inflates very slightly. Thread this end onto the horn of the sausage stuffer and continue to push the casing onto the horn until a section about 3 inches hangs off the end of the horn. Tie a knot in this end and place some of the filling in the hopper of the stuffer. Turn the machine on, and use the pusher to slowly push the filling into the auger. Hold the casing on the horn with a gentle pressure, allowing the filling to flow into and fill the casing. When you reach a length of about 5 inches, twist the sausage several times to form a link, and continue until you have filled the length of casing. Tie off the end and your first hank of sausages is completed. Keep repeating this process until all the sausages are made.

7. In a large pot, bring all the reserved stock just to a simmer. Add the sausage gently, 1 or 2 hanks at a time, then reduce the heat to medium. Allow the water to return to a temperature of 190°F to 200°F—steaming but not quite simmering.

It is important to maintain the heat at this temperature—anything lower will not heat the sausages thoroughly, but too high a heat will cause them to break, so adjust the heat as necessary. Continue to cook the boudin until it is heated through, about 20 minutes. Remove the boudin hanks gently, using a spatula or large spoon to support them, and continue until all the hanks are heated. This homemade boudin is quite soft and will break if treated roughly.

Garden Greens
and Andouille

Makes 6 main-course or 12 appetizer servings   *With all the greens, this stew is just as nutritious as it is delicious! A study of the ingredients—coriander, fenugreek, New Mexico chile peppers, turmeric, daikon, and andouille—is like a geography lesson. If you can't find fenugreek already ground, do as we do: Buy the seeds, which are more readily available, and grind them in a small coffee grinder. Daikon, also called Japanese radish, looks a little like a large white carrot and adds a wonderful texture to this dish. If you have some left over, leave it raw and grate it into your next salad for a tasty crunch.*

2 tablespoons vegetable oil
2 cups chopped onions
2 cups seeded and chopped green bell peppers
2 cups chopped celery
4 cups chopped daikon
1 pound andouille, or your favorite smoked
    pork sausage, quartered lengthwise, then
    cut into ½-inch pieces
7 quarts loosely packed mustard greens,
    washed well and stems removed
10 quarts loosely packed collard greens,
    washed well and stems removed
2 cups chicken stock
6 cups cooked white rice

1. Combine the seasoning mix ingredients in a small bowl.

2. In a heavy 4-quart pot, heat the vegetable oil over high heat just until it begins to smoke, about 3 to 4 minutes. Add

Seasoning Mix

2½ teaspoons salt

2 teaspoons paprika

1 teaspoon dried chervil

1 teaspoon ground coriander

1 teaspoon ground
   fenugreek

1 teaspoon garlic powder

1 teaspoon ground ginger

1 teaspoon dry mustard

1 teaspoon onion powder

1 teaspoon ground dried
   New Mexico chile peppers

1 teaspoon ground turmeric

¾ teaspoon cayenne

½ teaspoon black pepper

the onions, bell peppers, celery, daikon, andouille, and the seasoning mix. Cover and cook, uncovering to stir every 2 or 3 minutes, for 18 minutes, then remove the cover and cook for 8 minutes longer. Add the greens a few handfuls at a time—they will wilt down quickly—and cook, stirring constantly, for 15 minutes. Add the stock, bring just to a boil, reduce the heat to low, and simmer, uncovered, for 25 minutes. *When you first add the greens, of course they're still slightly tough and somewhat bitter, and the broth is still surprisingly mild. Later, though, the broth absorbs the taste of the greens—that great flavor that people who love greens call "pot likker."*

3. To serve as a main course, place 1 cup of the rice in a large serving bowl and ladle 2 cups of stew around it. For an appetizer, serve ½ cup rice with 1 cup of stew.

Magazine Street
Pork Stew

Makes 4 servings *Don't worry if you can't find pork stew meat— just buy boneless pork loin chops and cut them into the correct size yourself. You notice we call for "5 to 6 cups pork stock" because if your stove puts out a lot of BTUs and your food cooks fast, you may need an extra ½ or 1 cup, but if your stove is not a dragon, you won't. The important thing is to have the liquid at the right "stew" consistency, thicker than a soup but thinner than gravy. Getting it there is going to depend on you! This is great served over mashed potatoes, rice, or pasta. Add a green salad and you have a nutritious, complete meal.*

2 tablespoons vegetable oil
1 pound pork stew meat cut into
   ½-inch pieces
2½ cups chopped onions
2 cups seeded and chopped green bell
   peppers
¾ cup chopped celery
5 to 6 cups pork stock, in all
2 cups peeled yucca root cut into
   ½-inch pieces
2 teaspoons chopped garlic
½ cup seeded and chopped red bell peppers
½ cup seeded chopped yellow bell peppers

Seasoning Mix

1¼ teaspoons salt

1 teaspoon paprika

¾ teaspoon dried basil

¾ teaspoon garlic powder

¾ teaspoon onion powder

½ teaspoon black pepper

½ teaspoon ground ginger

½ teaspoon dry mustard

½ teaspoon dried tarragon

¼ teaspoon cayenne

¼ teaspoon ground cumin

¼ teaspoon ground allspice

¼ teaspoon white pepper

1. Combine the seasoning mix ingredients in a small bowl.

2. In a heavy 4-quart pot, heat the vegetable oil over high heat just until it begins to smoke, about 3 to 4 minutes. Add the pork evenly over the bottom of the pot and sprinkle

1 tablespoon of the seasoning mix over it. Cook for 2 minutes without stirring, to allow the meat to release some of its fat, which helps keep it from sticking. Now stir well, coating the meat on all sides with the oil, and cook for 4 minutes. You'll notice that the oil has combined with the meat fat and that the mixture is brown and bubbling. Remove the meat from the pot and set it aside. *Notice that the small amounts of ground ginger and mustard in the seasoning mix add a subtle hint of the exotic that really makes the meat taste great!*

3. To the same pot, add the onions, green bell peppers, celery, and the remaining seasoning mix. If necessary to keep the brown bits from burning, add ½ cup of the stock and use it to deglaze the pot. Stir well, then cover and cook for 5 minutes. Uncover, stir the mixture well, and scrape the bottom of the pot. *The vegetables now have acquired that wonderful caramelized sweetness that I like to achieve by cooking over high heat to add a rich, complex taste to the final dish.* Stir in 1 cup of the stock, re-cover, and cook until the vegetables wilt and stick slightly to the bottom of the pot and the liquid is absorbed, about 8 to 10 minutes. Uncover and add 1 cup of the stock and stir well. Re-cover and cook until the liquid is level with the vegetables, about 5 minutes. Uncover and stir in the yucca with a folding motion, mixing it with the other vegetables. Re-cover and cook until the mixture starts to thicken and bubble like little volcanoes, about 5 minutes. Uncover and stir in the garlic, re-cover, and continue to cook, uncovering to stir and scrape the bottom of the pot every 3 minutes, until the liquid is very thick and sticking to the bottom, about 7 to 8 minutes. Add 1 cup of the stock and the red and yellow bell peppers. Scrape the bottom of the pot, re-cover, and cook for 5 minutes, at which time *the peppers will have lost some of their bright color and "raw" taste.* Uncover and stir in 1½ cups of stock, the reserved meat, and any accumulated juices. Re-cover, bring to a boil, then reduce the heat to medium and simmer, uncovering to stir frequently, until the yucca is tender, about 15 minutes. Uncover, add ½ cup of the stock, and cook, uncovered, until the liquid is very thick and beginning to stick, and the yucca is cooked all the way through. To determine if the yucca is fully cooked, remove a piece and cut it in half—there will no longer be an opaque section in the center when it is done, for the entire piece will be translucent. This last step will take between 8 and 20 minutes, depending on the freshness (and therefore the water content) of the yucca. If it takes close to the 20 minutes for the yucca to be fully cooked, you may wish to add the final ½ cup stock. Serve hot.

Parsnip Hash

Makes 4 servings   Serve this as you would any other meat hash—as a light lunch or supper, or with a poached egg on top for a hearty breakfast. Unlike regular potato hashes, this hash begins with the aroma and taste of the parsnips. The hash brown flavor from the deeply caramelized vegetables follows in the middle, with a finishing taste that is lightly salty from the ham. Note the complex textures created by staging the vegetables.

3 tablespoons olive oil

3½ cups chopped onions, in all

1½ cups seeded and chopped green bell peppers, in all

½ pound cooked ham cut into ½-inch cubes (buy a little more than ½ pound, to allow for waste)

3 cups peeled parsnips cut into ½-inch cubes

1 tablespoon minced garlic

Seasoning Mix

1½ teaspoons paprika

1 teaspoon dillweed

1 teaspoon dry mustard

1 teaspoon onion powder

1 teaspoon salt

¾ teaspoon dried thyme leaves

½ teaspoon black pepper

½ teaspoon cayenne

½ teaspoon ground cumin

½ teaspoon garlic powder

¼ teaspoon white pepper

1. Combine the seasoning mix ingredients in a small bowl.

2. In a large nonstick skillet over high heat, heat the olive oil just until it begins to smoke, about 3 to 4 minutes. Add 2 cups of the onions and ½ cup of the bell peppers, and cook, stirring frequently, just until the vegetables brown on the edges, about 5 to 8 minutes. Move the vegetables to one side of the skillet and add the ham. Cook the ham for 2 minutes, stirring frequently, then add the parsnips and seasoning mix and stir the hash to combine all the vegetables with the ham. Spread the mixture evenly across the bottom of the skillet and cook without stirring for 3 minutes. Add the remaining onions, the remaining bell peppers, and the garlic. Scrape the skillet bottom thoroughly, then spread the mixture evenly across the bottom of the skillet again. Continue to cook, scraping and spreading the mixture

every 3 minutes, until the hash is a golden brown, about 12 minutes in all. The hash should regularly stick to the bottom of the skillet as it cooks, and the process of spreading, cooking, and scraping is very important for the hash to brown evenly and properly, and to loosen the sticking bits and prevent them from burning. Serve hot.

Paul's Portobellos
and Pork

Makes 6 servings *This hearty dish combines 2 wonderful flavors: portobello mushrooms and pork. If this is the first time you've used portobellos, you have a treat in store! Besides being great in recipes, they're terrific in salads, and some people even grill thick slices to use in sandwiches instead of meat. The amount of stock you need will depend partly on how fresh the mushrooms are—really fresh ones tend to be moister.*

2 pounds pork stew meat

2 tablespoons vegetable oil

2 cups chopped onions

8 cups portobello mushrooms cut
    into 1-inch pieces, in all

3 to 4 cups pork stock, preferably, or beef
    stock, in all

½ cup cane syrup or your favorite syrup
    (fruit or pure maple syrup)

5 cups peeled white potatoes cut into
    ½-inch cubes

2 cups chopped carrots

2 cups chopped celery

Seasoning Mix
1 tablespoon salt
2½ teaspoons ground dried Anaheim chile peppers
2 teaspoons dried basil
2 teaspoons onion powder
2 teaspoons paprika
1½ teaspoons garlic powder
1 teaspoon ground dried chipotle chile peppers
¾ teaspoon cayenne
¾ teaspoon black pepper
¾ teaspoon white pepper

1. Combine the seasoning mix ingredients in a small bowl.

2. Sprinkle the pork evenly with 2 tablespoons of the seasoning mix and rub it in well. In a heavy 5-quart pot, heat the vegetable oil over high heat just until it begins to smoke, about 3 to 4 minutes. Add the pork and cook, stirring every 2 minutes, until it begins to brown, about 6 minutes. Stir in the onions, 4 cups of the mushrooms, and the remaining seasoning mix. Cover and cook, uncovering to stir and scrape the pot to prevent sticking every 2 minutes, for 10 minutes.

If absolutely necessary to prevent scorching, especially if your mushrooms are a little old and dry, stir in ½ cup of the stock and use it to deglaze the pot.

3. Uncover and add the cane syrup, potatoes, carrots, and celery. Stir well and replace the cover. Cook for 20 minutes, uncovering to scrape the pot about every 2 minutes, especially toward the end of the cooking time, when the mixture will be browned and sticking hard. At this point, the texture is very thick, with only a little moisture. *The first highly seasoned stew flavor is replaced quickly by a spike of sweet flavor that carries the distinctive molasses-like flavor of the cane syrup. The later taste is almost like a roasted sweet potato. The illusion comes from the combination of the carrot, potato, and cane syrup flavors.*

4. Uncover and add 3 cups of the stock, scrape up all the browned bits on the pot bottom, then add the remaining mushrooms. Stir well, cover, and bring to a boil, then reduce the heat to medium and cook at a brisk simmer, uncovering to stir and scrape up any brown bits every 3 to 4 minutes, for 12 minutes. If you prefer your stew a little more liquid, stir in the remaining stock. Return just to a brisk simmer and remove from the heat. Serve pipping hot.

Perfect Pork Roast with
Roasted Vegetables

Makes 6 to 8 servings *Here's a great meal to set before a hungry man! The steaming roast, fragrant from the interesting mixture of seasonings, is complemented by roasted vegetables and a sauce made with those delicious vegetables.*

One 4- to 5-pound pork loin roast, bone in
3 sweet potatoes
2 Idaho potatoes
1 medium-size rutabaga
2 onions, sliced in half
2 ripe plantains, peeled

Sauce

1 tablespoon cornstarch
1 cup plus 2 tablespoons pork stock,
  preferably, or chicken stock, in all
¼ teaspoon salt (optional)

Seasoning Mix

2 teaspoons dillweed

2 teaspoons salt

1½ teaspoons dried basil

1½ teaspoons onion powder

1½ teaspoons paprika

1 teaspoon cayenne

1 teaspoon ground cumin

1 teaspoon garlic powder

1 teaspoon dry mustard

1 teaspoon ground dried
  New Mexico chile peppers

¾ teaspoon black pepper

½ teaspoon ground ginger

¼ teaspoon white pepper

1. Combine the seasoning mix ingredients in a small bowl.

2. Preheat the oven to 250°F.

3. Cut a 3-inch-deep pocket between each two-rib section of the roast. Sprinkle the roast evenly with all the seasoning mix, coating it well and working the seasoning into the pockets.

4. Peel the vegetables.

5. Place the roast in a large roasting pan—no rack is necessary—and arrange the plantains and vegetables around the roast. Place in the oven and roast until the internal temperature of the meat is 160°, about 3 to 4 hours. Remove from the oven, pour off and reserve the pan drippings, and allow the roast to sit for about 15 minutes before slicing. If you slice a roast immediately after taking it out of the oven, you lose a lot of the juice—but don't let it sit so long that it cools off.

6. Make the sauce while the roast is "resting." Chop 1 roasted onion half and 1 half of one roasted sweet potato. Dissolve the cornstarch in 2 tablespoons of the stock and set aside.

7. In a 1-quart saucepan, heat the pan drippings, the remaining 1 cup stock, the chopped onion and sweet potato, and the salt, if you're using it. Bring the mixture to a boil and whisk in the dissolved cornstarch. Return to a boil, whisking constantly, then remove from the heat.

8. Slice the remaining roasted vegetables. Serve the sliced roast accompanied by the sliced vegetables and the sauce.

Pork Roast with
Bay Leaves

Makes 8 servings *The honey, bacon, and seasonings add a wonderful flavor to this roast—one that's apparent, thanks to the great smell coming from the oven, for the last half of its cooking time. Notice that the roast is to be refrigerated overnight, allowing the incredible flavors of the vegetable mixture time to be absorbed, so you'll need to plan ahead. By the way, the size of the roast is important because of cooking time and seasoning, so be sure yours is between 6 and 7 pounds.*

6 cloves fresh garlic, peeled
½ pound sliced bacon cut crosswise into
    ½-inch-wide strips
1½ cups chopped onions
1 cup chopped celery
½ cup seeded and chopped green bell peppers
8 bay leaves
One 6- to 7-pound fresh pork shoulder roast
¼ cup honey

Seasoning Mix

1 tablespoon plus ½ teaspoon salt

2 teaspoons dry mustard

2 teaspoons dried oregano

2 teaspoons paprika

1½ teaspoons garlic powder

1½ teaspoons ground dried árbol chile peppers

1½ teaspoons dried thyme leaves

1 teaspoon cayenne

1 teaspoon ground cumin

1 teaspoon onion powder

½ teaspoon black pepper

½ teaspoon white pepper

1. Day 1: Combine the seasoning mix ingredients in a small bowl.

2. Remove the brown tip from each clove of garlic, then slice each clove lengthwise into slices about ⅛ inch thick. You should have about 24 slices.

3. Place the bacon in a 10-inch skillet over high heat. Stir the bacon, breaking it up as you stir. In about 5 minutes, the bacon will be soft and will have rendered a good bit of fat. Add the onions, celery, bell peppers, bay leaves, and 4 tablespoons of the seasoning mix. Continue to cook, stirring frequently, for 6 minutes. The mixture will be just beginning to brown, and the onions will be a pale gold color. Add the

garlic slivers and continue to cook and stir for another 6 minutes, until the vegetables are medium brown and soft, then remove from the heat and allow to cool. Remove the bay leaves and set them aside. *All the flavors of the stuffing must be very intense, because they will permeate and flavor the roast during cooking. In front is the salty-smoky flavor of the bacon, briefly suppressed by the sweet taste of the bell peppers and the piquant sweetness of the garlic. The seasonings reach full intensity in the later part of the taste, underscored by the relatively low but aromatic flavor of the bay leaves.*

4. With a small knife, cut 12 pockets in the top of the roast by inserting the knife about 2 inches and moving it back and forth—the pockets should be about 2 inches deep and about 1 inch across at the opening. Divide 1 tablespoon of the seasoning mix among the pockets, pushing the seasoning into each pocket, then sprinkle the remaining seasoning mix over the top of the meat. Place 1 teaspoon of the honey in each pocket and put 1 tablespoon of the bacon/vegetable mixture into each pocket, pushing it in so that the pocket is completely full—try to get 2 slivers of the garlic into each pocket. Spread the remaining mixture over the top of the pork roast and lay the reserved bay leaves on top of the mixture. Wrap the roast in plastic wrap and refrigerate overnight.

5. Day 2: Preheat the oven to 275°F.

6. Unwrap the roast, place it in a roasting pan, then place it in the oven. Roast for 1 hour, then cover the top of the roast with a sheet of aluminum foil and insert a meat thermometer through the foil, into the center of the meat. Continue to roast until the internal temperature of the roast is 155°F, about 2½ hours longer, for a total roasting time of 3½ hours. The roast will be medium-rare. Serve hot, but I have it on good authority that it's really great cold, especially with a little Creole mustard.

Pueblo Chili

Makes 6 main-course or 12 appetizer servings   *This version*
of an old favorite is guaranteed to put spikes on your cactus! Did you
know that if you get a bite that's too hot to handle, the best thing is
not to reach for a cold drink, which will only spread the capsaicin (the
hot stuff in chile peppers) around your mouth? A
little sugar will help dissipate the heat.

Vegetable oil for frying
Four 6-inch corn tortillas
3 cups chopped onions, in all
1½ cups seeded and chopped green bell
    peppers, in all
1 tablespoon unsalted butter
2 pounds ground pork
One 1-pound can roasted green chile
    peppers, drained and diced
1 tablespoon seeded and chopped fresh
    jalapeño chile peppers
7 cups pork stock, preferably, or chicken
    stock, in all
¼ cup all-purpose flour

Seasoning Mix

1 tablespoon salt

2 teaspoons ground dried
    chipotle chile peppers

1½ teaspoons ground cumin

1 teaspoon dried oregano

1 teaspoon dry mustard

1 teaspoon onion powder

1 teaspoon garlic powder

1 teaspoon ground dried
    árbol chile peppers

¾ teaspoon black pepper

¾ teaspoon white pepper

1. Combine the seasoning mix ingredients in a small bowl.

2. Add enough vegetable oil to a heavy 10-inch skillet to measure 1 inch deep and heat it to 350°F. (Use an electric skillet or a regular skillet and a cooking thermometer and adjust the heat as necessary to keep the oil temperature steady.) Fry the tortillas, one at a time, turning with tongs several times, until they are crisp and golden brown. Remove with the tongs, drain on paper towels, and, as soon as they are cool enough to handle, break up and grind them in a blender or food processor until they resemble coarse cornmeal. Set aside.

3. Preheat a heavy 4-quart pot over high heat until very hot, about 3 minutes. Add 1½ cups of the onions and ¾ cup of the bell peppers and cook, stirring almost constantly, until the onions are just beginning to brown on the edges, about 2 minutes. Add the butter and continue to cook, stirring almost constantly, until the onions are nicely browned on the edges, about 4 minutes, then add the pork and 2 tablespoons of the seasoning mix. Cook, stirring every 2 or 3 minutes and breaking up the meat, until the meat is lightly browned, about 8 to 10 minutes, then add the remaining onions, the remaining bell peppers, the ground tortillas, green chiles, jalapeños, and the remaining seasoning mix. Stir well and cook until the mixture sticks hard and there are brown spots on the bottom of the pot, about 15 to 20 minutes.

4. Add 1 cup of the stock, then cook, stirring and scraping the pot bottom vigorously, loosening the brown bits, for 10 minutes. *Before adding the stock, the meat mixture has very little chili flavor; the taste of the meat is dominated by the seasonings, but without any deep flavors. After the stock has been added and the mixture brought to a simmer, notice how all the rich flavors of the chili have been liberated into the mixture. The slightly acid edge from the canned chiles will cook out as the chili simmers.* Add the flour and stir until it is completely absorbed. Cook, scraping the pot bottom, for 5 minutes, then stir in 3 cups of the stock. Cook, stirring every 2 or 3 minutes, for 7 minutes. Add the remaining 3 cups stock, bring to a boil, then reduce the heat to low and simmer for 20 minutes. Stir well before serving.

Stuffed Anaheim Chiles

Makes 6 servings

The strong-flavored cheeses we've used, not to mention the fresh dill and dried chile peppers, take this pepper dish way out of the ordinary, yet look at how simple it is to put together. Because some Stilton cheese is very salty, we've used a little less salt than usual, so taste the mixture and, if necessary, add more salt to taste. For lunch or a light supper, serve this casserole with the most flavorful fresh tomatoes you can find and hot buttered corn bread or corn tortillas.

½ pound ground lean pork
2 tablespoons vegetable oil
1½ cups chopped onions
½ cup seeded and chopped green bell
    peppers
¾ cup seeded and chopped red bell peppers
¾ cup seeded and chopped yellow bell
    peppers
1 cup seeded and chopped fire-roasted
    Anaheim chile peppers
1½ cups chopped mirliton (chayote)
2 cups peeled and diced jicama
3 tablespoons all-purpose flour
1 cup pork stock
3 ounces sharp goat cheese
3 ounces Stilton cheese
¼ cup fresh dill leaves, stemmed
4 Anaheim chile peppers fire-roasted,
    split in half lengthwise, and seeded
    and stemmed
8 ounces Monterey Jack cheese, freshly grated

Seasoning Mix

1½ teaspoons salt

1½ teaspoons paprika

1½ teaspoons ground dried
    New Mexico chile peppers

1 teaspoon cayenne

1 teaspoon onion powder

½ teaspoon garlic powder

½ teaspoon ground dried
    Anaheim chile peppers

1. Combine the seasoning mix ingredients in a small bowl.

2. Place the pork in a heavy 12-inch nonstick skillet over high heat and sprinkle evenly with 2 teaspoons of the seasoning mix. Cook, stirring gently and breaking up the clumps of meat, until nicely browned, about 6 to 8 minutes. Remove the meat and set it aside. To the same skillet, add the vegetable oil and heat just until it begins to smoke, about 2 to 3 minutes. Add the onions, all the bell peppers, the chopped Anaheim peppers, the mirliton, jicama, and the remaining seasoning mix. Cook, stirring every 2 minutes, until the vegetables are well browned, about 15 minutes. *The first taste is the clear flavor of roasted Anaheim peppers, followed by seasoning and heat tastes combined with the starchy taste of the mirliton. Note the distinctive crunch, like a radish, which comes from the jicama.* Add the flour and stir until the white is no longer visible. Spread the mixture over the pan bottom, allowing it to absorb the heat and begin to brown. After 2 minutes, stir up the mixture and spread it out again. *Repeat this stirring and spreading 2 more times—it's a great technique for creating exciting new flavors in your cooking. As the crust is built, the tastes of the vegetables are underscored by an increasing brown flavor in the crust. The heat comes down and the sweetness comes up.* Add the stock and the reserved browned meat and stir or whisk until they are thoroughly blended. Continue to cook for 5 minutes, then remove from the heat.

3. Preheat the oven to 350°F.

4. In a small bowl, mix the goat cheese, Stilton cheese, and dill together.

5. Arrange the Anaheim chile pepper halves in a casserole dish or baking pan. Spoon the vegetable mixture over them, then spoon the cheese/dill mixture over the vegetable mixture. Sprinkle the grated Monterey Jack cheese evenly on top. Bake for 25 minutes, then increase the oven temperature to 500°F and bake until the cheese is golden brown, about 5 minutes longer. Serve hot.

Yam-n-Ham!

Makes 4 side-dish servings

We know that Louisiana sweet potatoes are not yams, botanically speaking, but we've always called them that, and we even have a "Yambilee" in Opelousas, Louisiana, my hometown. You can serve this dish any time you would serve potatoes or plain sweet potatoes—as a great accompaniment to roasted meat, especially pork—and I think it turns a good breakfast into a great breakfast! Drizzle with just a little honey or cane syrup for an exciting change of pace. Yummmmmmmmm!

Three 1-pound sweet potatoes
¼ cup vegetable oil
3 cups chopped onions, in all
8 ounces cooked ham cut into ¼-inch cubes
1 tablespoon minced fresh garlic
1 teaspoon finely chopped orange zest
1½ to 2 cups chicken stock, in all

Seasoning Mix

1¼ teaspoons onion powder
¾ teaspoon dry mustard
¾ teaspoon salt
½ teaspoon ground allspice
½ teaspoon cayenne
½ teaspoon garlic powder
½ teaspoon black pepper
½ teaspoon white pepper
½ teaspoon dried thyme leaves
¼ teaspoon ground cinnamon

1. Combine the seasoning mix ingredients in a small bowl.

2. Peel the sweet potatoes. Grate 2 of them, using the largest hole in the grater, and chop the third one into ½-inch pieces. Set aside.

3. In a heavy 12-inch nonstick skillet, heat the vegetable oil over high heat just until it begins to smoke, about 3 to 4 minutes. Add 2 cups of the onions and cook, stirring frequently, until they are translucent and beginning to brown on the edges, about 6 minutes. Add the ham, two thirds of the grated sweet potatoes, and the seasoning mix; stir well; then cook for 3 minutes.

4. Stir and scrape to loosen the brown bits, then add the remaining 1 cup onions, the remaining grated sweet potatoes, the diced sweet potatoes, garlic, orange zest, and ½ cup of the stock. Stir and scrape the skillet bottom, then bring the mixture just to a boil. Reduce the heat to medium and cook for 3 minutes. *You will see that the sweet potatoes are beginning to soften and lose their bright orange color, while the orange zest adds the distinctive sweet flavor and aroma of citrus, a natural complement to sweet potatoes. Here the heat is fairly intense, apparent on the roof of your mouth.* Add 1 cup of stock, then stir and scrape the skillet bottom. Continue to cook, stirring and scraping every 2 to 3 minutes, until the liquid evaporates and the hash becomes a rich golden brown, about 25 minutes. If, during this 25 minutes, the hash becomes too dry and starts to stick hard, add another ½ cup of stock. Increase the heat to high and cook, turning the hash frequently and spreading it over the pan bottom until it turns a medium brown, about 5 minutes. Serve hot.

Slow-Roasted Baby Back Pork Ribs

Makes 4 to 6 servings

Potato salad or coleslaw, baked beans, your favorite cold drink, and these ribs—heaven! One of my assistants, noticing that this recipe doesn't include a marinade or sauce, assumed the ribs would be dry. Was she wrong! They are juicy and absolutely delicious, as she discovered to her delight as soon as they came out of the oven. And look how easy they are to prepare!

4 to 5 pounds baby back pork ribs

1. Preheat the oven to 250°F.

2. Combine the seasoning mix ingredients in a small bowl.

3. Sprinkle all the seasoning mix evenly over both sides of the ribs and gently rub it in. Place in a roasting pan—you don't need a rack—and roast until the meat is tender and pulls away easily from the bone, about 2½ hours. They're great just as they are, or you can serve them with our Sweet and Sour Barbecue Sauce (page 98), developed especially to complement their flavor.

Seasoning Mix

2 teaspoons salt

1½ teaspoons ground cumin

1½ teaspoons dry mustard

1 teaspoon cayenne

1 teaspoon dillweed

1 teaspoon garlic powder

1 teaspoon ground ginger

1 teaspoon paprika

1 teaspoon ground dried ancho chile peppers

½ teaspoon onion powder

½ teaspoon black pepper

½ teaspoon white pepper

½ teaspoon dried thyme leaves

Veal-Stuffed
Poblano Chiles

Makes 6 servings *Serve as a hearty appetizer, or pair with a tomato and cucumber salad for a light lunch or supper. Poblanos are not as hot as other chile peppers, so you don't have to take special precautions when handling them.*

6 fresh poblano chile peppers

Stuffing

1 tablespoon vegetable oil
1 cup chopped onions
½ cup chopped celery
½ cup seeded and chopped green bell peppers
½ cup seeded and chopped fresh poblano
   chile peppers
1 pound ground veal
4 ounces Cheddar cheese, freshly grated
4 ounces Monterey Jack cheese, freshly grated
2 teaspoons olive oil

Sauce

5 tablespoons vegetable oil
½ cup all-purpose flour
1 tablespoon ground dried New Mexico chile
   peppers
1 tablespoon ground dried Anaheim chile
   peppers
3 cups chicken stock, in all
½ cup heavy cream
1 cup loosely packed chopped fresh cilantro
   leaves

continued

Seasoning Mix

1¾ teaspoons paprika

1¾ teaspoons salt

1¼ teaspoons cayenne

1¼ teaspoons ground
   coriander

1¼ teaspoons ground cumin

1¼ teaspoons ground ginger

1¼ teaspoons onion powder

1¼ teaspoons ground dried
   ancho chile peppers

½ teaspoon garlic powder

½ teaspoon black pepper

½ teaspoon white pepper

1. Combine the seasoning mix ingredients in a small bowl. Prepare the whole poblano chile peppers for stuffing: With a small, sharp knife, cut a circle around the stem of each pepper. Gently pull on the stem to remove the stem section and the attached seed pod. Cut off the seed pod, leaving the stem and the top of the pepper intact. Carefully scrape out the peppers with a spoon, removing all the seeds and fleshy ribs. Parboil the pepper shells and tops in boiling water to cover for 5 minutes, then drain and set them aside.

2. Make the stuffing: In a heavy 10-inch skillet over high heat, heat the vegetable oil just until it begins to smoke, about 3 to 4 minutes. Add the onions, celery, bell peppers, chopped poblanos, veal, and 2 tablespoons plus 2 teaspoons of the seasoning mix. Reserve the remaining seasoning mix for the sauce. Cook, stirring every 4 or 5 minutes and breaking up the clumps of meat, for 15 minutes, then remove from the heat and let cool. *The first taste is of the veal, which has a very light flavor enhanced by the browning process and the sweetness of the browned vegetables. The middle taste comes from the poblano chiles, with their flavor similar to that of uncooked bell peppers combined with a dark, almost grassy, taste. The finish comes from the seasoning and builds in heat as the other tastes fade. Note the special aroma of the cooked poblano chiles.*

3. Preheat the oven to 450°F.

4. When the stuffing is cool, stir in the two cheeses. Divide the stuffing among the peppers, packing it loosely, then replace the caps.

5. Brush the olive oil on the bottom of a small roasting pan, arrange the stuffed poblanos in it, and bake for 15 minutes. Reduce the oven temperature to 250°F (the actual temperature will not immediately be lowered to 250°F, but it will slowly go down from 450°F, which is what we want to happen here) and bake for 25 minutes longer. While the poblanos are baking, make the sauce.

6. In a 10-inch skillet over high heat, heat the vegetable oil just until it begins to smoke, about 3 to 4 minutes. Add the flour and whisk constantly to make a roux. When the roux is the color of light milk chocolate, whisk in the dried chile peppers. Immediately but carefully whisk in the stock. Add the remaining seasoning mix, bring just to a boil, reduce the heat to low, and simmer for 10 minutes. Whisk in the heavy cream and cilantro, raise the heat to high, bring to a boil, reduce the heat to low, and simmer for 2 minutes. Remove from the heat.

7. *Before boiling, the sauce has an intense earthy taste, with a bitter undertone. After the sauce comes to a full boil, the taste changes dramatically. There is a subtle sweetness on your lips, the other ingredients fall into balance, and the overall flavor is reminiscent of chocolate. The taste of the dry chiles comes forward; note the unique "enchilada" taste, which comes from their brief cooking in hot oil.*

8. To serve, drizzle about ¾ cup sauce over each stuffed pepper.

Stuffed Veal Flank Steaks

Makes 4 servings

All my Louisiana French ancestors would throw their hands in the air if they saw yucca root in a dish! "Qu'est-ce que c'est?" they'd ask—what is that? But I do believe that once they tasted it, they'd enjoy using it as much as I do. If you can't find yucca root where you shop, substitute the same amount of white potatoes and add 1 tablespoon sugar. Of course, you won't get the distinctive flavor of yucca, but the dish will have the same texture, and the rest of the seasonings are pretty terrific.

Four 6-ounce baby veal flank steaks
½ cup olive oil, in all
2 cups well-washed leeks, white parts only,
    cut into ¼-inch pieces
1 cup seeded and chopped green bell
    peppers
1 cup seeded and chopped red bell peppers
1 cup seeded and chopped yellow bell
    peppers
1 small yucca root, peeled and cut into
    ¼-inch cubes (about 3½ cups)
3½ cups beef stock
¼ cup heavy cream

Seasoning Mix

2 tablespoons salt

1 tablespoon onion powder

1¾ teaspoons cayenne

1¾ teaspoons ground cumin

1¼ teaspoons garlic powder

1¼ teaspoons ground ginger

1¼ teaspoons dry mustard

1¼ teaspoons dried oregano

½ teaspoon white pepper

1. Combine the seasoning mix ingredients in a small bowl.

2. Form a pocket in each steak by carefully cutting into each one horizontally, making about a 3-inch opening. Continue to cut horizontally, enlarging the pocket as much as possible without cutting all the way through the meat. Sprinkle each side of each steak with ½ teaspoon of the seasoning mix and gently rub it in. Set the steaks aside.

3. In a heavy 12-inch skillet or a 4-inch quart pot, heat ¼ cup of the olive oil over high heat just until it begins to

smoke, about 3 to 4 minutes. Add the leeks, all the bell peppers, the yucca root, and the remaining seasoning mix. Cover and cook, stirring and scraping the pan bottom as the mixture begins to stick, every 3 or 4 minutes, until the vegetables are golden brown, about 20 to 25 minutes. If your stove produces a lot of heat or if your pot is not very heavy, you may need to reduce the heat to medium to prevent burning—watch carefully. *At the beginning, there is a brief taste of salt, followed by a fairly intense seasoning taste, which builds through the middle and end. Also, the middle taste is the starchy flavor, contributed by the yucca, mixed with a slight sweetness from the leeks and peppers. Note that the heat from the seasoning stays in the front of the mouth, not in the throat.* Remove from the heat and reserve 2 cups of this mixture for the stuffing.

4. To make the sauce, return the mixture remaining in the pot to high heat and whisk in the stock. Cook, whisking every 2 or 3 minutes, and after 10 minutes or so start mashing with a potato masher, until the mixture has thickened to sauce consistency, about 16 to 18 minutes. *Like the stuffing, the sauce leads with a brief taste of salt. However, from this point the taste is dominated by a rich gravy flavor with an intense seasoning component. The taste finishes with a tingling heat in the front of the mouth. Notice that this is one of those times when the sauce is very similar to some other portion of the dish, in this case the stuffing—this duplication with only a small change is one way to build the flavors of a recipe, which you know I like to do.* Keep the sauce warm while you stuff and cook the steaks.

5. For the stuffing, mash the reserved vegetable mixture with a potato masher, then add the heavy cream and mash to combine it well. Divide the stuffing among the pockets, then rub each steak with ¼ teaspoon of olive oil.

6. In a heavy 12-inch skillet over high heat, heat the remaining olive oil just until it begins to smoke, about 3 to 4 minutes. Cook the stuffed veal flanks, in 2 batches if necessary, until the outsides are brown and the insides are thoroughly warmed, about 3 to 4 minutes per side. Divide the sauce evenly among the steaks and serve immediately.

Truck Farm Stew

This is another recipe that was a big hit with everyone who tasted it!

2 pounds veal stew meat, cut into 1-inch pieces
2 to 3 tablespoons vegetable oil, as needed
20 peeled small- and medium-size cloves garlic
1½ cups chopped onions
2½ cups beef stock, in all
2 cups carrots cut into ½-inch pieces
2 cups peeled white potatoes cut into
    ½-inch pieces
2 cups small cauliflower florets
2 cups peeled turnips cut into ½-inch pieces
2 medium-size portobello mushrooms,
    cut into ½-inch pieces (about 2 cups)

Seasoning Mix

2 teaspoons paprika

2 teaspoons salt

1¼ teaspoons garlic powder

1 teaspoon dillweed

1 teaspoon ground ginger

1 teaspoon dry mustard

1 teaspoon onion powder

1 teaspoon ground dried
    Anaheim chile peppers

1 teaspoon ground dried
    guajillo chile peppers

¾ teaspoon cayenne

½ teaspoon black pepper

1. Combine the seasoning mix ingredients in a small bowl. Sprinkle the meat evenly with 1 tablespoon plus 2 teaspoons of the seasoning mix and rub it in well. Set aside.

2. In a heavy 4-quart nonstick pot, heat 2 tablespoons of the vegetable oil over high heat just until it begins to smoke, about 3 to 4 minutes. Add as much of the meat as will fit in a single layer without crowding on the bottom of the pot, then add the garlic cloves and cook, turning with tongs every minute or so, until the meat is browned on all sides, about 3 to 5 minutes. Remove the browned meat, leaving the garlic, and brown the next batch, adding a little more oil if necessary.

3. When all the meat has been browned and removed, add the onions and ½ cup of the stock to the pot. Cook, stirring and scraping the pot every 3 or 4 minutes, until the onions are browned, about 15 minutes. Return the meat and the accumulated juices to the pot, and add the remaining 2 cups stock, the remaining seasoning mix, the carrots, potatoes, cauliflower, and turnips. Cover and cook for 5 minutes, then stir in the mushrooms. *The broth at this point is still quite thin, but it will thicken later from the vegetable starches. The broth tastes like a rich stock, just slightly bitter from the turnips. As the mushrooms cook, their flavor will infuse the broth, adding an earthy taste.* Reduce the heat to low and simmer, covered, uncovering to stir every 5 minutes, for 30 minutes. Remove from the heat and serve with rice or pasta.

Veal Cutlets with
Enoki Mushroom Sauce

Makes 4 servings   *Usually we tell you to drain fried food on paper towels, but not in this case. When you fry larger foods such as cutlets or fish fillets, it's better to drain them on a wire rack, because the steam from the hot fried food would be trapped by the towels and make the crusts soggy and more likely to fall off.*

Veal Cutlets

> **Eight 3- to 4-ounce cutlets**
> **1½ cups unseasoned dried bread crumbs**
> **2 large eggs, lightly beaten**
> **¼ cup olive oil**

Enoki Mushroom Sauce

> **2 tablespoons olive oil**
> **1 cup seeded and chopped red bell peppers**
> **1 cup seeded and chopped yellow bell peppers**
> **1 cup seeded and chopped green bell peppers**
> **6 tablespoons all-purpose flour**
> **7 ounces enoki mushrooms, stem bottoms trimmed off**
> **3 cups beef stock**

Seasoning Mix

1 tablespoon salt
2½ teaspoons dried basil
1½ teaspoons garlic powder
1½ teaspoons onion powder
1 teaspoon cayenne
1 teaspoon dry mustard
1 teaspoon dried oregano
1 teaspoon paprika
½ teaspoon ground cumin
½ teaspoon dillweed
½ teaspoon black pepper
¼ teaspoon white pepper

1. Combine the seasoning mix ingredients in a small bowl. Sprinkle each side of each cutlet with ¼ teaspoon of the seasoning mix and gently pat it in.

2. Combine the bread crumbs with 1 tablespoon of the seasoning mix and place them in a cake or pie pan. Remove the remaining seasoning mix for the sauce. Place the beaten eggs in a similar pan.

3. Make the sauce: Preheat an empty 10-inch skillet over high heat until it is very hot, about 4 minutes. Add the olive oil and all the bell peppers and cook, stirring every 30 seconds, for 4 minutes. Add the flour and stir constantly until the white is no longer visible. Scrape the brown crust off the bottom of the skillet, add the mushrooms, and stir gently until the mixture is well combined. Stir in the seasoning mix and the stock. Bring to a boil, then reduce the heat to medium and simmer briskly for 10 minutes. Keep warm while you cook the veal cutlets.

4. In a heavy 12-inch skillet, heat the olive oil over high heat just until it begins to smoke, about 3 to 4 minutes. Dip the cutlets into the eggs, evenly coating both sides. Transfer the cutlets to the bread crumbs and, turning several times, gently but firmly press the crumbs into the meat with your hands. Shake off the excess crumbs and transfer immediately to the hot oil. Cook, turning once, until the cutlets are golden brown on both sides, about 3 to 4 minutes per side. Drain on a wire rack and serve with the sauce.

Poultry

Some of my earliest memories involve the fantastic number of ways my mother cooked chicken! It seemed as though she never did it the same way twice, and each new dish she created was better than the one before. We're lucky that chicken is so economical these days, and if you skin it, it's also low in fat and cholesterol. I like to prepare it with traditional Louisiana favorites like tasso and with ingredients I hadn't heard of when I was a boy, such as parsnips and mangoes.

Best Country Chicken Pie

Makes 4 generous servings

Chicken pies have long been a favorite dish with families all over the country, but what's new here is the use of corn and cornmeal in the crust. You wouldn't think that such small amounts would make such a dramatic difference in taste and texture, but they do! I think the combination of two colors of bell peppers makes a great-looking dish, but if you prefer, you can use ¾ cup of either red or green bell peppers in the filling.

2¼ cups all-purpose flour
¼ cup yellow cornmeal
1 tablespoon sugar
¾ cup very cold vegetable shortening
One 8½-ounce can creamed corn, Green
    Giant brand preferably, in all
2 large egg yolks
5 tablespoons unsalted butter, in all
1 large or 2 small parsnips, peeled
1 small head garlic, peeled
9 ounces boneless, skinless chicken breast,
    cut into ¾-inch cubes
1½ cups peeled white potatoes cut into
    ½-inch cubes
2 cups chicken stock, in all
1 tablespoon olive oil
1 cup chopped onions
½ cup chopped celery
½ cup seeded and chopped red bell peppers
¼ cup seeded and chopped green bell
    peppers
½ cup seeded and chopped fresh
    Anaheim chile peppers
1 cup peeled fresh tomatoes cut into ½-inch
    pieces

Seasoning Mix

2¼ teaspoons salt
1¼ teaspoons paprika
1¼ teaspoons dried savory
1¼ teaspoons dried thyme
    leaves
¾ teaspoon onion powder
½ teaspoon cayenne
½ teaspoon garlic powder
½ teaspoon ground nutmeg
½ teaspoon black pepper
¼ teaspoon white pepper

1. Combine the seasoning mix ingredients in a small bowl.

2. Make the dough: In a kitchen mixer equipped with a dough hook, combine the flour, cornmeal, sugar, and 1 tablespoon of the seasoning mix. Process briefly to combine the dry ingredients, then add the shortening. Process at slow speed until the ingredients combine—the dough will look very lumpy. With the mixer running, slowly add ½ cup of the creamed corn and the egg yolks and pulse until the dough just combines, then mix at low speed for 3 minutes. Wrap the dough in plastic wrap and refrigerate until cold.

3. Roast the vegetables: Preheat the oven to 350°F. Melt 2 tablespoons of the butter. Place the parsnip(s) and garlic on a baking sheet and brush them with the melted butter. Place them in the oven and roast, checking frequently and turning as needed, until they brown evenly on all sides, about 20 minutes. When cool enough to handle, chop the parsnip(s) into ¼-inch pieces, and mince the roasted garlic. Set both aside.

4. Make the filling: Sprinkle the chicken evenly with 1 tablespoon of the seasoning mix and gently pat it in. In a blender, purée ¾ cup of the potato cubes with 1 cup of the stock until smooth and set aside. In a 5-quart pot, heat the olive oil over high heat just until it begins to smoke, about 3 to 4 minutes. Add the seasoned chicken and spread the pieces evenly over the bottom. Loosen the pieces from the bottom with a spatula and turn. Continue to cook, turning the meat frequently, until it is lightly browned on all sides, but not cooked through, about 2 minutes. Remove the chicken with a slotted spoon and set aside.

5. To the same pot, add 2 more tablespoons of the butter and when it's almost melted, add the onions, celery, both bell peppers, the Anaheim peppers, the roasted garlic, and 1 tablespoon of the seasoning mix. Stir well, then spread the vegetables evenly over the bottom of the pan and cook, stirring frequently and scraping the bottom of the skillet, until the vegetables are faded in color and slightly browning in places, but still crunchy, about 6 to 8 minutes. *This part of the cooking process is the most important step, because it develops the sweetness and deep flavors of the vegetables. This process changes the tastes of the dish dramatically. The vegetables cooked in this way have complex flavors, which change as you chew them.*

6. Continue to cook, scraping constantly to counteract the sticking, for 3 more minutes, then stir in the puréed potatoes, the remaining cubed potatoes, and 1 tablespoon of the seasoning mix. Scrape well and continue to cook, stirring frequently, until the color of the mixture is a gravy-like brown, and large volcano-

like bubbles burst on the surface, about 10 minutes. *The taste at this point is very rich with deep vegetable flavor, a strong taste of salt, and a medium taste from the seasonings. You may notice that the mixture appears slightly stringy, the action of the potato starch, which will disappear when the pie is cooked.*

7. Add the roasted parsnips, the tomatoes, the remaining canned corn, and the remaining 1 cup stock. Continue to cook, stirring and scraping the bottom and sides of the pot constantly, until the mixture returns to a boil. Stir in the reserved chicken and any accumulated juices until evenly mixed, then remove from the heat. Refrigerate if not using immediately, but reheat to 120°F before using. *The flavor of the finished filling is a rich, browned stew taste, balanced with chicken flavor and a generous infusion of herbs and spices, which spreads in your mouth as you taste. Following these flavors are the softer starchy potato and sweet parsnip flavors. These tend to cut off the other flavors abruptly when you bite into them. The seasoned crust, on the other hand, works with the other flavors and extends them.*

8. To assemble and bake: Preheat the oven to 350°F. Roll out two thirds of the dough about ¼ inch thick, sprinkling the work surface and the dough lightly with flour as you work, and use it to line an 8-inch square baking dish or casserole. Refrigerate the remaining dough until ready to use. If necessary to loosen the dough from the rolling surface, use a broad spatula. If any of the dough breaks while you are working, patch it with a little of the remaining dough. Trim the edges flush with the top of the pan, and pierce the dough on the bottom and sides with the tines of a fork. Bake until the dough is slightly crisp to the touch, about 20 minutes, then let cool to room temperature.

9. Rewarm the filling to 120°F if necessary. Place the filling in the crust, roll out the remaining dough, and shape it to cover the pie. Seal and trim the edges flush with the top of the dish—a crimped edge will burn—and bake until the crust is golden and the edges are beginning to darken, about 20 minutes. Serve hot, and if you have any left over, it's really great the next day, too!

Chicken Roulades with a Vegetable Stuffing

Makes 4 servings

"Roulade" comes from the French verb "to roll," and usually refers to a slice of meat rolled around a filling before cooking. In this case, the filling or stuffing is cooked alongside, not inside, the rolled-up chicken. Unless you're experienced at deboning poultry, have your butcher do this, then check to be sure all the pieces of bone and cartilage have been removed.

The chicken and stuffing can be reheated in a microwave or conventional oven, but because the sauce is mostly heavy cream, please keep its wonderful texture and flavor intact by reheating gently in a heavy saucepan on top of the stove. Leaving the skin on all the quarters adds great flavor, but if you want to lower the fat a little, you can remove the skin.

3 tablespoons olive oil
1½ cups chopped onions
1½ cups chopped celery
1 cup seeded and chopped green bell peppers
1 tablespoon minced fresh garlic
1¾ cups chicken stock, in all
2 cups eggplant, peeled and cut
    into ½-inch cubes
2 cups unpeeled zucchini cut into ½-inch cubes
2 cups portobello mushrooms cut into ½-inch
    cubes
One 3- to 4-pound chicken, deboned, then
    quartered
½ cup unseasoned dried bread crumbs
3 tablespoons unsalted butter, melted
1¼ cups heavy cream

Seasoning Mix

2½ teaspoons salt

1½ teaspoons dried basil

1½ teaspoons onion powder

1½ teaspoons paprika

1¼ teaspoons cayenne

1 teaspoon black pepper

1 teaspoon garlic powder

1 teaspoon dried thyme
    leaves

¾ teaspoon dried oregano

½ teaspoon white pepper

181

1. Combine the seasoning mix ingredients in a small bowl and mix well.

2. Preheat the oven to 300°F.

3. Heat the olive oil in a large skillet over high heat just until it begins to smoke, about 3 to 4 minutes. Add the onions, celery, and bell peppers and cook until the onions begin to brown, about 5 minutes. Add 2 tablespoons plus ½ teaspoon of the seasoning mix and cook, stirring and scraping the bottom of the skillet constantly and being careful not to let the seasonings burn, for 2 minutes. Add the garlic and cook, continuing to stir and scrape, for 3 minutes. By now, the wonderful fragrance of the browning vegetables is starting to fill the entire house, and those waiting for dinner are beginning to salivate! Tell 'em it's way too early and to go find something useful to do!

4. Stir in 1 cup of the stock and scrape the skillet bottom well, loosening any brown bits that stick. Add the eggplant, zucchini, and mushrooms. Cook, stirring occasionally, for 7 minutes, then stir well and transfer the contents of the skillet to a 9 × 13-inch baking pan. *The first flavor is of the cooked vegetables—the eggplant and zucchini—followed by the more subtle, dark taste of the portobellos and the mild sweetness of the onions. The finishing taste is lightly salty and well seasoned with a pleasant lingering heat in the front of the mouth.* Bake for 45 minutes, opening the oven (be careful!) to stir the stuffing 2 or 3 times.

5. While the stuffing is baking, season each breast piece evenly with 1 teaspoon of the seasoning mix. Sprinkle each leg/thigh piece evenly with 2 teaspoons of the seasoning mix. Place the leg/thigh pieces on your work surface, skin sides down. Place 1 breast piece in the middle of each leg/thigh piece and roll up tightly, allowing the meat to overlap. Place the seam sides down and smooth each roulade into an even shape—no need to pin or tie the roulades, as they will hold their shape on their own.

6. At the end of the 45 minutes, remove the pan of stuffing from the oven, stir in the bread crumbs, and scrape the pan bottom well. Push the dressing to one side, then place the roulades on the other side of the pan. Return to the oven and bake for 15 minutes, then add the butter to the dressing and stir well. Return the pan to the oven and bake for 15 more minutes. Stir the dressing, which is now a rich brown color, mixing in the juices from the chicken, then place a meat thermometer into 1 of the roulades so that the tip is right in its center. Return to the oven and continue to bake until the internal temperature reaches 170°F, 35 to 45 minutes. Remove from the oven and remove ¾ cup of the now dark brown stuffing from the pan to make the sauce. *This recipe produces an extremely complex and fla-*

vorful dressing. Among the many flavors present are the cooked mushrooms, roasted eggplant, and bread crumbs.

7. Combine the ¾ cup stuffing, the heavy cream, and the remaining ¾ cup chicken stock in a blender. Process until smooth, 1 or 2 minutes, then reheat briefly in a small pan.

8. To serve, cut each roulade in half. For each portion, serve half a roulade, one quarter of the stuffing, and a generous ½ cup of the sauce.

Chicken Breasts with Vegetables

Makes 4 servings

Multicolored fresh vegetables—broccoli, cauliflower, zucchini, tomatoes, red and yellow bell peppers—give this one-dish chicken recipe a variety of flavors as well as textures. You can prepare this dish without any oil—just be sure to use a nonstick pan, and don't scrape the pan after adding the vegetables but add an extra ¼ cup stock at that time to steam them. With or without the oil, the chicken-and-vegetable combination is beautiful to look at and nourishing as well as delicious. To keep the vegetables as bright and fresh-tasting as possible, be sure not to overcook them.

Eight 4-ounce boneless, skinless chicken
　　breast halves
2 cups broccoli florets
2 cups cauliflower florets
2 cups unpeeled zucchini cut to the same size
　　as the florets
1½ cups chopped fresh tomatoes
1½ cups chopped onions
1½ cups seeded and chopped red bell peppers
1½ cups seeded and chopped yellow bell
　　peppers
2 tablespoons vegetable oil
½ cup chicken stock

Seasoning Mix
1¾ teaspoons salt
1½ teaspoons dry mustard
1½ teaspoons paprika
1 teaspoon cayenne
1 teaspoon ground dried Anaheim chile peppers
¾ teaspoon garlic powder
¾ teaspoon onion powder
½ teaspoon ground cumin
½ teaspoon ground dried guajillo chile peppers
¼ teaspoon black pepper

1. Combine the seasoning mix ingredients in a small bowl.

2. Sprinkle the chicken breasts evenly with 2 tablespoons plus 1 teaspoon of the seasoning mix and gently pat it in. Combine the vegetables in a large bowl, sprinkle the remain-

ing seasoning mix over them, and mix gently just until the seasonings are evenly distributed.

3. In a heavy 12-inch skillet or a 4-quart pot with a cover, heat the vegetable oil just until it begins to smoke, about 3 to 4 minutes. Add the seasoned breast halves, in batches if necessary, and cook, turning once, until they are browned on both sides, but not fully cooked, about 4 minutes per side. Remove the chicken from the pan and set it aside.

4. To the same pan, add the seasoned vegetables and the stock. Scrape the pan thoroughly, then cover immediately. Cook, uncovering to stir and scrape about once a minute, for 5 minutes, then return the chicken and the accumulated juices to the pan. Re-cover and cook until the chicken is cooked through, about 4 to 6 minutes more. For each serving, place 2 breast halves on a plate and divide the vegetables evenly among the portions.

Chicken with a
Green and White Taste

Makes 4 servings

Think how many "green and white" tastes go great together: turnips and greens, spinach and cream, potatoes and green beans, peas and pearl onions, mint and yogurt, to name a few.

When the peas are fresh, they have an awesome, very sweet taste that is fantastic with the white of the cheeses. Sugar snap peas are very much like snow peas—you eat both varieties whole, pods and all, and they can be used interchangeably. Be careful not to overcook them, though, or they'll lose their wonderful crunch and delicate flavor. You'll find they add just the right texture contrast to the tangy chicken and smooth cheese sauce in this recipe.

One 3- to 4-pound chicken, cut into 8 pieces
2 tablespoons vegetable oil
3 cups chopped onions
¼ cup seeded and minced fresh jalapeño chile peppers
¼ cup all-purpose flour
4 cups chicken stock
1 cup heavy cream
4 ounces white Cheddar cheese, freshly grated
4 ounces Monterey Jack cheese, freshly grated
1 pound sugar snap peas, ends trimmed and strings removed

Seasoning Mix
2 teaspoons salt
1¾ teaspoons onion powder
1¾ teaspoons dried oregano
1½ teaspoons ground cumin
1 teaspoon paprika
1 teaspoon ground dried New Mexico chile peppers
¾ teaspoon garlic powder
¾ teaspoon ground dried ancho chile peppers
½ teaspoon cayenne
½ teaspoon ground cinnamon
½ teaspoon ground nutmeg
½ teaspoon black pepper
½ teaspoon white pepper

1. Combine the seasoning mix ingredients in a small bowl.

2. Sprinkle the chicken evenly with 1 tablespoon plus 1 teaspoon of the seasoning mix and rub it in well.

3. Heat the vegetable oil in a heavy 4-quart pot over high heat just until it begins to smoke, about 3 to 4 minutes. To the pot add the chicken, large pieces first and skin sides down first, and cook, turning frequently, until golden brown on both sides, about 10 minutes per batch. Remove the chicken from the pot and set it aside.

4. To the pot add the onions, jalapeños, and the remaining seasoning mix. Cook, stirring and scraping the pot every 2 or 3 minutes, until the vegetables begin to brown, about 7 minutes. *Even the jalapeños will have a tinge of slightly sweet flavor, believe it or not!* Add the flour and stir until the white is no longer visible.

5. Spread the mixture evenly over the bottom of the pot and cook until a brown crust forms, about 2 to 3 minutes. Scrape up the crust, which should be a pretty light brown with a reddish tinge and will be very sweet and flavorful, then add the stock and stir until the crust dissolves. Reduce the heat to medium-low, add the heavy cream and the two cheeses, and return the chicken and the accumulated juices to the pot. Cook, stirring every 3 to 4 minutes, until all the cheese melts (*taste the incredible richness now!*), about 10 minutes. Add the sugar snap peas and simmer until they are just cooked but still sweet and crunchy, about 12 minutes. Serve on a mound of your favorite pasta or rice.

Chicken Palawan

Makes 4 servings Just about everybody likes a one-dish meal because it's so easy to prepare and cook, the flavors blend beautifully, and it's easy to transport if you're going to a covered-dish supper. Adding daikon, yucca root, and lemongrass takes this dish out of the ordinary, without messing with its old-time virtues.

One 3½- to 4-pound chicken, cut into 8 pieces
2 cups chopped onions
2 cups peeled and chopped daikon
2 cups peeled and chopped yucca root
½ cup lemongrass, ground very fine in a
    blender
1 cup chopped celery
4 cups chicken stock, in all

Seasoning Mix

2½ teaspoons salt
1½ teaspoons garlic powder
1½ teaspoons dry mustard
1½ teaspoons onion powder
1 teaspoon dried basil
1 teaspoon ground cumin
1 teaspoon ground paprika
1 teaspoon ground dried
    Anaheim chile peppers
¾ teaspoon cayenne
¾ teaspoon dried oregano
½ teaspoon black pepper
½ teaspoon ground dried
    árbol chile peppers

1. Combine the seasoning mix ingredients in a small bowl.

2. Sprinkle the chicken pieces evenly with 1 tablespoon plus 1 teaspoon of the seasoning mix and rub it in well.

3. Preheat a heavy 4-quart pot over high heat until it is very hot, about 4 minutes. To the pot, add the chicken, skin side down first and large pieces first, and cook, turning every 1 or 2 minutes, until the chicken is golden brown, about 8 minutes. If your pot is not large enough to cook all the chicken at one time, add the remaining pieces as the pieces in the first batch are removed.

4. When the chicken has been removed, add the onions, daikon, yucca, lemongrass, celery, and the remaining seasoning mix. Stir and scrape well, then cover and cook, uncovering every 2 minutes to stir and scrape the bottom of the pot, until the mixture sticks hard to the bottom, 8 to 10 minutes. *At this time, the vegetables have a dark, almost bitter flavor, with a noticeable crunch from the daikon and yucca.* Add 1 cup of the stock and scrape the bottom of the

pot well, loosening all the brown bits sticking to the bottom. Re-cover and cook, uncovering every 2 minutes to stir and scrape, for 12 more minutes. Add 1 cup of the stock, re-cover the pot, and continue to cook, uncovering to scrape and stir every minute or so, for an additional 4 minutes. Uncover, add the remaining 2 cups stock, scrape the bottom well, then return the chicken and the accumulated juices to the pot. Re-cover and cook until the chicken is cooked through and the vegetables are tender, about 15 minutes. Serve hot.

Chicken Smothered
in Black Beans

Makes 4 generous servings   *Notice that the beans are to be soaked overnight, a step that shortens the cooking time. If you forget, or if you're in a hurry, you can cook them, in water to cover, on high in the microwave for about 30 minutes, which will produce a similar result. If you do it this way, cook the beans first, then prepare the seasoning mix, then the vegetables, and the beans should be ready for use by then. Don't be afraid of the several hot peppers in the seasoning mix. This dish is spicy, but with the full pound of beans, and especially if it's served over rice, even my wimpy friend Mrs. Podunk enjoys it!*

This dish makes a great presentation—the fresh tomato garnish, if you use it, adds just the right contrast of color, temperature, flavor, and texture.

1 pound dried black beans, rinsed and
    picked over
One 3- to 4-pound chicken, cut into 8 pieces
2 tablespoons vegetable oil
2 cups chopped onions
2 cups seeded and chopped bell peppers, all
    one color if you like, or use about ⅔ cup
    each of red, yellow, and green bell peppers
1 cup chopped celery
4 to 4½ cups chicken stock, in all
1 cup peeled and diced fresh tomatoes
    (optional)

Seasoning Mix

1 tablespoon salt

2 teaspoons paprika

1¾ teaspoons dry mustard

1¾ teaspoons onion powder

1½ teaspoons dried basil

1½ teaspoons ground cumin

1½ teaspoons garlic powder

1 teaspoon dried oregano

1 teaspoon black pepper

1 teaspoon ground ancho
    chile peppers

1 teaspoon ground árbol
    chile peppers

1 teaspoon ground dried
    Anaheim chile peppers

½ teaspoon cayenne

1. *Day 1:* Add enough water to the beans to cover them by 3 to 4 inches and soak overnight in the refrigerator. Or see headnote above to prepare them the same day.

2. *Day 2:* Drain but do not rinse the beans and set them aside. Combine the seasoning mix ingredients in a small bowl. Sprinkle the chicken pieces evenly with 1 tablespoon plus 1 teaspoon of the seasoning mix and rub it in well.

3. In a heavy 4-quart pot, heat the vegetable oil over high heat just until it begins to smoke, about 3 to 4 minutes. Brown the chicken in batches, large pieces first and skin side down first, turning once a minute, until nicely browned, about 8 minutes per batch. Remove the chicken from the pot and set it aside.

4. To the pot, add the onions, bell peppers, celery, and the remaining seasoning mix. Cook for 10 minutes, stirring and scraping the pot every 2 minutes to prevent sticking (and, if absolutely necessary during this time to prevent burning, add a little bit of the stock—no more than ½ cup—to deglaze the pot). Stir in 3 cups of the stock and the beans, cover, and bring just to a boil. *At this early point, the seasonings don't taste balanced and have a flavor very much like their uncooked state.* Reduce the heat to medium-low and simmer, stirring and scraping the pot every 5 minutes, for 45 minutes, stirring more often toward the end of the cooking time. Add ½ cup of the stock, and cook, still stirring and scraping every 3 to 5 minutes, for 15 minutes. If the beans start to stick hard to the pot bottom, add the remaining ½ cup stock and scrape the bottom carefully.

5. Return the chicken and the accumulated juices to the pot and submerge the chicken pieces in the beans and liquid. Return just to a boil, reduce the heat to low, and simmer until the beans are soft and their liquid is thick and creamy, about 15 minutes. *You'll notice that now the seasonings are well balanced and the beans have absorbed their flavor, producing a very rich, complex finished taste.* If you're like me, toward the end of the cooking time you'll want to smash some of the beans against the side of the pot to thicken the sauce and release even more of the wonderful flavor of the beans. Remove from the heat, garnish with the diced fresh tomatoes, if desired, and serve immediately with hot rice.

Chicken Stuffed with Chiles

The wonderfully fragrant, browned vegetable mixture, used as stuffing in the cavity and under the skin, subtly flavors every bit of the chicken. Even though there are several chile peppers—both dried and fresh—they do not overwhelm the bell peppers and onions. What results is a sophisticated yet basically simple dinner that would be welcome any time of year. Well-buttered rice tinted and flavored with turmeric or saffron, along with one of our crispy chowchows (page 90 or page 92), would be great accompaniments.

1 cup peeled sweet potatoes
    cut into ¼-inch cubes
3 cups chicken stock, in all
2 tablespoons olive oil
1½ cups chopped onions
1½ cups chopped celery
1 cup seeded and chopped yellow bell
    peppers
1 cup seeded and chopped red bell peppers
½ cup seeded and chopped fresh banana
    peppers (also called wax peppers)
½ cup seeded and chopped poblano chile
    peppers
½ cup seeded and chopped fresh red
    jalapeño chile peppers
1 tablespoon minced fresh garlic
One 3-pound chicken
2 tablespoons all-purpose flour

Seasoning Mix

2½ teaspoons salt

1¼ teaspoons garlic powder

1¼ teaspoons paprika

1¼ teaspoons ground cumin

1 teaspoon dry mustard

1 teaspoon onion powder

1 teaspoon ground dried
    pasilla chile peppers

1 teaspoon dried oregano

1 teaspoon ground coriander

1 teaspoon dried thyme
    leaves

½ teaspoon white pepper

½ teaspoon cayenne

½ teaspoon ground dried
    New Mexico chile peppers

¼ teaspoon black pepper

1. Combine the seasoning mix ingredients in a small bowl.

2. Purée the sweet potatoes and 1½ cups of the stock in a blender until smooth, then set aside.

3. Heat the olive oil in a 14-inch skillet or a 4-quart pot with a lid just until the oil begins to smoke, about 3 to 4 minutes. Add the onions, celery, all the bell peppers, and 3 tablespoons plus 2 teaspoons of the seasoning mix. Stir well, then cover and cook for 5 minutes. Uncover and scrape the bottom of the pan to loosen any material sticking to the bottom. Add all the banana peppers and chile peppers, stir well, add the sweet potato purée, and stir until well combined. Re-cover and cook for 3 minutes. Remove the cover and stir in the garlic. *Taste now and get the unfocused sweet flavor from the sweet potato, with a well-seasoned taste and a smooth mouth feel, with heat building rapidly from the chiles.* Cook, uncovered, stirring and scraping the bottom of the pan frequently, until the mixture becomes a thick paste, about 15 minutes. *Now notice how the earlier flavors, which were pleasant but unfocused, have become rich and deep. The seasoning is now at a high intensity and the vegetables are rich and sweet. The chile heat spreads in the mouth, lingering for a long time without burning.* Remove from the heat and allow to cool.

4. Preheat the oven to 300°F.

5. *When the mixture reaches room temperature, you'll notice that all the previous flavors remain in play, but they've mellowed as they cooled. When the stuffing is cooked in the bird, the natural flavor of the chicken and its fat will enrich these flavors and baking will add a browned flavor for a deep and complex taste.*

6. Now make a pocket between the skin and the breast of the chicken by pushing your fingers underneath the skin to loosen it. Stuff this pocket with half the vegetable mixture, pushing it in evenly so that it makes a layer about ½ inch thick. Stuff the cavity of the bird with the remaining mixture, then sprinkle the outside of the bird with the remaining seasoning mix. Place the bird, breast side up, in a roasting pan (you don't need a rack), insert a meat thermometer into the thickest part of the chicken but not touching a bone, and place it in the oven. Roast until the internal temperature of the chicken reaches 170°F, about 1½ hours.

7. Take the chicken from the roasting pan and remove 1 cup of stuffing from the bird (Keep the chicken warm while you make the sauce.) Place the roasting pan over high heat on top of the stove, add the flour, and stir until the white is no longer visible. Add the 1 cup stuffing and stir and scrape the bottom of the pan to loosen all the brown bits. Stir in the remaining 1½ cups stock and bring the mixture to a boil. Cook, stirring constantly, until the sauce thickens slightly, about 1 minute.

8. To serve, cut the chicken into quarters, drizzle each portion with some of the sauce, and pass the remaining sauce separately.

Chicken in "Tomato Sugar"

Makes 4 servings

Every cook needs a wide repertoire of chicken recipes, and this good-looking, great-tasting chicken dish is one you'll be glad to add to your list. Served over rice or pasta, and fairly brimming with delicious fresh vegetables, this is a one-dish meal.

One 4- to 5-pound chicken, cut into 8 pieces
2 tablespoons vegetable oil
1½ cups seeded and chopped green bell peppers
1½ cups seeded and chopped red bell peppers
1½ cups seeded and chopped yellow bell peppers
1½ cups peeled turnips cut into ½-inch cubes
One 15-ounce can tomato sauce, in all
1 tablespoon minced fresh thyme leaves
2 teaspoons minced fresh garlic
One 15-ounce can diced tomatoes
2 cups chicken stock

Seasoning Mix

2 teaspoons salt
1 teaspoon ground cumin
1 teaspoon garlic powder
1 teaspoon dry mustard
1 teaspoon onion powder
1 teaspoon paprika
1 teaspoon ground dried chipotle chile peppers
¾ teaspoon cayenne
½ teaspoon black pepper
¼ teaspoon white pepper

1. Combine the seasoning mix ingredients in a small bowl. Sprinkle the chicken evenly with 1 tablespoon plus 1 teaspoon of the seasoning mix and rub it in well.

2. In a heavy 4-quart pot, heat the vegetable oil over high heat just until it begins to smoke, about 3 or 4 minutes. Add the chicken in batches, large pieces first and skin sides down first. Cook, turning several times, until the chicken is browned, but not cooked through, about 8 minutes per batch. Remove the chicken from the pot and set it aside.

3. To the pot, add all the bell peppers, the turnips, and the remaining seasoning mix. Cook, stirring every 2 to 3 minutes, until the vegetables wilt and start to brown, about 12 minutes. *At this point, the vegetables will have lost their "raw" taste and be slightly sweet. You'll also notice some of the heat of the*

chile peppers, but this will subside as other ingredients are added. Add 1 cup of the tomato sauce and cook until the sauce is dark and thick, the vegetables are soft and brown, and the mixture begins to stick, about 7 minutes. *Reducing the tomato sauce with dry heat and allowing it to brown gives it color and depth and the sweetness that we call "tomato sugar." You'll experience a wonderful flavor and aroma unlike anything else—your nose will tell you when you reach this stage! This process also gives the vegetables a fire-roasted taste.* Now add the thyme and garlic and continue cooking. When the mixture is dry and sizzling (watch the pot, not the clock, especially here), stir in the remaining tomato sauce, the diced tomatoes, and the stock. Return the chicken and the accumulated juices to the pot and bring just to a boil. Reduce the heat to medium and simmer until the chicken is cooked through, about 20 to 25 minutes. Remove from the heat and serve over rice or pasta.

Chicken with Tasso

Makes 4 servings   Tasso, a dense, highly seasoned smoked ham, is very popular with the Acadian French people of south Louisiana because it adds a rich flavor, which contrasts nicely with the natural sweetness of the browned vegetables in this dish. Busy cooks have always liked one-pot recipes because they're so easy, and this one is no exception. Chop the vegetables, brown the chicken—dinner's almost ready! The vegetables cook in plenty of stock, so their flavors are incorporated into the sauce, but they're still firm enough to give a good texture to the dish.

One 3½-pound chicken, cut into 8 pieces
¼ cup olive oil
2 cups chopped onions
2 cups chopped celery
½ cup seeded and chopped green bell peppers
½ cup seeded and chopped red bell peppers
½ cup seeded and chopped yellow bell peppers
½ pound finely diced tasso or premium-quality cooked ham
1 tablespoon minced fresh garlic
3 cups chicken stock, in all
3 tablespoons all-purpose flour

Seasoning Mix

1 tablespoon salt
2¼ teaspoons dried cilantro
1¾ teaspoons ground ginger
1¾ teaspoons dry mustard
1¾ teaspoons paprika
1¼ teaspoons onion powder
1 teaspoon garlic powder
¾ teaspoon cayenne
½ teaspoon ground star anise
½ teaspoon black pepper
½ teaspoon white pepper

1. Combine the seasoning mix ingredients in a small bowl.

2. Sprinkle the chicken pieces evenly with 2 tablespoons of the seasoning mix and rub it in well with your hands.

3. In a heavy 4-quart pot, preferably nonstick, heat the olive oil over high heat just until it begins to smoke, about 3 to 4 minutes. Add the chicken, in batches if necessary, skin sides

down first and large pieces first, and cook until the skin is brown, about 4 minutes. Turn the pieces over and cook just until the other sides are brown but the chicken is not cooked through, about 4 minutes. Remove the chicken from the pot and set it aside.

4. To the same pot, add the onions, celery, all the bell peppers, and the tasso. Stir well and scrape the bottom of the pot to loosen the brown bits left from the chicken. Continue to cook, stirring frequently, for 3 minutes—the colors are so bright they're almost glowing—then add the remaining seasoning mix and the garlic. Stir well, then cover and cook for 5 minutes. Uncover and stir well—you'll see that the vegetables are beginning to brown and stick slightly. Scrape the bottom of the pot to loosen any sticking material, then re-cover and cook for 4 minutes. At this point the vegetables are medium brown and may be sticking hard, so add ½ cup of the stock and deglaze the pot by scraping to loosen all the material on the bottom. Add the flour and stir until the white is no longer visible, adding a little more stock if necessary to help absorb the flour. Scrape the bottom of the pot one more time, then cover and let the mixture cook for 3 minutes. *Warning: Do not do this if your pot does not have a good thick bottom. A thin pot will heat too quickly and your mixture will definitely burn, so reduce the heat and watch closely to be sure that doesn't happen. Your cooking time may have to be a little longer to make up for using less heat. But if you do have a good heavy-bottomed pot, you'll discover that flour moistened with the juices from the vegetables and tasso creates a wonderful flavor when it is allowed to brown in this way.*

5. Uncover, add the remaining 2½ cups of stock, and scrape the bottom of the pot well. Bring to a boil, return the chicken and any accumulated juices to the pot, and return the liquid just to a boil. *At this time, the broth is reminiscent of gumbo, but very salty from the seasonings.* Reduce the heat to medium, re-cover, and cook, stirring and scraping the pot occasionally, until the chicken is fully cooked, about 25 minutes. *Now the rich gravy flavor is enhanced by the round pepper taste—look for the subtle flavors of anise, which appear at the back end of the taste.* Serve over rice.

Palmetto Chicken

Makes 4 servings *This is one of my very favorite recipes in this book, and you'll understand why the moment you taste your first bite! If you're familiar with Louisiana gumbo, this dish might remind you of that, with its okra, andouille, and chicken, especially if you serve it over rice as we suggest. It's not a soup, though, but a knife-and-fork dinner simmered in a dark, spicy sauce. The red and yellow bell peppers can be expensive, so unless you have them on hand or will use them for another purpose, you can use green peppers instead, or all red or all yellow peppers.*

One 3-pound chicken, cut into 8 pieces
2 tablespoons olive oil
1 cup chopped onions
¾ cup chopped celery
¼ cup seeded and chopped red bell peppers
¼ cup seeded and chopped yellow bell peppers
½ pound andouille, or good quality smoked sausage, quartered lengthwise, then each length cut into ½-inch pieces
6 ounces okra, ends trimmed and cut into ½-inch-thick rounds
2 tablespoons all-purpose flour
1 cup chicken stock

Seasoning Mix

1¾ teaspoons paprika
1¾ teaspoons salt
1¼ teaspoons dry mustard
1¼ teaspoons onion powder
¾ teaspoon cayenne
¾ teaspoon garlic powder
½ teaspoon ground cumin
½ teaspoon black pepper
½ teaspoon white pepper

1. Combine the seasoning mix ingredients in a small bowl.

2. Sprinkle the chicken evenly with 1 tablespoon plus 1 teaspoon of the seasoning mix and rub it in well with your hands.

3. In a heavy 4-quart pot, preferably nonstick, heat the olive oil over high heat just until it begins to smoke, about 3 to 4

minutes. Add the chicken, large pieces first and skin sides down first, and cook until the skin is brown, about 4 minutes. Turn the pieces over and cook until the other side is brown but the chicken is not cooked through, about 4 minutes. Remove the pieces from the pot as soon as they are done and set them aside, then add the remaining pieces as soon as there is room in the pot.

4. To the pot, add the onions, celery, all the bell peppers, and 1 tablespoon plus 2 teaspoons of the seasoning mix. Stir well and scrape the bottom of the pan, loosening all the brown bits from the chicken. If necessary, deglaze the pot by adding a little of the stock and stirring and scraping thoroughly. Add the andouille and okra, stir well, and cook, stirring frequently, for 4 minutes. Sprinkle the flour evenly over the top of the mixture in the pot and stir until the white is no longer visible, about 1 minute. Stir in the stock and scrape the bottom of the pot again to loosen any new brown bits, then return the chicken and the accumulated juices to the pot. As soon as the liquid just begins to boil, reduce the heat to medium, cover, and simmer until the chicken is fully cooked, about 15 to 20 minutes.

5. Serve hot, allowing 2 pieces of chicken and a quarter of the vegetable mixture (about 1 cup) per serving. A cup of hot rice for each portion will make the meal complete.

Roast Chicken
Stuffed with Parsnips

Makes 4 servings

Stuffing a chicken before roasting is an easy, efficient way to add great flavor, and a bonus is that you have your vegetables already cooked! Notice that we've used a cup of the stuffing as an important ingredient in the sauce—the flavors and textures will be a little different, but complementary.

One 4- to 5-pound chicken
2 tablespoons vegetable oil
1½ cups chopped onions
1 cup seeded and chopped red bell peppers
1 cup seeded and chopped yellow bell peppers
3½ cups parsnips, peeled and cut into ½-inch cubes
2½ cups chicken stock, in all
1 medium-size sweet potato (about ½ pound)

Seasoning Mix

2¼ teaspoons paprika

2¼ teaspoons salt

1¼ teaspoons garlic powder

1¼ teaspoons onion powder

1¼ teaspoons dried oregano

1¼ teaspoons ground dried Anaheim chile peppers

1 teaspoon ground cumin

1 teaspoon ground ginger

1 teaspoon dry mustard

1 teaspoon ground dried New Mexico chile peppers

1 teaspoon ground sage

¾ teaspoon cayenne

½ teaspoon black pepper

¼ teaspoon white pepper

1. Combine the seasoning mix ingredients in a small bowl.

2. Sprinkle the chicken evenly with 1 tablespoon plus 2 teaspoons of the seasoning mix on the outside, and with 1 teaspoon on the inside.

3. Make the stuffing: In a 12-inch nonstick skillet, heat the vegetable oil over high heat just until it begins to smoke, about 3 to 4 minutes. To the skillet, add the onions, the bell peppers, the parsnips, and 3 tablespoons of the seasoning mix. Cover and cook, stirring occasionally, until the vegetables are somewhat browned and the parsnips turn a lovely yellow gold color, about 15 to 18 minutes. *Now the vegetables will taste sweet from the browning. The seasoning flavor*

seems quite low until the other flavors fade, then becomes more apparent. Uncover and add ½ cup of the stock and scrape the bottom of the skillet well. Continue to cook, uncovered, stirring and scraping about once a minute, for 5 minutes, then add another ½ cup of the stock. Scrape the skillet bottom well and continue to cook, stirring and scraping vigorously, for 2 minutes, then remove from the heat. *At this stage, the sweetness of the vegetables is much more pronounced, the parsnips are far less starchy, and the seasoning level is more noticeable than before.* Reserve 1 cup of the stuffing for the sauce.

4. Preheat the oven to 250°F.

5. Stuff the chicken with the remaining stuffing and place it, breast side up, in a roasting pan—no rack is necessary. Place the sweet potato in the pan, and roast until the chicken is cooked through and the skin is crisp, and the interior reaches 165°F on a cooking thermometer, about 1½ to 2 hours. Reserve the pan drippings and the sweet potato for the sauce, and keep the chicken warm while you make the sauce.

6. Make the sauce: As soon as the sweet potato is cool enough to handle, peel and measure it. You'll need 1 cup; discard the rest or just enjoy its goodness on the spot! In a large skillet, combine the reserved stuffing, the 1 cup baked sweet potato, the remaining seasoning mix, the reserved pan drippings, and the remaining 1½ cups stock. Place over high heat and cook, whisking constantly, until the sauce is combined. Bring just to a boil, then reduce the heat to low and simmer, whisking once a minute, for 6 minutes. Remove from the heat and serve with the chicken.

Squash-Stuffed Chicken Breasts

Makes 6 servings

These stuffed chicken breasts are just as beautiful in your mouth as they are on the serving platter. As you can see from reading the recipe, they're not a bit tricky to prepare, but they look as though you spent all day in the kitchen. To make the dicing go as fast as possible, use the best knife you have that's a comfortable size for you to work with, and keep it well sharpened. And remember, never, ever use the sharp blade to move the food you're chopping—that will ruin it in no time. Use the dull side of the blade to scrape the cubes wherever you want to put them. Most people who want to get the preparation out of the way in a hurry keep a sharpening steel right on the counter where they're working and use it often.

6 boneless, skinless chicken breast halves,
    trimmed of fat
¼ cup olive oil, in all
2 cups chopped onions
2 cups unpeeled zucchini
    cut into ¼-inch cubes
2 cups unpeeled yellow squash cut into ¼-inch
    cubes
2 cups butternut squash cut into ¼-inch cubes
1 cup chicken stock
½ pound Cheddar cheese, freshly grated
1½ cups whole milk

Seasoning Mix

1¼ teaspoons salt

¾ teaspoon garlic powder

¾ teaspoon dry mustard

¾ teaspoon onion powder

½ teaspoon dried basil

½ teaspoon ground cumin

½ teaspoon dried oregano

½ teaspoon ground paprika

½ teaspoon ground dried
    Anaheim chile peppers

¼ teaspoon cayenne

¼ teaspoon black pepper

¼ teaspoon ground dried
    árbol chile peppers

1. Combine the seasoning mix ingredients in a small bowl.

2. With the flat surface of a meat mallet, pound the chicken breasts until they are very thin, then season them evenly on both sides with 2 teaspoons of the seasoning mix.

3. Make the stuffing: In a heavy 4-quart pot, heat 3 tablespoons of the olive oil over high heat just until it begins to smoke, about 3 to 4 minutes. Add the onions, zucchini, yellow and butternut squashes, and the remaining seasoning mix. Cook, stirring and scraping the pot bottom every 2 minutes, until the mixture begins to stick hard, about 20 minutes. Add the stock, then scrape up all the browned bits from the bottom and sides of the pot—*those bits are one of the things that give this dish its rich goodness! And notice how wonderful it smells right now—a sure sign that it will taste great. In fact, go ahead and taste it! You'll first notice the squash flavor in the broth, followed closely by the sweet caramelized flavor of those browned bits.* Continue to cook, stirring and scraping every 2 minutes, until the vegetables are soft, the mixture thickens, and the liquid is almost completely evaporated, about 10 minutes. Remove from the heat, add the cheese, and stir until the cheese melts. *Now the flavor reminds you of a grilled cheese sandwich, an effect that softens all the earlier flavors.* Set aside to cool.

4. To make the sauce, combine the milk with ¾ cup of the stuffing in a blender and process until smooth, about 2 minutes. Transfer the mixture to an 8-inch skillet and bring to a full boil. Remove from the heat and set aside.

5. Spread ½ cup of the stuffing on each breast half. Roll up and secure with toothpicks or tie with clean kitchen twine.

6. In a 10-inch skillet, heat the remaining 1 tablespoon olive oil over high heat just until it begins to smoke, about 3 to 4 minutes. Add the stuffed breasts to the skillet and cook them, turning every 1 or 2 minutes, until they are golden brown on all sides, about 7 minutes. Add the sauce to the skillet and bring to a full boil. Reduce the heat to low and simmer for 3 minutes, then remove from the heat. Divide the sauce evenly among the portions and serve immediately.

Tropical Fruit Salad
with Bronzed Chicken

Makes 6 servings *If you're the type of person who likes to gild the lily, you could top this with toasted grated coconut. You can serve this great combination two different ways. The first would be to make the salad first, then bronze the chicken and serve the chicken hot with the cool salad alongside it. If you follow this plan, you'll need to measure out the proper amount of seasoning mix for the chicken (6 teaspoons) and set it aside. Or you can cook the chicken first, chill it, and cut into bite-size pieces to toss with the fruit salad. You'll like it either way!*

6 boneless, skinless chicken breast halves
  (about 4 to 5 ounces each), trimmed of fat
2 tablespoons olive oil
2 tablespoons firmly packed light brown
  sugar
1 cup sour cream
1 ripe mango (about 6 ounces), peeled,
  seeded, and chopped
1 ripe papaya (about 6 ounces), peeled,
  seeded, and chopped
1 small pineapple, peeled, cored, and
  chopped
1 cup crushed raw macadamia nuts

Seasoning Mix

1½ teaspoons paprika

1½ teaspoons salt

1¼ teaspoons garlic powder

1¼ teaspoons black pepper

¾ teaspoon dill seeds

¾ teaspoon onion powder

½ teaspoon dried basil

½ teaspoon ground ginger

½ teaspoon dry mustard

½ teaspoon white pepper

1. Combine the seasoning mix ingredients in a small bowl.

2. Bronze the chicken: Sprinkle ½ teaspoon seasoning mix evenly on each side of each breast half and gently pat it in.

3. Preheat a heavy 12-inch skillet, preferably nonstick, over high heat until very hot, about 3 to 4 minutes. Add the olive oil and heat it for 1 minute, then add the chicken and cook, turning once or twice, until nicely browned and just cooked through, about 6 minutes in all.

4. Make the salad: In a large bowl, whisk the brown sugar and remaining 3 teaspoons seasoning mix into the sour cream until it is thoroughly combined. Add the mango, papaya, pineapple, and nuts. You should have about 4 cups.

5. Serve the chicken either hot or cold, with the fruit salad, as described above.

Vegetables and
Chicken Olé!

Makes 4 generous servings *Once you have the seasoning mix combined and the vegetables prepared, just about all you have to do is toss everything into a pan and bake—it really is that simple! This is one case in which the herbs and spices combine so well with the various vegetables that it takes absolutely no skill to prepare an unusual and tasty dish. If you work outside the home, you can prepare the seasoning mix and vegetables the night before, refrigerate them in plastic zipper bags, and be ready to put a delicious, nutritious dinner on the table in no time!*

6 tablespoons (¾ stick) unsalted butter
½ cup seeded red bell peppers cut into julienne strips
½ cup seeded yellow bell peppers cut into julienne strips
½ cup seeded green bell peppers cut into julienne strips
1 cup onions cut into julienne strips
½ cup celery sliced diagonally into ½-inch pieces
½ cup small broccoflower florets
½ cup carrots sliced diagonally into ½-inch pieces
½ cup mirlitons (chayote) cut into 2½ × ½ × ½-inch pieces
2 boneless skinless chicken breast halves (about 4 ounces each), trimmed of fat and sliced into 1½-inch-wide pieces
½ cup thinly sliced pitted dates
1 cup dry-roasted peanuts

Seasoning Mix

1½ teaspoons salt
1 teaspoon dried basil
1 teaspoon ground coriander
1 teaspoon paprika
1 teaspoon ground dried ancho chile peppers
1 teaspoon ground dried guajillo chile peppers
1 teaspoon ground dried New Mexico chile peppers
¾ teaspoon onion powder
½ teaspoon ground cumin
½ teaspoon garlic powder
½ teaspoon dry mustard
½ teaspoon black pepper
¼ teaspoon white pepper

3 tablespoons cane vinegar, or your
favorite vinegar

1. Preheat the oven to 400°F.

2. Combine the seasoning mix ingredients in a small bowl.

3. Place the butter in a 9 × 13-inch baking pan or casserole dish and put the pan in the oven just until the butter melts. Remove the pan from the oven and add all the vegetables, mirlitons, chicken, dates, and peanuts. Sprinkle with the seasoning mix. Stir well to distribute the seasonings and coat all the ingredients with the melted butter. Cover with a sheet of aluminum foil and bake for 10 minutes. Remove from the oven, uncover, and stir again, then re-cover and continue cooking just until the chicken is cooked through, about 15 minutes longer. Remove from the oven, sprinkle evenly with the vinegar, stir, and serve hot with pasta or rice.

Stuffed Turkey Breasts

Makes 6 servings

What's happening here? The turkey is so lean that it wants the fat of the chorizo? That must be it, plus the sausage has so much flavor that it brings the turkey to a crescendo of taste excitement! What's also happening here is that you cook the sausage with spices, fresh garlic and ginger, and the onions and jicama to make a great stuffing, then use some of the same mixture, plus heavy cream, goat cheese, and fresh spinach, for the sauce. I like to repeat and modify flavors like this, to add variety to a dish while keeping everything related and complementary.

2 tablespoons vegetable oil
2 cups chopped onions
½ pound chorizo sausage, cut into
    ¼-inch pieces
1 tablespoon minced fresh garlic
1 tablespoon peeled and minced fresh ginger
2 cups peeled jicama cut into ¼-inch pieces
3 cups turkey or chicken stock, in all
¼ cup all-purpose flour
Two 8-ounce whole turkey breasts, trimmed
    of fat
1 cup heavy cream
¾ cup crumbled goat cheese
¼ cup chopped fresh cilantro leaves
6 ounces fresh spinach, washed well and
    stemmed

Seasoning Mix

2 teaspoons paprika
2 teaspoons salt
1½ teaspoons dried basil
1½ teaspoons garlic powder
1½ teaspoons onion powder
1 teaspoon cayenne
¾ teaspoon black pepper
¾ teaspoon ground sage
¾ teaspoon dried thyme
½ teaspoon white pepper

1. Combine the seasoning mix ingredients in a small bowl.

2. In a heavy 4-quart pot, heat the vegetable oil over high

heat just until it begins to smoke, about 3 to 4 minutes. Add the onions, chorizo, garlic, ginger, jicama, and 2 tablespoons plus 1 teaspoon of the seasoning mix. Stir well, then cover and cook, uncovering to stir and scrape the pot bottom every 2 minutes, until the vegetables are wilted and beginning to stick to the pot, about 10 minutes. *At this point, the first taste is the quick hit of sweet caramelized onions, followed immediately by the very salty and slightly sour and smoky-garlic taste of the chorizo. Underneath the other flavors is the barest hint of fresh ginger.* Add 1 cup of the stock, scrape the pot, and cook, uncovered, stirring and scraping every minute or so, for another 10 minutes, then add the flour. Mix it in well until the white is no longer visible. Stir in the remaining 2 cups stock and scrape well to loosen the brown bits on the bottom of the pot. Remove 1 cup of this mixture for the stuffing, and set aside the pot with the remaining mixture to make the sauce.

3. Preheat the oven to 350°F.

4. In each breast section, cut a horizontal pocket with a 2- to 3-inch opening. Without enlarging the opening, and being very careful not to pierce the sides of the breast, extend the pocket into the breast as far as possible in all directions. Divide the reserved 1 cup stuffing between the breast pockets. Place the stuffed breasts in a roasting pan and roast until the breast surfaces are golden brown, about 30 minutes.

5. While the breasts are roasting, make the sauce. To the mixture remaining in the pot add the heavy cream, goat cheese, cilantro, spinach, and the remaining seasoning mix. Bring to a boil. Let it boil for 2 minutes, then remove from the heat.

6. To serve, slice each stuffed breast into 3 sections and divide the sauce among the portions.

Fish and Seafood

We may not have had talapia or tuna in my house when I was young, but believe me we had plenty of crawfish, oysters, trout, and other Louisiana products. Some of the recipes in this section are very close to the way we cooked them back then, whereas others have been developed with a more contemporary approach. Shrimp in Tropical Fruit Cream provides a good example. Even though in my youth we ate a lot more crawfish than shrimp, we did enjoy shrimp once in a while. We generally boiled, fried, or smothered them, or added them to gumbo. In those days it would have been unheard of to serve crawfish or shrimp in a rich, fruity sauce, never mind the fact that mangoes and papayas were totally unknown to our community.

Bronzed Redfish
with a Gingersnap Gravy

Makes 4 servings *Each time we tested this recipe, we used a different brand of gingersnaps, and they all had different tastes and thickening properties, so you may need to add a little more or less stock to the sauce to obtain the thickness you want.*

3 tablespoons unsalted butter
1 cup chopped onions
½ cup seeded and chopped red bell peppers
½ cup seeded and chopped yellow bell peppers
1 teaspoon minced fresh garlic
2 teaspoons peeled and minced fresh ginger
About 2 cups seafood stock, preferably, or vegetable stock, in all (see headnote above)
⅓ cup gingersnap cookies broken into pieces
1 cup heavy cream
4 redfish fillets (about 4 ounces each), or other firm, mild-flavored fish
2 tablespoons vegetable oil

Seasoning Mix

2½ teaspoons salt
2 teaspoons paprika
1¾ teaspoons ground ginger
1½ teaspoons onion powder
1 teaspoon cayenne
1 teaspoon ground coriander
1 teaspoon dry mustard
1 teaspoon dried oregano
¾ teaspoon ground cumin
¾ teaspoon garlic powder
¾ teaspoon black pepper
½ teaspoon white pepper

1. Combine the seasoning mix ingredients in a small bowl.

2. Heat the butter in a 10-inch skillet over high heat. As soon as it melts, stir in 1 tablespoon plus 1 teaspoon of the seasoning mix. When the butter is sizzling and foamy, add the onions and all the bell peppers. Stir well, then cover and cook for 6 minutes. Uncover, stir, and scrape up any brown bits sticking to the bottom of the skillet. The vegetables will be brightly colored and just beginning to brown. Re-cover, cook for 4 more minutes, stir, and scrape again, then re-cover and cook for 2 more minutes. *The onions are now golden* *brown—edged with dark brown—the bell peppers are slightly crunchy, and the flavors of all the ingredients are well defined, with a creamy sweetness at the end.*

3. Stir in the garlic, ginger, and 1 teaspoon of the seasoning mix. Stir well, then add 1 cup of the stock and stir and scrape well until all the browned material is dissolved. The mixture should be a red-brown color. Re-cover and cook for 8 minutes, then whisk in the gingersnaps and the remaining 1 cup stock. Cook, whisking frequently, until the mixture is smooth, about 3 minutes. Gradually whisk in the heavy cream, bring to a boil, then reduce the heat to medium and simmer, whisking frequently, until the gravy has thickened to the consistency of heavy cream, about 10 minutes. Keep hot. (Makes about 3 cups.) *The finished sauce should be a rich brown color and the flavor dominated by the ginger flavors— both fresh and ground—and the sweetness of the gingersnap cookies.*

4. Season each side of each fillet evenly with ½ teaspoon of the seasoning mix.

5. Place the vegetable oil in a 12-inch nonstick skillet over high heat just until the oil just begins to smoke, about 3 to 4 minutes. Place the fillets in the pan and cook, turning once, until they are just cooked through, about 2 to 3 minutes per side. The fillets are cooked when they flake easily. Serve immediately, dividing the sauce evenly among the portions.

Buckwheat
Batter–Fried Shrimp

Makes 8 to 12 appetizer servings   *If you think buckwheat flour is good just for frontier-style pancakes, what a happy surprise is in store for you! Its rich flavor combines really well with regular flour and corn flour to give these shrimp a coating with substantial character. The honey adds a touch of complementary sweetness, and the bell peppers and onions perk things up considerably.*

**2 pounds raw shrimp, 20 to 25 shrimp per
    pound**

Cane Syrup–Creole Mustard Relish

**One 11-ounce can corn, preferably Green Giant
    brand**
¼ cup minced onions
¼ cup seeded and minced red bell peppers
¼ cup seeded and minced green bell peppers
1 cup minced fresh tomatoes
**¼ cup red wine vinegar, or your favorite
    vinegar**
1 tablespoon minced fresh garlic
**¼ cup cane vinegar, or your favorite sweet
    vinegar**
**3 tablespoons Chef Paul Prudhomme's
    Magic Pepper Sauce, or other
    medium-hot pepper sauce**
1 tablespoon Creole mustard
**¼ cup cane syrup, or your favorite syrup
    (fruit or pure maple syrup)**

Seasoning Mix

1¾ teaspoons salt

1 teaspoon dried oregano

¾ teaspoon dried basil

¾ teaspoon garlic powder

½ teaspoon cayenne

½ teaspoon onion powder

½ teaspoon ground dried
    Anaheim chile peppers

½ teaspoon ground dried
    New Mexico chile peppers

½ teaspoon ground dried
    pasilla chile peppers

¼ teaspoon ground bay
    leaves

¼ teaspoon dry mustard

¼ teaspoon black pepper

¼ teaspoon white pepper

Sweet Vinegar Mayonnaise

> **2 large eggs**
> **2 cups vegetable oil**
> **¾ cup liquid reserved from relish preparation**
> **1 cup relish**

Batter

> **½ cup corn flour**
> **¼ cup all-purpose flour**
> **¼ cup buckwheat flour**
> **1 teaspoon baking soda**
> **½ cup milk**
> **1 large egg**
> **¼ cup honey**
> **3 tablespoons Creole mustard**
> **¼ cup seeded and minced green bell peppers**
> **¼ cup seeded and minced red bell peppers**
> **¼ cup minced onions**

For Frying

> **Vegetable oil for frying**

1. Combine the seasoning mix ingredients in a small bowl. Set aside 1¼ teaspoons of the seasoning mix for the mayonnaise.

2. Peel and devein the shrimp, leaving the tails on. Season the shrimp with 1 tablespoon of the seasoning mix, working it in evenly with your hands.

3. Prepare the relish: In a 1-quart measuring cup or a bowl with a pouring spout, combine all the ingredients and mix until well combined—you should have 4 cups. Strain off and reserve ¾ cup of the liquid (here's where you'll be glad you mixed the relish in a cup or bowl with a spout) and set aside 1 cup of the relish for use in the mayonnaise.

4. Prepare the mayonnaise: Process the eggs in a blender until they are light yellow, about 30 seconds. With the blender running, slowly add the vegetable oil in a thin stream until the mixture is the consistency of thick mayonnaise. Add the 1¾ teaspoons seasoning mix and the ¾ cup reserved liquid. Process briefly just until the ingredients are combined. Transfer the mixture to a bowl and stir in the 1 cup relish.   *continued*

5. Prepare the batter: In a small bowl, combine the flours and baking soda and whisk until they are well mixed. In a medium-size bowl, combine the milk and egg and whisk until they are well combined, then whisk in the flour mixture to form a paste. Whisk in the honey, mustard, bell peppers, onions, and the remaining seasoning mix. Stir until combined, then refrigerate the shrimp, batter, relish, and mayonnaise until cold.

6. When the shrimp, batter, relish, and mayonnaise are cold, prepare to fry the shrimp. In a 12-inch skillet over high heat, pour enough vegetable oil to measure 2 inches deep and heat it to 325°F, about 15 minutes. Use a cooking thermometer and adjust the heat so that the temperature of the oil stays as close to 325°F as possible—an electric skillet, if you have one, works well. When the oil reaches 325°F, remove the shrimp and batter from the refrigerator. Dip a few shrimp at a time in the batter, then hold them up momentarily to allow the excess batter to drain off. Immediately put the battered shrimp into the hot oil and fry, turning them almost constantly, until the coating is a rich mahogany brown, about 3 to 4 minutes per batch. Remove with a slotted spoon, drain on paper towels, and repeat with the remaining shrimp until all have been fried. Serve immediately, accompanied by the relish and mayonnaise.

Stuffed Flounder

Makes 4 servings

We've included instructions for preparing whole flounders for stuffing, but if the people at your fish market will do this for you, great! Just be sure to select the fish when they're whole, so you can check to be certain they're fresh, with firm flesh and clear eyes. Really fresh, healthy fish never have an unpleasant "fishy" odor.

This kind of recipe is very popular in New Orleans, with visitors as well as locals, so when you prepare it for guests, they're going to be mightily impressed! If you want to get fancy-schmancy, use some of the feathery fennel leaves, called anise, as garnish.

4 whole flounders (each about 1 pound)
1 pound peeled Louisiana crawfish tails, in all,
    or 1 pound peeled shrimp
2 tablespoons vegetable oil
2 cups chopped onions
2 cups peeled sweet potatoes cut
    into ½-inch cubes
2 cups peeled white potatoes cut
    into ½-inch cubes
2¾ cups seafood stock, in all
1 cup chopped celery
1 cup chopped fennel bulb
1 tablespoon minced fresh garlic
1 tablespoon peeled and minced fresh ginger
½ cup seeded and chopped fresh chile peppers
    (your choice of mild, medium, or hot
    peppers)
1 tablespoon lightly packed light brown sugar
4 tablespoons (½ stick) unsalted butter, plus
    2 tablespoons (optional)
One 13½-ounce can unsweetened coconut milk
¼ teaspoon ground dried chipolte chile
    peppers
4 ounces smoked Cheddar cheese, freshly grated

Seasoning Mix

1 tablespoon plus ¼
    teaspoon salt

2½ teaspoons paprika

1¾ teaspoons dried basil

1¼ teaspoons ground dried
    Anaheim chile peppers

1¼ teaspoons garlic powder

1¼ teaspoons ground
    coriander

1 teaspoon cayenne

1 teaspoon dillweed

1 teaspoon ground ginger

1 teaspoon dry mustard

1 teaspoon onion powder

1 teaspoon dried oregano

½ teaspoon black pepper

½ teaspoon white pepper

1. Combine the seasoning mix ingredients in a small bowl.

2. Prepare a pocket for stuffing each flounder, one at a time: Reach into the semi-circular openings behind the eyes and remove the gills, stomach, and liver. They are connected and should come out all in 1 piece, but if not, poke your fingers in again and be sure to get all the material. Removing the head is optional—some people don't want the fish looking back at them, so if that's the case at your house, cut it off. Remove the scales by scraping from the back of the fish to the front with a sharp knife. Rinse the fish under running water—the skin should feel very smooth—and pat dry. On the top (dark) side of the fish, make an incision lengthwise, following the backbone (which is indicated by a darker line right down the center) deep enough to reach the bone. Widen the cut by running your finger down the length of it—you'll feel the backbone. Working from this incision, gently cut the meat from the bones by running the knife under the flesh to separate it from the bones, keeping the knife blade slanted toward the bones rather than the skin and flesh, and cutting as close to the bones as possible. Continue working in this way until you almost reach the outside edge of the bones, then cut through the outer edges of all the bones with kitchen shears or a small sturdy pair of scissors. Turn the flounder around and repeat this process on the other half. Carefully remove the bones, then prepare the other 3 fish in the same manner. There will still be the tiny end pieces of the bones, so look out for them when eating the fish. The flounders are now ready to stuff. Sprinkle ½ teaspoon seasoning mix evenly inside each flounder and set the fish aside in a cool place.

3. Reserve 40 of the best-looking crawfish tails or shrimp for garnish and set aside the remainder.

4. Make the stuffing. Heat the vegetable oil in a heavy 4-quart pot over high heat just until it begins to smoke, about 3 to 4 minutes. Add the onions, sweet potatoes, and white potatoes. Stir well, cover, and cook, uncovering to stir every 2 minutes, for 6 minutes, then stir the pot again, checking to make sure that the vegetables are not sticking. Cover and cook until the mixture begins to stick to the bottom of the pot, about 5 minutes, then uncover and add ½ cup of the stock. Add the celery, fennel bulb, garlic, ginger, chile peppers, and 2 tablespoons of the seasoning mix. Stir well, then re-cover and cook until the mixture begins to stick again, about 5 minutes. Uncover and add ½ cup of the stock and scrape the bottom of the pot. Re-cover and cook until the coating on the bottom of the pot is a nice deep brown, about 5 minutes, then uncover and add ½ cup of the stock. Scrape the bottom of the pot very well, turning several times so that all the sides of the pot are completely scraped. As you stir and scrape, the potatoes will begin to break up. Cover the pot and continue to cook for 5 minutes. Remove the cover,

add ½ cup of the stock, and scrape the sides and bottom of the pot. Reduce the heat to medium and stir until the mixture becomes a thick paste. Using a potato masher, break up the large vegetable pieces until the mixture becomes a thick red-brown paste with small pieces of vegetables in it. Stir in 3 tablespoons of the seasoning mix—*the stuffing flavor is very intense at this point. Outstanding is the strong spice note, especially pepper, with fennel and dill tastes up front and saltiness behind. The deep potato flavor follows*—and continue to cook, uncovered, for 4 minutes, then stir thoroughly. Cook for 3 minutes longer, then stir in the brown sugar. *When the brown sugar is added, a noticeable reduction in the intensity of the seasoning occurs. The strong flavors of the stuffing will come into balance when the crawfish, which are also naturally sweet, are added to the mixture.* Continue to cook for 5 minutes, then mash the mixture again with the potato masher. Cook for 5 more minutes, then scrape the bottom. Remove from the heat, then stir in 2 tablespoons of the butter until it melts. Stir in the non-garnish crawfish or shrimp. Transfer 3 cups of this mixture to a sheet pan and set it aside to cool.

5. Make the sauce: Place the remaining mixture in a food processor with the coconut milk and process until smooth. Return this mixture to a 10-inch skillet over high heat and add the remaining ¾ cup stock, the chipotle chile pepper, and the remaining seasoning mix. Whisk to combine thoroughly, bring to a full boil, whisking constantly, then remove from the heat. *Because the sauce is made with the stuffing, the flavors of the stuffing are the first flavors to come through, followed by the background taste of the coconut milk. Note how the chipotle and coconut flavors create a different direction of flavor for the sauce, while tying the flavors to those of the main dish.*

6. Preheat the oven to 350°F.

7. Thinly slice 2 tablespoons of the butter. Place the prepared and seasoned flounders in a large baking pan and place 1½ teaspoons of the thinly sliced butter under each fish. Open the 2 flaps on top of each fish. Divide the smoked Cheddar cheese among the fish, placing it in the middle of each fish, covering the bottom, then place ¾ cup of the stuffing on top of the cheese. Close the flaps and place 10 of the reserved crawfish tails or shrimp in the seam of each flap. If desired, divide 2 tablespoons butter, cut into small pieces, over the crawfish or shrimp on each fish. Bake until the fish are done, but still moist and tender, and the stuffing is cooked through and nicely browned on the surfaces, about 20 minutes.

8. Serve some of the sauce with each flounder, and pass the rest separately.

Chile-Laden
Swordfish Steaks

Makes 4 servings

Mirin is a Japanese rice wine, similar to sake but somewhat sweeter and more golden than pale yellow. It is usually available in Asian specialty shops, but you if you absolutely can't find it, you can substitute sake plus a little sugar (about 1 tablespoon plus 1 teaspoon) and a dash of salt with much the same result. This recipe works great with any fish large enough to cut into steaks, such as tuna, salmon, or red snapper.

Four 8-ounce swordfish steaks, about
   ½ inch thick
2 tablespoons olive oil
1 cup chopped onions
½ cup seeded and chopped fresh poblano chile
   peppers, in all
½ cup seeded and chopped fresh Anaheim chile
   peppers, in all
½ cup seeded and chopped fresh banana
   peppers (also called wax peppers), in all
1 cup loosely packed, coarsely chopped
   bok choy leaves
2 tablespoons freshly squeezed lemon juice
2 tablespoons freshly squeezed lime juice
5 tablespoons mirin, in all
2 tablespoons unsalted butter
1 tablespoon all-purpose flour
2 cups thinly sliced shiitake mushroom caps
1 cup chopped bok choy stalks
1½ cups heavy cream

Seasoning Mix

2 teaspoons salt

1½ teaspoons onion powder

1 teaspoon cayenne

1 teaspoon garlic powder

1 teaspoon ground dried
   New Mexico chile peppers

1 teaspoon paprika

¾ teaspoon ground dried
   Anaheim chile peppers

½ teaspoon ground dried
   árbol chile peppers

1. Combine the seasoning mix ingredients in a small bowl.

2. Sprinkle both sides of the swordfish steaks evenly with a total of 1 tablespoon of the seasoning mix and gently pat it in. Cover with plastic wrap and refrigerate until cold.

3. Heat the olive oil in a 14-inch skillet over high heat just until it begins to smoke, about 3 to 4 minutes. Place the cold swordfish steaks in the pan and cook, turning once, until the steaks are brown on the outside but not cooked through, about 1½ minutes per side. Remove the steaks from the heat and set aside.

4. To the hot pan, add the onions; ¼ cup each of the poblano, Anaheim, and banana peppers; and 1 tablespoon of the seasoning mix. Stir well, cover, and cook for 4 minutes. Uncover and stir. The vegetables will be pale brown with *a slightly hot taste from the chiles, combined with a strong saltiness from the seasoning mix.* Re-cover and continue to cook until the vegetables are medium brown, about 2 to 4 minutes longer. Add all the remaining chile peppers and the bok choy leaves. Re-cover and continue to cook until the leaves are dark green, from 2 to 4 more minutes. Stir in the citrus juices and continue to cook until the juices are almost evaporated, about 1 to 2 minutes. Add 3 tablespoons of the mirin and 2 teaspoons of the seasoning mix and stir well. The mixture will be a dark earthy brown *with a succession of intense flavors—first sour from the citrus, then sweet from the vegetables, and finishing with a strong herb and spice taste and a deep brown flavor that is almost at the edge of being burned.*

5. Add the butter and, as it melts, sprinkle the flour over the mixture and stir until the white is no longer visible. By this time the mixture should be sticking to and glazing the bottom of the pan. Scrape the bottom well, then add the remaining 2 tablespoons mirin and continue scraping until the brown bits are loosened. Add the mushrooms, the bok choy stalks, and the remaining seasoning mix. Continue to cook until the mushrooms are coated and beginning to darken, about 2 minutes. Add the heavy cream and any juices that have accumulated from the fish. Stir well, bring to a boil, and remove from the heat immediately. You should have about 2¾ cups.

6. Move as much as possible of the sauce to the outer edge of the skillet and place the fish steaks in the cleared portion. Baste all the steaks evenly with the sauce for 1 minute—the heat from the sauce will begin to cook the fish—then let sit until the fish is completely cooked, when it flakes easily, about 2 minutes longer. Serve at once, dividing the sauce among the portions.

Cilantro Fried Shrimp

You may never have thought of putting fresh herbs in your batter, but why not? The taste of cilantro should be sturdy enough to withstand the oil's high temperature, but the flavor can vary, depending on its freshness and the time of the year. So taste your cilantro, and if its flavor seems a little weak, sprinkle a little extra on the shrimp just before serving. This dish makes a great appetizer, and if you want to serve it as finger food, just leave the tails on.

Vegetable oil for deep frying
2 pounds raw shrimp, 21 to 25 shrimp per
   pound, peeled
1½ cups all-purpose flour, in all
3 large eggs
½ cup milk
½ cup plus 1 tablespoon lightly packed finely
   chopped fresh cilantro leaves
Four Pack Chile Dip (page 86)

Seasoning Mix

2 teaspoons salt
1¼ teaspoons cayenne
1¼ teaspoons dry mustard
1¼ teaspoons onion powder
1¼ teaspoons dried oregano
¾ teaspoon ground cumin
¾ teaspoon garlic powder
¾ teaspoon paprika
¾ teaspoon black pepper
½ teaspoon white pepper

1. Combine the seasoning mix ingredients in a small bowl.

2. In a deep fryer with a thermostat, pour enough vegetable oil to measure about 3 inches deep and heat it to 350°F. If you don't have a deep fryer, you can use a large pot and a cooking thermometer.

3. Season the shrimp evenly with 1 tablespoon of the seasoning mix.

4. Place ½ cup of the flour in an 8-inch square pan or casserole dish. In a similar pan, whip the eggs and milk together until combined. In a third dish, combine the remaining 1 cup flour, the cilantro, and the remaining seasoning mix, and mix well.

5. Line up the pans in the order in which you'll use them—the seasoned flour, egg wash, then the unseasoned flour. You'll save a lot of hand washing if you use one hand for the dry batters and the other for the egg wash. You can let the shrimp sit in the seasoned flour or egg wash for more than a few seconds if you have to, but don't let them remain in the unseasoned flour any longer than absolutely necessary—fry them as soon as possible. The number of shrimp that can be fried at one time depends upon the size of your fryer or pot. Don't try to fry too many at one time because if the pot becomes too crowded, the oil will cool down and the coating will be soggy. Keep the temperature of the oil as close to 350°F as possible, especially between batches.

6. When the oil reaches 350°F, fry the shrimp in several batches. To fry, dredge 1 batch of shrimp in the seasoned flour, coating them evenly. Shake off the excess flour and transfer them to the egg wash, coating them evenly. Remove the shrimp from the egg wash and shake off any excess liquid, then transfer them to the unseasoned flour. Working quickly, mound the flour over the shrimp and press it in with your hands, until they are thoroughly coated. Immediately shake off the excess flour and transfer the shrimp to the hot oil. Fry until golden brown, about 2½ to 3 minutes. Remove with a slotted spoon and drain on paper towels. Repeat this process until all the shrimp are cooked. Serve immediately, sprinkling the shrimp with additional cilantro if desired, with our Four Pack Chile Dip on the side.

Cilantro Salmon with Roasted Onions and Garlic

Makes 4 servings

It would be easier to cook fish if each piece were exactly the same size and the same thickness throughout, but nature doesn't package food that way. Your salmon fillets are going to be thicker in the middle than they are at the ends, so you want to strike a balance between undercooking the thick center and overcooking the thinner ends. It's not a big deal—just watch the fish carefully and be ready to zap it out of the pan just as soon as the thickest parts lose their color and flake easily.

Four 6-ounce salmon fillets, about 1 inch at
   the thickest part
4 tablespoons (½ stick) unsalted butter
1 tablespoon all-purpose flour
1 cup chopped fire-roasted onions
2 tablespoons minced fire-roasted garlic
¼ cup minced fresh cilantro leaves
2 cups heavy cream
4 cups cooked pasta—penne or rotelli,
   or your favorite variety

Seasoning Mix
2½ teaspoons paprika
1½ teaspoons salt
1¼ teaspoons dried basil
1¼ teaspoons garlic powder
1¼ teaspoons onion powder
1 teaspoon dry mustard
¾ teaspoon dried oregano
¾ teaspoon black pepper
¾ teaspoon white pepper
½ teaspoon ground nutmeg

1. Combine the seasoning mix ingredients in a small bowl.

2. Sprinkle each side of each salmon fillet evenly with ½ teaspoon of the seasoning mix, patting it in gently so that the seasoning is moistened by the natural juices of the fish.

3. Make the sauce: Melt the butter in a 12-inch nonstick skillet over high heat. As the butter melts, whisk in the flour and the remaining seasoning mix. As soon as the seasoning mix is incorporated into the butter, add the onions and garlic. Reduce the heat to medium and cook, stirring frequently, until the onions soften and the mixture resembles hash browns. *The vegetables have a fairly intense flavor with a deep taste of roasted onions and a top note from the roasted garlic. The herbs and spices provide a rich and flavorful finish to the taste.* Stir in the cilantro and cook just until it wilts slightly, then add the heavy cream. Increase the heat to high and bring to a boil, whisking constantly. Whisking prevents the flour from settling and possibly burning, and helps dissolve and distribute the seasonings and brown bits into the cream. When the mixture reaches a boil, continue to cook for 1 more minute, then remove from the heat. You will have about 2½ cups sauce.

4. Place a 12-inch nonstick skillet over high heat until it is very hot, about 360°F, about 5 to 6 minutes. Reduce the heat to medium and place 2 of the fillets in the dry pan. Cook, turning once, until the fillets are just cooked through, about 4 minutes total. As they cook, a white line will form between the portion of the fish closest to the skillet, indicating that it has cooked (it will be noticeably more opaque), and the still raw fish. Turn the fish over when this line reaches about a third of the way up the fish. Cook just until the white line that forms on this side reaches about a third of the way up the fish—there will still be a small section of raw fish between the two cooked portions, but most of that will cook from the heat transferred from the cooked parts. This will produce a tender, tasty piece of fish. If you're in doubt about when the fish is sufficiently cooked, take a fork and try to flake off a portion of the fish at its thickest part—if it flakes easily, it's done. It's better to undercook than overcook, because, if necessary, you can always put the fish back into the skillet for a few more seconds. Remove the fillets from the heat and keep them warm while repeating the process for the remaining 2 fillets.

5. Serve 1 fillet per person, accompanied by 1 cup of the pasta and a generous ½ cup of the sauce over the pasta and fish.

Oysters Florentine

Makes 4 serving

"Florentine" implies spinach, and indeed this dish combines tender oysters with that wonderful green. Cooked in a savory cream sauce and served over pasta, oysters have never had it so good! We used baby spinach, which has leaves only 1 to 3 inches long and very small stems, but if it's unavailable, use regular spinach and simply remove all the stems and tear the leaves into 1-inch pieces.

1 gallon water
1 teaspoon salt
1 tablespoon olive oil
8 ounces uncooked pasta (penne or your
    favorite pasta)
1 pint shucked oysters in their liquor
3 tablespoons unsalted butter
1 cup chopped fire-roasted onions
2 tablespoons chopped fire-roasted garlic
10 ounces fresh baby spinach
2 cups heavy cream

> ## Seasoning Mix
>
> 1½ teaspoons paprika
>
> 1½ teaspoons salt
>
> 1 teaspoon garlic powder
>
> ¾ teaspoon dried basil
>
> ¾ teaspoon onion powder
>
> ¾ teaspoon ground dried
>   Anaheim chile peppers
>
> ½ teaspoon dried oregano
>
> ½ teaspoon black pepper
>
> ¼ teaspoon white pepper

1. Combine the seasoning mix ingredients in a small bowl.

2. In a large pot over high heat, bring the water to a rolling boil. Add the salt and olive oil, then add the pasta. Stir the pasta briefly to keep it from sticking together, then cook to the *al dente* stage. Drain the pasta in a colander, then run cold water over it until it is cool to the touch. Drain off all excess water, then sprinkle the pasta with 2 teaspoons of the seasoning mix and toss until evenly coated. Set aside.

3. Drain the liquid from the oysters and reserve the oysters and the liquid.

4. In a 5-quart pot, melt the butter over high heat. When the butter melts and begins to sizzle, add the roasted onions and garlic and the remaining seasoning mix. Cook, stirring

frequently, until the onions are brown and have a glazed appearance, about 4 to 5 minutes. *All the flavors hit at once, with a strong taste of salt. Note the rich undertone of roasted flavors from the garlic and onions.* Stir in ½ cup of the reserved oyster liquor, then add the spinach. Continue to cook, stirring frequently, until the spinach cooks down and the liquid bubbles like little volcanoes, about 4 minutes. *Note the sweetness of the onions and garlic, and the developing brown color and flavor from the caramelizing process. Also present is a faint taste of oyster from the cooking liquid.*

6. Add the heavy cream and bring to a boil. If the cream thins out as it heats, continue cooking until it thickens again before proceeding. If it remains thick, go immediately to the next step. Reduce the heat to medium and add the oysters. Watch the oysters carefully, which is a bit hard to do, as they are somewhat hidden in the sauce. Pick one up with a slotted spoon to check the progress. When they begin to curl and show a series of pleated folds on their sides, about 2 minutes, they are cooked. Remove from the heat and serve over the pasta.

Pan-Roasted
Soft-Shell Crabs

Makes 6 servings *Soft-shell crabs, which have recently shed their old hard shells after having outgrown them, are considered a real delicacy in my part of the world.*

6 soft-shell crabs
4 tablespoons (½ stick) unsalted butter
3 small ripe Roma tomatoes, peeled and
    finely chopped
1 cup heavy cream
2 large egg yolks, lightly beaten

Seasoning Mix

¾ teaspoon onion powder

¾ teaspoon black pepper

¾ teaspoon salt

½ teaspoon dried basil

½ teaspoon cayenne

½ teaspoon dry mustard

½ teaspoon paprika

¼ teaspoon ground anise

¼ teaspoon garlic powder

¼ teaspoon white pepper

1. Combine the seasoning mix ingredients in a small bowl.

2. Clean the crabs. Place one in front of you, legs down. Cut off the eyes and the tip of the mouth. Gently lift up one side of the shell, exposing the gills, which are a row of feather-like objects. Some people in Louisiana call them "dead men" or "dead men's fingers." Remove the gills and close the shell. Repeat this process on the other side. Turn the crab over and locate the "apron," which is a piece shaped like a handle on male crabs and like a bell on females. Pull off the apron and the membranes that attach it to the crab. Repeat with the remaining crabs.

3. Preheat the oven to 350°F.

4. Sprinkle the crabs evenly with 3 to 5 teaspoons of the seasoning mix, according to your own taste, and gently pat it in.

5. Melt the butter in a large ovenproof skillet. When it begins to sizzle, place the crabs in the skillet, top side down. Cook, turning once, until the crabs are brown on both sides, about 3 to 4 minutes per side. Add the tomatoes to the skillet and place the skillet in the oven. Bake until the crabs are cooked through and the shells are slightly crisp, about

20 minutes. Remove the skillet from the oven and transfer the crabs to a plate. Place the skillet over high heat and add the heavy cream. Bring to a boil, whisking frequently and scraping up the brown bits from the bottom of the skillet, then whisk in the egg yolks. You will notice little bits of cooked egg yolk in the sauce, which is exactly what we want to happen, as they add the desired texture and flavor to the sauce. Continue to whisk vigorously for 1 minute, then remove from the heat.

6. To serve, place 1 crab on a plate and divide the sauce among the portions.

Pepper Patch Shrimp

Makes 4 servings

When I was growing up near Opelousas, Louisiana, we used several kinds of chile peppers, but we didn't have nearly as wide a variety as is found in today's supermarkets. Shallots were unheard of, though we had plenty of yellow and white onions. Because we had cows on our farm, we didn't consider butter and heavy cream the luxury many people do these days, and we had never heard of cholesterol! We could harvest our own crawfish from rice fields, but we bought Gulf shrimp, iced down in an old tin tub, from the back of a pickup truck down the road. So, all in all, this dish represents the best of traditional Louisiana cooking, with just a few touches that were unavailable to us back then.

3 tablespoons unsalted butter
1 tablespoon olive oil
½ cup minced shallots
¼ cup seeded and minced fresh red jalapeño
   chile peppers
¼ cup seeded and minced fresh green
   jalapeño chile peppers
¼ cup seeded and minced fresh
   Anaheim chile peppers
¼ cup seeded and minced fresh poblano
   chile peppers
1½ cups heavy cream
½ cup shrimp stock
1 pound raw shrimp, 21 to 25 shrimp
   per pound, peeled

Seasoning Mix

1½ teaspoons salt
1 teaspoon dillweed
1 teaspoon paprika
¾ teaspoon cayenne
¾ teaspoon dry mustard
¾ teaspoon onion powder
¾ teaspoon ground dried
   New Mexico chile peppers
½ teaspoon garlic powder
½ teaspoon black pepper
¼ teaspoon white pepper

1. Combine the seasoning mix ingredients in a small bowl.

2. Place the butter and olive oil in a heavy 10-inch skillet, preferably nonstick, over high heat. As soon as the butter begins to melt, add the shallots, all the fresh chile peppers, and the seasoning mix. Cook, stirring frequently, until the vegetables are starting to get tender (test by poking them with the times of a fork, or pull out a piece and taste it) but still have a good crunch and bright color, about 4 minutes. *The flavor of the vegetables at this stage is very intense. The first taste is a quick note of browned butter, followed by a jolt of salt and the chile peppers. There is a slight suggestion of bitterness, and the seasoning continues to build. The heat from the chiles concentrates on the back of the mouth and the throat, and both tastes last for quite a while.*

3. Stir in the heavy cream and stock and bring just to a boil. Warning: the mixture will boil up very fast and might overflow the pan unless you keep a whisk handy to knock down the foam. Reduce the heat to medium and continue to cook, whisking frequently. As the mixture simmers rapidly, notice that an orange "slick" from the shrimp fat appears on the surface. Continue to cook and whisk until this slick is reabsorbed into the sauce and little drops of oil appear on the edges of the mixture, about 8 to 10 minutes. *The flavor of the sauce seems very salty until the shrimp are added. Taste carefully for a very slight bitter flavor, which can just be detected beneath the creamy flavors of the sauce. The heat is quite subdued from the earlier levels, but still quite noticeable in the back of the throat.* Add the shrimp, then gently scrape the sides of the pan and stir very gently toward the center of the pan, which helps to keep the sauce from breaking. Cook until the shrimp are pink, plump, opaque, and starting to curl, about 3 minutes. Remove from the heat and let sit for 5 minutes before serving over rice or pasta.

Portobello Tuna

Makes 4 servings *Here's an unusual fish dish that can earn you a reputation for creativity. The dusky flavor of portobello mushrooms contrasts nicely with the crisp tuna taste, while the creamy sauce ties everything together.*

1 tablespoon black poppy seeds
Four 1-pound tuna steaks, each about
  4½ × 5 inches across, and about
  1½ inches thick
Up to 5 tablespoons butter, in all
4 portobello mushroom caps, each at least
  5 inches in diameter, larger if possible
1 cup heavy cream

Seasoning Mix

2 teaspoons salt
1 teaspoon paprika
1 teaspoon onion powder
½ teaspoon dillweed
½ teaspoon garlic powder
½ teaspoon dry mustard
½ teaspoon black pepper
½ teaspoon ground dried árbol chile peppers
¼ teaspoon white pepper

1. Combine the seasoning mix ingredients in a small bowl.

2. To toast the poppy seeds: Place them in an 8-inch skillet over high heat, shaking the skillet often to keep the seeds moving, just until the seeds produce a toasted aroma and you see smoke rising, about 2 minutes. Cover the skillet, if necessary, to keep the seeds from popping out as they toast. As soon as they're toasted, remove the seeds from the skillet and combine them with the seasoning mix.

3. Sprinkle ½ teaspoon of the seasoning mix evenly over one side of each tuna steak and gently pat it in. Use slightly less or a bit more if your steaks are smaller or larger than ours. Set aside.

4. Place a 10-inch skillet over high heat, add 1 tablespoon of the butter, and, when it melts, add the mushrooms, gill sides down. Move them around in the skillet to coat them with the butter, then turn them over and move them around again to coat the other sides. Sprinkle the top side of each mushroom with ½ teaspoon of the seasoning mix and cook just until the tops appear wet, about 2 to 3 minutes. Turn over, sprinkle each of these sides with ½ teaspoon of the sea-

soning mix, and cook until these sides appear wet, about 3 to 4 minutes longer. As the mushrooms cook, add up to 2 additional tablespoons of the butter if necessary to keep some in the bottom of the skillet at all times, and tilt the pan if necessary to move the melted butter to all parts of the pan. You want to use as little butter as necessary to hold the seasonings in place. Turn the mushrooms one last time and remove them from the pan. To this same skillet, add the heavy cream and reduce the heat to medium. Cook, whisking constantly, until little bubbles appear around the outside of the skillet. Add all but 2 teaspoons of the seasoning mix and continue to cook and whisk until the cream boils. Reduce the heat so that the cream does not boil too vigorously and continue to cook, whisking constantly, until the seasonings are thoroughly incorporated and the sauce thickens somewhat, about 8 to 10 minutes longer. A good way to determine when the sauce reaches the right consistency is to spoon some up and release it back into the pan—it should form a solid "ribbon" of sauce, rather than separate drops as plain cream does. When the ribbon forms, remove the sauce from the heat—you'll have about ¾ cup. Keep warm while you cook the tuna.

5. Preheat a large heavy skillet, preferably made of cast iron, over high heat until very hot, about 4 to 5 minutes. Cut 2 tablespoons of the butter into 4 pieces and place 1 of these pieces on each of the seasoned sides of the tuna. Place the steaks in the hot skillet, buttered and seasoned sides down. Then sprinkle another ½ teaspoon of the seasoning mix evenly on top of each tuna steak. In this next step it's really important to watch the fish, not the clock. To cook the tuna to medium-rare, which will produce the tastiest, most tender result, cook just until you can see that the fish has lost its red color about one-third of an inch up from the surface of the skillet, about 2 to 3 minutes. As the heat rises, you'll see a white line between the cooked and uncooked portions of the fish. Turn and continue cooking just until the white line on that side rises to about one-third of an inch, about 3 to 4 minutes longer. Remove from the heat—the tuna will continue to cook from its own heat.

6. To serve, place the mushrooms on serving plates, gill sides up, and center a tuna steak on each. Divide the sauce among the portions.

Salmon Cakes

Makes 12 patties; 6 main-course or 12 appetizer servings

If you've cooked my recipes before, you know that the first thing I usually do is to brown or caramelize some of the vegetables over high heat. In this case, though, we use medium or even medium-low heat to start the vegetables because too much browning would interfere with the naturally sweet taste of the salmon, and also could intensify the slight oily taste of some salmon.

1½ pounds fresh salmon fillets
6 tablespoons (¾ stick) unsalted butter, in all
1 cup chopped onions, in all
½ cup chopped celery, in all
¼ cup seeded and chopped green bell peppers, in all
¼ cup seeded and chopped red bell peppers, in all
¼ cup seeded and chopped yellow bell peppers, in all
1 tablespoon peeled and minced fresh ginger
2 teaspoons minced fresh garlic
One 10-ounce sweet potato, baked in a 350°F oven until tender and peeled
½ cup unseasoned dried bread crumbs
½ cup chopped green onions or scallions
4 tablespoons olive oil, in all
1 cup seafood stock, preferably, or vegetable stock
2 cups heavy cream

> ## Seasoning Mix
>
> 1¾ teaspoons salt
> 1 teaspoon dried basil
> 1 teaspoon ground coriander
> 1 teaspoon garlic powder
> 1 teaspoon onion powder
> ¾ teaspoon dry mustard
> ½ teaspoon cayenne
> ½ teaspoon ground ginger
> ½ teaspoon dried oregano
> ½ teaspoon paprika
> ½ teaspoon dried thyme leaves
> ¼ teaspoon ground cinnamon
> ¼ teaspoon ground nutmeg
> ¼ teaspoon white pepper

1. Combine the seasoning mix ingredients in a small bowl.

2. Remove any skin and or pin bones from the salmon and cut it into ¼-inch cubes.

3. In a 10-inch skillet over medium heat, melt 2 tablespoons of the butter and, as soon as it sizzles, add ½ cup of the

onions, ¼ cup of the celery, 2 tablespoons each of the bell peppers, and 1 table-spoon of the seasoning mix. Stir well, cover, and cook—reducing the heat to medium-low if the vegetables start to brown—for 4 minutes. Uncover and stir well, then re-cover and cook for another 4 minutes. Stir and scrape the bottom of the skillet, then add the remaining onions, celery, bell peppers, and 2 teaspoons of the seasoning mix. *The first taste is the green taste, slightly bitter, of the bell peppers, followed by the herb and spice flavors, mixed with a fainter brown taste from the bottom of the pan.* Stir well, reduce the heat to low if necessary to prevent too much browning, then re-cover and cook for 4 more minutes. Uncover and add 2 tablespoons of the butter, stir until it's almost melted, then add the ginger and garlic. Stir and scrape well, then re-cover and cook for 5 minutes. Uncover, stir and scrape well, then re-cover and cook for 5 minutes. Remove from the heat and set aside. *The vegetables are now somewhat dark and faded and speckled with dark brown bits. The taste is first a light caramelized sweetness, followed by an intense herb and spice flavor.*

4. Combine ½ pound of the salmon, the vegetable mixture, and the baked sweet potato in a food processor and process until smooth.

5. In a large bowl, combine the puréed mixture with the remaining 1 pound salmon, 1 tablespoon of the seasoning mix, the bread crumbs, and the green onions. Fold gently until well combined. Set aside 1 cup of this mixture for making the sauce. Spread the remaining mixture on a baking sheet and refrigerate until the mixture is very cold.

6. Preheat the oven to 350°F.

7. When the mixture is cold, shape it into patties, using a heaping ¼ cup of the mixture for each, making each patty about 2½ inches in diameter and 1 inch thick. Place 2 large ovenproof skillets over high heat, with 2 tablespoons of the olive oil and 1 tablespoon of the butter in each skillet. When the oil begins to crackle, after about 2 minutes, place 6 patties in each skillet. Fry the patties until golden brown on one side, about 3 minutes, then turn all the patties over with a spatula and place the skillets in the oven until the patties are just cooked through, about 6 to 8 minutes. If you only have 1 skillet, or your skillets are not large enough to hold all the patties, you can prepare the salmon cakes in 2 batches, keeping the first batch warm while making the second.

8. To make the sauce, purée the reserved salmon mixture with the stock and remaining seasoning mix in a food processor until fairly smooth, about 30 seconds, then transfer to a skillet over high heat. Whisk in the heavy cream and bring to a full boil, whisking frequently. Remove from the heat and serve at once.

Seafood and
Eggplant Jambalaya

Unless you have seafood stock on hand, buy 2 pounds of unpeeled shrimp and use the shells, heads, and tails to make the stock. Like most jambalaya recipes, this one is peppery; if you don't care for so much heat, reduce the amounts of árbol chile pepper, cayenne, and black and white peppers. Notice that we said to reduce the amounts, not the number of pepper types, because a variety gives you a rounded, complex flavor.

2 tablespoons vegetable oil
2 cups chopped onions
½ pound andouille, or your favorite
    smoked pork sausage, quartered
    lengthwise, then cut into ½-inch pieces
½ pound tasso, preferably, or smoked ham,
    cut into ¼-inch cubes
1 cup chopped celery
2 cups seeded and chopped green bell
    peppers
1 medium-size unpeeled eggplant or 2 small
    eggplant (about 1 pound total), cut
    into ½-inch cubes
1 tablespoon minced fresh garlic
3½ cups seafood stock (see headnote above)
1¾ cups rice
½ pound firm white-fleshed fish fillets,
    such as orange roughy, tilapia, or
    trout, cut into bite-size pieces
1 pound peeled medium-size raw shrimp,
    21 to 25 shrimp per pound
    (see headnote above)

Seasoning Mix

1¼ teaspoons paprika

1¼ teaspoons salt

1 teaspoon dried basil

1 teaspoon garlic powder

1 teaspoon onion powder

½ teaspoon cayenne

½ teaspoon ground cumin

½ teaspoon ground ginger

½ teaspoon dry mustard

½ teaspoon ground dried
    árbol chile peppers

½ teaspoon dried thyme
    leaves

¼ teaspoon black pepper

¼ teaspoon white pepper

1. Combine the seasoning mix ingredients in a small bowl.

2. In a 4-quart pot, heat the vegetable oil over high heat just until it begins to smoke, about 3 to 4 minutes. Add the onions, andouille, tasso, celery, bell peppers, and eggplant. Cover (the eggplant will steam in the covered pot and cook down while picking up the flavors of the other ingredients) and cook, uncovering to stir and scrape the bottom of the pot after 7 minutes and again after 14 minutes, until the eggplant is cooked down, about 20 minutes. Uncover and add the garlic and the seasoning mix. Scrape vigorously and cook, uncovered, to allow the moisture to evaporate, for 10 minutes. *The eggplant has absorbed the seasonings, not only from the seasoning mix but from the tasso and bell peppers. All the vegetables are rich and sweet-tasting.* Stir in the stock and scrape the sides and bottom of the pot thoroughly. Re-cover and bring to a boil, then uncover and stir in the rice. Cover again and bring to a boil over high heat, then reduce the heat to low. Stir once very carefully, then re-cover and cook until the rice is cooked, about 20 minutes. *Taste the rice—it would be wonderful by itself! But the finished jambalaya will boast the flavors of the vegetables, fish, and shrimp, too.* Add the fish and shrimp, and let the pot sit off the heat, covered, for 10 minutes—the heat of the other ingredients will cook the seafood—before serving.

Seafood-Smothered Potatoes

Makes 8 side-dish or 4 main-course servings *If you prefer, you can use all chicken stock or all fish stock instead of the two different stocks. And you certainly can use all one color of bell peppers, instead of the three colors, but I like the way the three colors look. I really like this dish, too—it goes great with just about any kind of seafood and is wonderful all by itself! This recipe is completely traditional, with nothing new to it—just typical south Louisiana fare. It's a perfect example of not fixing something that's not broken.*

1 tablespoon plus 1 teaspoon olive oil
1½ cups chopped onions, in all
¾ cup seeded and chopped green bell
   peppers, in all
¾ cup seeded and chopped red bell peppers,
   in all
¾ cup seeded and chopped yellow bell
   peppers, in all
1½ cups fish stock, in all
1½ cups chicken stock, in all
1½ teaspoons minced fresh garlic
1½ pounds white potatoes, peeled and
   cut into ½-inch cubes
½ pound peeled raw shrimp, 21 to 25
   shrimp per pound (about 1 pound
   unpeeled)
1 pint shucked oysters in their liquor

Seasoning Mix

1¼ teaspoons salt
1 teaspoon onion powder
1 teaspoon paprika
¾ teaspoon dried basil
¾ teaspoon garlic powder
½ teaspoon cayenne
½ teaspoon dry mustard
½ teaspoon dried oregano
½ teaspoon black pepper
¼ teaspoon white pepper

1. Combine the seasoning mix ingredients in a small bowl.

2. Heat the olive oil in a heavy 4-quart pot, preferably non-stick, over high heat just until it begins to smoke, 3 to 4 min-

utes. Add 1 cup of the onions, ½ cup of each color bell peppers, and 1 teaspoon of the seasoning mix. Cover and cook, uncovering every 2 minutes to stir and scrape the bottom of the pot, until the colors of the vegetables have faded and they are just beginning to brown, about 6 to 8 minutes. Add ½ cup of the fish stock and the remaining seasoning mix. Stir, re-cover, and cook, uncovering every 2 minutes to stir, until the mixture begins to stick to the bottom of the pot, about 4 to 6 minutes. Uncover and add ½ cup of the chicken stock, then scrape the bottom of the pot well to loosen any of the brown bits and dissolve them into the liquid. Re-cover and cook until the mixture begins to stick again, about 3 to 4 minutes. Uncover and stir in the remaining ½ cup onions, the remaining ¼ cup each color bell pepper, and the garlic. Re-cover and cook until the liquid has almost evaporated and what remains has tiny steam vent holes all over the surface, about 4 minutes. Scrape the bottom well, loosening any brown bits that stick to it. Re-cover and cook for 2 more minutes, then uncover and add ½ cup of the fish stock. Cook, uncovered, stirring every 2 minutes and scraping the bottom of the pot, until the vegetables are soft and have absorbed color from the seasoning mix and the liquid has almost evaporated, 8 to 10 minutes. Add the remaining ½ cup fish stock and the remaining 1 cup chicken stock. The liquid is a beautiful deep brown and the vegetables are brightly colored, *but the taste is very bitter at this point, with a very high level of seasonings, overpowering the milder vegetable taste.*

3. Scrape the bottom of the pot well, then add the potatoes. Stir well and cover, then reduce the heat to medium. Cook, uncovering every 5 minutes to stir and scrape the bottom of the pot, until the potatoes are fully cooked and soft, and the sauce is very thick, about 35 to 40 minutes. During this time there will be a lot of bubbling going on! And the potatoes will be so soft that they will begin to disintegrate and thicken the liquid—but that's great, because they add wonderful flavor and texture. At the end of the 35 to 40 minutes, *the sauce has a faint seafood taste and a light brown gravy flavor softened by the starchy potato taste, which spreads across the tongue. The seasonings are still pronounced.* Now add the shrimp, oysters, and oyster liquor. Cover and cook just until the seafood is cooked through but still tender, about 3 to 4 minutes. Watch the shrimp as a guide—they will become plump and opaque when they're done—and don't overcook, or they'll be tough. The final appearance is very much like a stew, and *the final taste is of fully balanced potato and seafood gravy flavors.* Serve piping hot.

Semolina-Battered
Fried Soft-Shell Crabs

Makes 6 servings

Semolina flour, often used to make pasta and sometimes labeled "pasta flour," is available at many supermarkets. You can substitute all-purpose flour, but semolina produces a distinctive, slightly crunchy crust. Corn flour is readily available at Latin markets, and in Louisiana it's sometimes labeled "fish fry." Make sure you buy it unseasoned, or you can use yellow cornmeal.

6 soft-shell crabs
Vegetable oil for frying
1 cup all-purpose flour
2 large eggs
1½ cups milk
1 cup semolina flour
½ cup corn flour
Four Pack Chile Dip (page 86)

Seasoning Mix

2 teaspoons dillweed
2 teaspoons salt
1½ teaspoons cayenne
1 teaspoon garlic powder
1 teaspoon dry mustard
1 teaspoon onion powder
1 teaspoon paprika
¾ teaspoon black pepper
½ teaspoon white pepper

1. Combine the seasoning mix ingredients in a small bowl.

2. Clean the crabs: Place one in front of you, legs down. Cut off the eyes and the tip of the mouth. Gently lift up one side of the shell, exposing the gills, which are a row of feather-like objects. Some people in Louisiana call them "dead men" or "dead men's fingers." Remove the gills and close the shell, then repeat this process on the other side. Turn the crab over and locate the "apron," which is a piece shaped like a handle on male crabs and like a bell on females. Pull off the apron and the membranes that attach it to the crab. Repeat with the remaining crabs.

3. In a deep fryer or large pot using a cooking thermometer, pour enough oil to measure 3 inches deep and heat it to 350°F.

4. Season each side of each crab with ½ teaspoon of the seasoning mix and set aside.

5. Place the all-purpose flour in an 8-inch square baking pan or casserole dish.

6. In a blender, process the eggs and milk together until combined, about 30 seconds, and place this mixture in a similar pan.

7. In a third pan, combine the semolina flour, corn flour, and the remaining seasoning mix. Mix well.

8 As soon as the oil reaches 350°F, fry the crabs according to the instructions in the next paragraph. Be very careful when placing the crabs in the hot oil. The moisture in the crabs can cause the oil to sputter heavily, so use caution and long tongs or a long slotted spoon. This step should be done in several batches, and the number of crabs that can be fried at one time depends on the size of your fryer or pot. Don't try to fry too many crabs at one time because if the pot becomes too crowded, the oil will cool down and the coating will be soggy. Keep the temperature of the oil as close to 350°F as possible, especially between batches. Gentle handling of the crabs when battering will help the coating stick.

9. Dredge 2 crabs in the all-purpose flour, coating them evenly. Shake off the excess flour and transfer them to the egg wash, coating them evenly. Remove the crabs from the egg wash, letting any excess drip off, and gently transfer them to the seasoned semolina flour mix. Working quickly, mound the mixture over the crabs and press it in with your hands until the crabs are thoroughly coated. Pick up the crabs, allowing any excess flour to fall off, and immediately transfer to the hot oil. Fry until golden brown, about 3 to 4 minutes. Remove using tongs or a slotted spoon and drain on paper towels. Repeat this process until all the crabs are cooked. Serve immediately, accompanied by our Four Pack Chile Dip.

Sesame-Crusted Catfish

Makes 4 servings

Adding sesame seeds to the dry batter of this old standard Louisiana recipe gives it a wonderful new taste and crunch, and the grape juice adds a delicate sweetness to the sauce. We liked it so much when we developed it in our Research and Development Kitchen that we determined it would be a great addition to our restaurant menu at K-Paul's. There's nothing the slightest bit complicated about the method, so you can have it at home any time you like.

Four 3- to 4-ounce fresh catfish (or other
   firm-fleshed fish) fillets, cut into pieces
   about 2 × 2½ inches
Peanut oil, preferably, or vegetable oil,
   for frying
1 large egg
¼ cup heavy cream, in all
¼ cup sesame seeds
½ cup yellow cornmeal
2 tablespoons all-purpose flour
1¼ cups white grape juice
2 teaspoons freshly squeezed lemon juice
2 teaspoons freshly squeezed lime juice
1 tablespoon plus 1 teaspoon soy sauce
1 tablespoon Chef Paul Prudhomme's
   Magic Pepper Sauce, or other
   medium-hot pepper sauce
1 tablespoon lightly packed light brown
   sugar

Seasoning Mix

1¾ teaspoons salt

1¼ teaspoons paprika

1 teaspoon onion powder

¾ teaspoon garlic powder

½ teaspoon dried basil

½ teaspoon cayenne

½ teaspoon ground dried
   chipotle chile peppers

½ teaspoon ground
   coriander

½ teaspoon dried thyme
   leaves

½ teaspoon black pepper

½ teaspoon dry mustard

¼ teaspoon ground anise

¼ teaspoon ground
   cinnamon

¼ teaspoon white pepper

1. Combine the seasoning mix ingredients in a small bowl.

2. Sprinkle both sides of all the pieces of fish evenly with 1 tablespoon plus 2 teaspoons of the seasoning mix and gently pat it in.

3. Pour enough peanut or vegetable oil into a 12-inch skillet to measure ½ inch and place over high heat. Bring the temperature of the oil to 350°F. It's important to keep the temperature of the oil as close to 350°F as possible, for if it drops too much, your fish will be oily instead of crisp. If the temperature does drop too much (25°F or more), try frying smaller batches.

4. While the oil is heating, prepare the wet and dry batters. Place the egg and 1 tablespoon of the heavy cream in an 8-inch square baking pan or casserole dish and whisk until well combined. In a similar dish, combine the sesame seeds, cornmeal, and 2 teaspoons of the seasoning mix.

5. When the oil reaches 350°F place the pieces of fish in the wet batter and turn until coated on all sides—do not discard the leftover wet batter, because you will use it later in the recipe. Transfer the pieces, a few at a time, to the dry batter. Mound the dry batter over the fish pieces and press with your hands until the pieces are evenly coated. Immediately but gently shake off the excess and transfer to the hot oil. Fry the pieces, turning them several times, until they are light golden brown on both sides, about 6 to 7 minutes in all. Remove with a slotted spoon, drain on paper towels, and keep warm while you make the sauce.

6. Pour out all but 1 tablespoon of the oil from the skillet. Return the skillet to high heat and add the flour. Whisk constantly until the flour darkens slightly to the color of caramel, about 2 minutes. Add the grape juice, lemon juice, lime juice, soy sauce, pepper sauce, brown sugar, and the remaining seasoning mix. Bring to a boil, whisking constantly, then add the reserved wet batter and the remaining 3 tablespoons heavy cream. Whisk well, remove the skillet from the heat, and continue to whisk constantly until the mixture has cooled down slightly, about 30 seconds. You should have about 1½ cups of sauce.

7. Divide the fried fish and sauce into 4 portions and serve at once.

Shrimp and Potato Stew
with Fresh Fennel

Makes 6 servings *I think fennel bulb is underused, even though it's available in supermarkets all over the country these days. It adds a fresh, dynamic flavor to foods, and its texture (which we keep crispy by adding it in two stages) goes especially well with the shrimp and potatoes in this stew. The basil and cumin in the seasoning mix really complement the fresh vegetables, and the chile peppers give the dish just the right amount of punch.*

¼ cup all-purpose flour
1 teaspoon ground dried Anaheim chile
    peppers
1 tablespoon vegetable oil
1 cup chopped onions
1 cup seeded and chopped green bell
    peppers
½ cup chopped celery
2½ cups peeled white potatoes cut into
    ½-inch cubes, in all
4 cups shrimp stock, in all
1½ cups chopped fennel bulb, in all
1 teaspoon peeled and minced fresh ginger
    (optional)
½ pound peeled raw shrimp, 21 to 25 shrimp
    per pound

Seasoning Mix

1 teaspoon salt
¾ teaspoon dried basil
½ teaspoon cayenne
½ teaspoon ground cumin
½ teaspoon dry mustard
½ teaspoon ground dried
    New Mexico chile peppers
¼ teaspoon garlic powder
¼ teaspoon onion powder
¼ teaspoon dried oregano
¼ teaspoon black pepper
¼ teaspoon white pepper

1. Combine the seasoning mix ingredients in a small bowl.

2. In a small skillet over high heat, brown the flour, stirring and shaking constantly to prevent burning, until the flour is the color of light milk chocolate. Immediately remove the flour from the skillet to stop the browning and stir in the ground chile pepper until fully blended. Set aside. *After the flour has cooled, taste it and note the effect that the browning has on its flavor. The combination of flavors, which we often describe as a "brown" flavor, is very subtle and combines slight tastes of sweet and bitter with a complex aromatic roasted flavor. As this dish progresses, remember this flavor and see how it changes.*

3. In a 5-quart pot, heat the vegetable oil over high heat just until it begins to smoke, about 3 to 4 minutes. Add the onions, bell peppers, celery, 1½ cups of the potatoes, and 1 tablespoon of the seasoning mix. Cover and cook, uncovering every 2 minutes to stir and scrape the pot (add ¼ cup stock now if the mixture seems about to burn on the bottom) until the mixture sticks hard, about 12 minutes. Stir in ½ cup of the stock and the flour/chile pepper mixture and continue to stir until the color of the flour is no longer visible, about 30 seconds. If necessary to absorb the flour mixture, add a little more stock. *Notice the almost mocha flavor created by the browned flour combined with the starchy taste of the potatoes and the caramelized taste of the onions. The flavor balances in center of the mouth, not moving too far in any direction.* Add the remaining seasoning mix, the remaining 1 cup potatoes, 1 cup of the fennel, 1 cup of the stock, and the ginger, if using. Cook, stirring and scraping every 2 to 3 minutes, for 15 minutes. Stir in the remaining stock and the remaining ½ cup fennel, reduce the heat to medium, and simmer briskly, scraping every 2 to 3 minutes if the mixture seems sticky—you don't want it to burn—for 10 minutes. *All the tastes are now bound into a rich "brown gravy" flavor, filled with subtle notes from the seasonings, a delicate sweetness from the browned vegetables and flour, and an almost undetectable whiff of anise from the fennel. Adding the shrimp makes the perfect finishing touch, with a very rich and sweet seafood component.* Stir in the shrimp and cook just until they are pink and opaque, about 3 to 4 minutes. Serve hot.

Shrimp Ratatouille

Makes 4 to 6 servings

The name ratatouille, pronounced RAT-a-TOO-ee, comes from a French word that means "to stir," and refers to a traditional vegetable stew. But just like good cooks everywhere, the Acadian French people of south Louisiana have always cooked with all the good things that were abundant in the fields and waters around them. Here we've added shrimp, which are available all year. Try this recipe as written, or make it totally vegetarian by leaving out the shrimp and using a vegetable stock. Either way, it satisfies your spirit as well as your taste buds.

By the way, if your pot is not really heavy, you'll have to be very careful during the first few minutes of cooking—you're using a very high heat, and you can't see what's going on because the pot is covered. If your pot bottom is so thin that there's a chance the chopped vegetables might burn instead of caramelize, reduce the heat slightly, be sure to check more often than suggested, and, if necessary, add a little stock at this time to replace the liquid that evaporates from the vegetables.

Seasoning Mix

2 teaspoons salt

1½ teaspoons paprika

¾ teaspoon dried oregano

½ teaspoon dried basil

½ teaspoon garlic powder

½ teaspoon dry mustard

¼ teaspoon cayenne

¼ teaspoon black pepper

¼ teaspoon white pepper

¼ teaspoon dried thyme leaves

2 tablespoons olive oil
½ cup chopped onions
½ cup seeded and chopped bell peppers
½ cup chopped celery
1 cup shrimp stock
2 cups unpeeled eggplant cut into 1-inch cubes
1 cup seeded red bell peppers cut into
    1-inch pieces
1 cup seeded yellow bell peppers cut into
    1-inch pieces

1 cup seeded green bell peppers cut into 1-inch pieces

1 medium-size onion, cut into 1-inch cubes

1 cup unpeeled zucchini cut into 1-inch cubes

1 cup unpeeled yellow squash cut into 1-inch cubes

2 cups peeled and chopped fresh tomatoes

1 pound peeled raw shrimp, 21 to 25 shrimp per pound

1. Combine the seasoning mix ingredients in a small bowl.

2. In a heavy 4-quart pot, heat the olive oil over high heat just until it begins to smoke, about 3 to 4 minutes. Add the chopped onions, chopped bell peppers, and celery and stir well to combine. Cover and cook for 3 minutes, then uncover and stir the vegetables, which should be brightly colored and glistening with oil. Re-cover and cook for 2 minutes—the vegetables will be starting to brown on the edges. Uncover and stir in 1 tablespoon of the seasoning mix, re-cover, and cook for 3 minutes. By this time, a crust is starting to form on the bottom of the pot, the vegetables are caramelized, and their aroma is sweet and pungent. Uncover and scrape the pot bottom until you feel no resistance, then add the stock and scrape the bottom completely, stirring to dissolve the crust and any coating that clings to the vegetables. *The brown liquid will have a strong salty taste, about the same level as seawater, and all the seasoning levels are very high at this point. The vegetables are noticeably sweet, with a light crunch.* Re-cover and cook for 1 minute, then add the eggplant, 3 colors of bell pepper pieces, onion cubes, and 2 teaspoons of the seasoning mix. Stir well, re-cover, and cook until the eggplant takes on some of the color from the seasoning mix, about 3 minutes. Add the zucchini, yellow squash, tomatoes, and the remaining seasoning mix. Stir the vegetables into the mixture with a folding motion, lifting the brown bits and liquid off the bottom and combining with the vegetables. Re-cover and cook for 5 minutes. Uncover and stir. *The mixture is now fading in color and softening. The eggplant is beginning to cook but is still chewy and the outside is flavored with the broth and seasoning.* Re-cover and cook for 3 minutes. Now the liquid should be at a full boil and level with the vegetables, and the tomatoes are beginning to break up into the liquid. Uncover, stir well, and reduce the heat to low. Re-cover and cook for 4 minutes. At this point, the liquid has both the color and *the taste of minestrone, or rich vegetable soup,* and the vegetables are almost fully cooked. *The seasoning is still somewhat high, as is the salt level, both of which are corrected after adding the shrimp—but let the shrimp cook before tasting again!* Uncover and stir in the shrimp. Re-cover and cook just until the shrimp are done, about 5 minutes. Remove from the heat and let sit, covered, for 10 minutes. Serve with rice.

Shrimp in Tropical Fruit Cream

Makes 6 servings

I've been eating shrimp all my life, but not until recently would I have thought of combining it with tropical fruit—or any fruit, for that matter. But the more I travel and enjoy the foods of other cultures, the more I realize that there are thousands of combinations that may sound unusual to us here in Louisiana, but that work great. This is certainly one of them.

2 tablespoons vegetable oil
1 cup chopped onions
1 cup chopped celery
2 tablespoons unsalted butter
1½ cups peeled, pitted, and chopped ripe
   peaches, in all
1½ cups peeled, seeded, and chopped ripe
   mangoes, in all
1½ cups peeled, seeded, and chopped ripe
   papayas, in all
¾ cup seafood stock, in all
1 cup heavy cream
1 pound peeled and deveined raw shrimp
½ cup plain yogurt

Seasoning Mix

¾ teaspoon paprika

¾ teaspoon salt

½ teaspoon ground
   coriander

½ teaspoon ground cumin

½ teaspoon garlic powder

½ teaspoon ground ginger

½ teaspoon dry mustard

½ teaspoon onion powder

½ teaspoon ground dried
   chipotle chile peppers

¼ teaspoon ground
   cardamom

¼ teaspoon ground
   cinnamon

¼ teaspoon black pepper

¼ teaspoon ground turmeric

1. Combine the seasoning mix ingredients in a small bowl.

2. Heat the vegetable oil in a 12-inch skillet over high heat just until the oil begins to smoke, about 4 minutes. Add the onions, celery, and the seasoning mix and cook, stirring frequently, until the onions are rich brown, the celery is faded and beginning to brown, and both have a slightly yellow tinge from the seasonings, about 5 to 7 minutes. Add the butter and stir until it is completely melted. *Here you can taste the beginnings of the curry flavor that is at the heart of*

this dish. The flavor is mild, but coming on. The caramelized vegetables are becoming sweet and have a silky texture and mouth feel from the butter. Add ¾ cup each of the peaches, mangoes, and papayas and cook, stirring frequently, until the mixture is pasty and bubbling, about 7 to 9 minutes. *As the fruit mixture cooks down, note how the flavors develop. They change from very tart to mild and somewhat sweet, and the final taste of the seasoning changes from very hot to a milder and richer flavor.*

3. Add ¼ cup of the stock and whisk well, breaking up the chunks of fruit, then whisk in the heavy cream. Bring the cream just to a simmer and add the remaining ½ cup stock. Whisk well to combine, then add the remaining ¾ cup each peaches, mangoes, and papayas and stir well. Continue to cook until the mixture reduces slightly, about 4 minutes. Add the shrimp and cook until the shrimp are just cooked, about 2 minutes, then remove the skillet from the heat. Measure out 1 cup of the cooking liquid and place it in a bowl. Whisk the yogurt into it until fully blended, then stir this mixture back into the skillet. Serve immediately over rice or pasta.

Speckled Trout with
Spinach Cream Sauce

Makes 8 servings   *Speckled trout is delicious any way you cook it, but here's a brand-new recipe with a rich, creamy sauce to enhance the fish's delicate flavor without overpowering it. The spinach in the sauce adds nutrients and taste, plus it means you don't really have to serve another green vegetable—noodles and some beautiful carrots would round out the meal and provide a nice color balance.*

3 pounds speckled trout (or your favorite trout) fillets, cut into sixteen 2- to 3-ounce pieces about 3 inches square
1½ cups vegetable oil
2 cups all-purpose flour
4 large eggs
2 cups milk
2 cups corn flour

Spinach Cream Sauce

¼ cup minced shallots
2 teaspoons minced fresh garlic
2 tablespoons unsalted butter
3 cups heavy cream, in all
One 10-ounce bag fresh spinach, washed well and stemmed
4 ounces Romano cheese, freshly grated
4 ounces Parmesan cheese, freshly grated

Seasoning Mix

1 tablespoon plus 1 teaspoon salt

1 tablespoon dried basil

2½ teaspoons onion powder

2 teaspoons ground cardamom

2 teaspoons dried oregano

2 teaspoons ground dried Anaheim chile peppers

2 teaspoons ground dried ancho chile peppers

1½ teaspoons cayenne

1½ teaspoons dried chervil

1½ teaspoons garlic powder

1½ teaspoons dry mustard

1 teaspoon ground nutmeg

1 teaspoon black pepper

½ teaspoon white pepper

1. Combine the seasoning mix ingredients in a small bowl.

2. Sprinkle all the fish pieces evenly with a total of 2 tablespoons plus 2 teaspoons of the seasoning mix and gently pat it in.

3. In a heavy 12-inch skillet over high heat, heat the vegetable oil to 350°F. Use a cooking thermometer and adjust the heat so that the oil stays as close to 350°F as possible. An electric skillet works well, too. If the temperature drops too much (25°F or more), try frying in smaller batches. Oil that isn't hot enough will cause your fish to be oily rather than crisp. Combine the all-purpose flour with 2 tablespoons of the seasoning mix in a cake pan or pie pan. Combine the eggs and milk in a similar pan and whisk until combined. Combine the corn flour with 2 tablespoons of the seasoning mix in a third pan. Line up the batters in the order in which you'll use them: seasoned all-purpose flour, egg wash, then the seasoned corn flour. You'll save a lot of hand washing if you use one hand for the dry batters and the other for the egg wash. The fish pieces can sit in the all-purpose flour or the egg wash for a couple of minutes, but don't let them sit in the final batter—take them out and fry them as soon as possible.

4. When the oil reaches 350°F, dredge some of the fillets in the seasoned all-purpose flour, gently shaking off the excess. Transfer them to the egg/milk wash, letting the excess drip off, then place them in the seasoned corn flour. Working quickly, put a handful of corn flour over the fillets and pat it in gently. Immediately transfer the fillets to the hot oil and fry, turning once, until the fish is just cooked through and tender, about 2 minutes per side. Keep the fish warm while you make the sauce.

5. Drain off and discard the oil from the pan, saving as much of the browned flour on the bottom as possible. Return the heat to high and add the shallots, garlic, butter, and 2 cups of the heavy cream. Whisk constantly until the cream begins to thicken, about 1 to 2 minutes, then add half the spinach leaves and stir constantly until the leaves are wilted. Add the remaining 1 cup cream and the remaining spinach leaves and stir constantly until the leaves are wilted. Add the remaining 2 tablespoons seasoning mix. Stir well, then stir in the Romano and Parmesan cheeses. Bring to a boil, reduce the heat to low, and simmer for 4 minutes. Remove from the heat. For each portion, serve 2 pieces of fish and ¾ cup sauce.

Spicy Fried Fish Sticks

Makes 4 servings *What a wonderful way to enjoy fish—kids will love eating this as finger food! A helpful hint when frying any food is to use one hand for the dry batter and the other hand for the wet.*

1 pound drum, tilapia, or other firm-fleshed white fish, cut into 2½ × ½-inch pieces

Sauce

½ cup mayonnaise

½ cup plain yogurt

1 tablespoon Creole mustard, or your favorite mustard

¼ cup ketchup

2 teaspoons prepared horseradish (not horseradish sauce)

1 tablespoon Chef Paul Prudhomme's Magic Pepper Sauce, or other medium-hot pepper sauce

1 tablespoon lightly packed light brown sugar

2 teaspoons ground dried chipotle chile peppers (optional)

Vegetable oil for frying

Batter

¾ cup all-purpose flour

1 large egg

1 cup milk

¾ cup corn flour

Seasoning Mix

2¼ teaspoons salt

1¾ teaspoons garlic powder

1¾ teaspoons paprika

1¼ teaspoons ground dried chipotle chile peppers

¾ teaspoon ground dried New Mexico chile peppers

¾ teaspoon onion powder

¾ teaspoon black pepper

¾ teaspoon dried thyme leaves

½ teaspoon white pepper

½ teaspoon ground cumin

½ teaspoon ground ginger

¼ teaspoon dry mustard

1. Combine the seasoning mix ingredients in a small bowl.

2. Place the fish pieces in a medium-size bowl and season them with 1 tablespoon plus 1 teaspoon of the seasoning mix. Work the seasoning in well with your hands until it is evenly distributed. Refrigerate while preparing the rest of the recipe.

3. Make the sauce by combining all the sauce ingredients with 1 teaspoon of the seasoning mix. Stir until evenly blended, then refrigerate until ready to use.

4. Place a 5-quart pot over high heat and add enough vegetable oil to measure about 3 inches deep. Heat the oil to 350°F. If you have one, a deep fryer with a good thermostat would work well, or use a regular large heavy pot and cooking thermometer and adjust the heat so that the temperature of the oil stays as close to 350°F as possible, or the fish sticks will be oily instead of crisp. If the temperature drops too much (25°F or more), try frying in smaller batches.

5. Make the batter: Place the all-purpose flour in a cake or pie pan. In a similar pan, whisk the egg and milk together until they are well blended. Place the corn flour in a third pan, add the remaining 2 tablespoons seasoning mix, and stir until evenly blended. Now line the pans up in the order in which you'll use them—the all-purpose flour, the egg wash, and the seasoned corn flour.

6. Before you start to fry, let me emphasize this: For best results, don't let the strips sit in the corn flour. The fish can sit in the all-purpose flour, or even the milk-egg mixture, for a few minutes, but once they're coated with the corn flour, you should fry them immediately!

7. When the oil reaches 350°F place a handful of the fish strips in the all-purpose flour. Turn and press the strips until they are fully and evenly coated. Shake off any excess flour and transfer the fish to the milk-egg mixture. Turn the strips in the liquid until they are well coated on all sides. Let any excess drip off. Transfer the strips to the corn flour, quickly cover them with a generous handful of the corn flour, and press down gently, coating them completely; then shake off any excess corn flour and immediately and very carefully drop the strips into the hot oil. Fry until golden brown, 2 to 3 minutes, turning the pieces as they cook. Remove with a slotted spoon and drain on paper towels. Repeat the process, working in small batches, until all the fish is cooked. Serve as quickly as possible, accompanying each portion with some of the sauce for dipping.

Stuffed Tilapia

Makes 4 servings

Good, fresh fish is wonderful all by itself, of course, but for variety it's good to have ways to dress it up, and this is one of my favorites. The bell peppers look so pretty, and the cream makes the sauce so rich, that you're going to serve a dish fit for royalty!

Elephant garlic, which we specify, is much larger than regular garlic, and also milder. If you use regular garlic, you might want to reduce the amount.

Four 6- to 8-ounce tilapia fillets
1½ cups chopped onions
½ cup seeded and chopped green bell peppers
½ cup seeded and chopped red bell peppers
½ cup seeded and chopped yellow bell peppers
1 cup chopped celery
1 tablespoon plus 1 teaspoon olive oil, in all
2 tablespoons unsalted butter, in all
½ cup heavy cream
4 cups fish stock, in all
4 cups peeled potatoes cut into ½-inch cubes
1 cup chopped fire-roasted elephant garlic, preferably, or roasted regular garlic
Vegetable oil cooking spray
¾ cup plain yogurt

Seasoning Mix
1 tablespoon salt
2 teaspoons garlic powder
1½ teaspoons dried basil
1½ teaspoons dry mustard
1½ teaspoons onion powder
1 teaspoon cayenne
1 teaspoon ground ginger
1 teaspoon dried oregano
¾ teaspoon black pepper
¾ teaspoon dried thyme leaves
½ teaspoon dill seeds
½ teaspoon white pepper

1. Combine the seasoning mix ingredients in a small bowl.

2. Season the tilapia fillets with 2 teaspoons of the seasoning mix per side.

3. In a heavy 8-inch nonstick skillet over high heat, combine the onions, all the bell peppers, the celery, and 1 tablespoon of the olive oil. Cook, stirring frequently, until the

vegetables just begin to brown and stick to the pot, about 8 minutes. Reduce the heat to medium-low and add the remaining 1 teaspoon olive oil—cooking the vegetables slowly like this gives them a sweet taste that is perfect for this dish. Stir well, then add 2 teaspoons of the seasoning mix. Continue to cook, stirring frequently, for 5 minutes, then remove from the heat. *The taste begins with the mild flavor of the cooked vegetables, followed by a combination of gentle sweetness and a hint of white pepper from the seasoning. The vegetables are still slightly crunchy at this point.* Set the vegetables aside.

4. In a heavy 4-quart saucepan, combine 1 tablespoon plus 1 teaspoon of the butter and the heavy cream over high heat and bring to a boil. Add 3 cups of the stock, the potatoes, roasted garlic, and 1½ teaspoons of the seasoning mix. Cover and return to a boil, then remove the cover and cook until the potatoes are tender, about 8 minutes. Remove ½ cup of the cooking liquid and set it aside. Mash the potato mixture, then add ½ cup of the stock and the slow-cooked vegetables (don't wash the skillet in which the vegetables were cooked—you'll use it for the sauce) and stir until well blended. Remove and reserve ¾ cup of this mixture and set aside to cool.

5. Place a sheet pan in the oven and preheat the oven to 350°F. When the pan is hot, remove it from the oven, spray it lightly with the vegetable oil, and arrange the tilapia fillets on it. Mound 1 cup of the stuffing mixture on top of each fillet and bake until the fish is white and opaque all the way through and the stuffing is nicely browned around the edges, about 20 minutes. Keep warm while you make the sauce.

6. Deglaze the 8-inch skillet with the remaining ½ cup stock, then add the reserved cooking liquid from the potatoes, the reserved potato mixture, the yogurt, and the remaining 2 teaspoons butter. Bring just to a boil, reduce the heat to low, simmer for 5 minutes, and remove from the heat. Makes about 1½ cups. Pour the sauce over the fillets and serve immediately.

Vegetarian Main Courses

I have to admit that the idea of "healthful food" was totally foreign to our way of thinking. When you worked on a farm, all food was healthful because it gave you the strength and energy to put in twelve-hour days, or longer. If our meals were loaded with fat, believe me, we worked it off! And as farmers, a vegetarian lifestyle would never have occurred to us. Sure, we ate many vegetable dishes, but they were likely to be flavored with ham, sausage, a beef bone, or rich chicken stock. Times change. We don't work as hard physically, and we give thought to the nutritional content of our dishes. So we have developed these wonderful main-course recipes that are so hearty and satisfying that the absence of meat will be completely overlooked.

St. Joseph's Vegetables

Makes 8 side-dish servings

St. Joseph's Day, March 19, is a big day in New Orleans' Italian-American community. The patron saint of Sicily, St. Joseph was especially honored for having miraculously ended a famine there centuries ago. Now, among those who migrated here, churches and families set up elaborate three-tiered altars, loaded with good things to eat, as well as religious statues and candles, in thanksgiving to St. Joseph for favors granted. The public is invited, everyone attending makes a donation for the poor, and at the end of the celebration the food is distributed to guests, with an abundance set aside for various charitable institutions.

There are several traditional foods prepared for these altars—fish (never meat!), large loaves of crusty bread, pasta dishes, fig cookies, and fresh fennel cooked in a wonderful tomato sauce. This last was the springboard for the creation of this recipe. We didn't intend for it to be an actual vegetable dish for a St. Joseph's altar, but we were inspired by the combination of fennel and tomato.

Seasoning Mix

1½ teaspoons salt

1¼ teaspoons ground cardamom

1¼ teaspoons cayenne

1¼ teaspoons onion powder

1 teaspoon ground cumin

¾ teaspoon garlic powder

¾ teaspoon dry mustard

½ teaspoon dried oregano

½ teaspoon dried thyme leaves

¼ teaspoon ground allspice

¼ teaspoon white pepper

4 tablespoons (½ stick) unsalted butter, in all
2 tablespoons olive oil
1½ cups onions cut into ½-inch pieces
1 cup seeded red bell peppers cut into ½-inch pieces

1 cup seeded yellow bell peppers cut into
    ½-inch pieces
1 cup seeded green bell peppers cut into
    ½-inch pieces
2 large parsnips, peeled and cut into
    ½-inch pieces (about 1½ cups)
1 medium-size butternut squash, cut into
    ½-inch pieces (about 3 cups)
5 stalks celery, cut into ½-inch pieces (about
    1½ cups)
1 fennel bulb, cut into ½-inch pieces (about
    2 cups)
1 tablespoon minced fresh garlic
One 15-ounce can tomato sauce
1 cup vegetable stock
1 tablespoon lightly packed dark brown
    sugar

1. Combine the seasoning mix ingredients in a small bowl.

2. Melt 2 tablespoons of the butter with the olive oil in a 14-inch skillet or
5-quart pot, preferably nonstick, over high heat. As soon as the butter begins to
sizzle, add all the vegetables, the garlic, and the seasoning mix. Stir well, then
cover and cook, uncovering to stir and scrape the bottom of the pan frequently,
for 4 minutes. You will see that the vegetables' colors are a little brighter, their
texture is somewhat more tender, and the fragrance is crisp and earthy. Continue
to cook, still uncovering to stir and scrape, until the vegetables begin to brown,
about 4 minutes longer. Now the fennel will be wilted, transparent, and tender
and the bottom of the pan will be dry. At this point the vegetables are partially
cooked but still retain some of their crunch. *Along with the vegetables' natural
taste, there is a subtle taste of anise from the fennel and the beginning of a brown flavor. The finish is a light herbal taste from the seasonings, which almost sparkle on
the tongue.*

3. Add the tomato sauce, stir, re-cover and cook, uncovering every 2 or 3 minutes—to stir, scrape, and check to be sure the mixture is not going to scorch—
just until the vegetables are pasty and thickly coated with sauce and the liquid
has evaporated, about 7 to 8 minutes. If you feel that there might be a risk of
overbrowning, then reduce the heat slightly. Add the stock, brown sugar, and
the remaining 2 tablespoons butter. *This red sauce will have a lovely sweet taste;*

notice how the brown sugar counteracts and balances the acidity of the tomatoes. The undertone is like browned flour. In a few minutes, each of the tastes will blend together to make a rich and complex set of flavors for the final dish. Stir very well and cook just until the butter is thoroughly melted into the sauce and the vegetables are tender, except for the celery, which should still have a little crunch, about 2 to 3 minutes. Serve hot over pasta.

Eggplant with a Tomato Filling

Makes 4 servings

The vegetables are cut into different sizes and cooked for differing periods of time, giving the finished dish a variety of textures that, along with the cheese topping, produces a satisfying "feel" to this casserole.

2 large eggplants (about 1 pound each)
1 small eggplant (about 10 ounces)
1 medium-size zucchini
1 medium-size yellow squash
1 cup freshly grated Muenster cheese
 (about 4 ounces)
1 cup freshly grated Monterey Jack cheese
 (about 3 ounces)
5 tablespoons olive oil, in all
¾ cup chopped onions
¼ cup chopped celery
¼ cup seeded and chopped green bell peppers
¼ cup seeded and chopped red bell peppers
¼ cup seeded and chopped yellow bell peppers
2 cups chopped fresh tomatoes
1 tablespoon minced fresh garlic
1 cup tomato sauce
1 cup water

Brown Rice

1 tablespoon firmly packed light brown sugar
½ teaspoon salt
1 tablespoon good quality olive oil
2 tablespoons rice vinegar, or your favorite
 vinegar
½ cup chopped green onions or scallions
3 cups hot cooked brown rice

Seasoning Mix

1¾ teaspoons salt

1 teaspoon paprika

¾ teaspoon dried basil

¾ teaspoon onion powder

¾ teaspoon ground dried
 New Mexico chile peppers

½ teaspoon garlic powder

¼ teaspoon ground fennel
 seeds

¼ teaspoon dry mustard

¼ teaspoon black pepper

¼ teaspoon white pepper

1. Combine the seasoning mix ingredients in a small bowl.

2. Preheat the oven to 350°F.

3. Roast the 2 large eggplants (they may burst open and drip a little, so put them on a sheet pan or sheet of aluminum foil to keep the bottom of your oven clean) until they are soft to the touch, about 30 to 40 minutes. Remove and set them aside to cool. When the eggplants are cool enough to handle, cut them in half lengthwise, trim off the stem end, and scoop out the meat, leaving the shell about ½ inch thick. Reserve the scooped-out meat.

4. Peel the small eggplant and cut it lengthwise into ¼-inch-thick slices. Cut the zucchini and yellow squash in half lengthwise, then slice each into ¼-inch-thick half rounds. Set aside.

5. Mix the 2 cheeses in a small bowl and set aside.

6. Sprinkle all the surfaces of the eggplant slices evenly with 1 tablespoon of the seasoning mix, then drizzle 1 tablespoon of the olive oil on one side of the slices.

7. Place a heavy 5-quart pot over high heat until it is very hot, about 4 minutes. Add the eggplant slices, oiled side down (if not all the slices fit in the pot, do this step in 2 batches), and drizzle 1 tablespoon of the olive oil on the tops of the slices. Cook, turning several times, until the slices are light bronze in color with darker spots, about 4 minutes. Remove the eggplant and let cool, then chop and set aside.

8. To the same pot, add the onions, celery, and all the bell peppers. Stir well, then add the remaining 3 tablespoons olive oil. Stir well until the oil is evenly distributed, then add the tomatoes, garlic, the reserved chopped eggplant, and the remaining seasoning mix. Stir well, then cover and cook, stirring and scraping every 5 minutes, for 20 minutes. *As the tomatoes begin to cook, there is a light acid front that rises and falls in the mouth, followed by the flavors of the vegetables, with a mild finish of eggplant and herb flavors.* Add the tomato sauce, water, and ¾ cup of the reserved scooped-out eggplant meat. Reduce the heat to medium-low, re-cover, and simmer, stirring and scraping every 5 minutes, until the sauce is thick and the tomatoes have lost their acid edge, about 1 hour. *Note how the flavors develop during this cooking process. The tomato taste changes from acid to sweet, the eggplant taste develops into a rich but delicate undertone, and the seasonings mellow and blend to become a mild glowing finish to the sauce. You could stop right now and have a great sauce for pasta, with a rich taste and "meaty" texture.*

9. During this slow cooking process, you can prepare the brown rice. Mix the brown sugar and salt together, stir in the olive oil, vinegar, and green onions, then combine with the cooked rice. Keep warm until ready to serve.

10. Add the zucchini and yellow squash slices to the tomato mixture. Cook, stirring and scraping frequently, until the squash turns bright in color, about 4 minutes, then remove the pot from the heat.

11. Preheat the oven again to 350°F.

12. Place the eggplant shells in an 8 × 13-inch baking dish and divide the tomato mixture among the shells. Top evenly with the mixed cheeses and bake until the cheese melts and begins to brown, about 20 minutes. I like to serve the rice, molded with a cup, alongside the stuffed eggplant, but you can place it underneath if you prefer.

Stuffed Acorn Squash

Makes 4 servings

Pretty is as pretty does, and this gorgeous dish tastes as great as it looks! Mirin is a rice wine, similar to sake, and generally available in Asian markets. If you can't find it, you can substitute the same amount of vermouth plus ½ teaspoon sugar.

2 acorn squashes
10 cups water
1½ cups chopped onions, trimmings reserved
¾ cup chopped celery, trimmings reserved
5 tablespoons unsalted butter, in all
½ cup seeded and chopped green bell peppers
½ cup seeded and chopped red bell peppers
½ cup seeded and chopped yellow bell peppers
2 tablespoons sesame seeds
2 tablespoons peeled and finely chopped fresh ginger
1 tablespoon finely chopped fresh garlic
3 cups fresh corn kernels, in all
½ cup mirin, in all (see headnote above)
3 tablespoons all-purpose flour
¼ cup soy sauce
¼ teaspoon dark sesame oil
4 cups cooked brown rice
¼ cup chopped fresh cilantro leaves

> ### Seasoning Mix
>
> 1¾ teaspoons salt
> 1¼ teaspoons paprika
> 1¼ teaspoons ground ginger
> 1¼ teaspoons ground coriander
> ¾ teaspoon ground dried New Mexico chile peppers
> ¾ teaspoon onion powder
> ¾ teaspoon black pepper
> ½ teaspoon ground dried árbol chile peppers
> ½ teaspoon garlic powder
> ½ teaspoon white pepper

1. Combine the seasoning mix ingredients in a small bowl.

2. Cut the squashes in half crosswise, then scoop out and discard the seeds and pulp. Cut a thin slice off the tops and bottoms so the halves will stand upright.

3. In a 6-quart pot, bring the water to a boil over high heat. Add the trimmings from the onions and celery and add the squash halves. Reduce the heat so that the water is just simmering. Poach the squashes for 10 minutes, remove from the pot, drain, then carefully peel them. If you want to make them especially pretty, leave a thin line of the green peel running down each indentation. Set squash halves aside.

4. Return the squash peels to the pot, reduce the heat to medium, and continue to simmer the liquid and the trimmings, letting the liquid reduce while you continue the recipe.

5. Melt 3 tablespoons of the butter in a 12-inch nonstick skillet over high heat. When the butter sizzles, add the chopped onions, the celery, all the bell peppers, sesame seeds, ginger, garlic, and 1 cup of the corn. Cook, stirring and scraping occasionally, for 5 minutes. *Before the onions develop their sweet, cooked flavor, they have a slightly acidic taste, which works against the sweet tastes from the other vegetables. Notice the faint but growing sesame flavor in the background.* Stir in the seasoning mix and continue to cook, stirring and scraping frequently, until the color of the vegetables resembles autumn leaves, about 4 to 6 minutes. Now you'll see that brown bits are forming—pure flavor! *The taste of the seasoning has changed dramatically, although the flavor is still very intense. Note how the addition of the seasoning changes all the other flavors and also how the sweetness of the corn develops as it cooks.*

6. Add the remaining 2 tablespoons butter. Stir well, then add 3 tablespoons of the mirin. Continue to cook until the butter melts and disappears and the mirin is absorbed, about 2 minutes. Remove ¾ cup of the cooked mixture and set it aside. Add the flour to the skillet and stir until the white is no longer visible. Strain 3 cups of the poaching water and add it to the skillet. Stir in well, then add the remaining 2 cups corn, the remaining 5 tablespoons mirin, and the soy sauce. Continue to cook, stirring and scraping frequently, until the liquid thickens to a sauce consistency, about 18 minutes. Add the sesame oil, stir in well, then remove from the heat. Yields about 4 cups of sauce.

7. Carefully, to prevent their breaking up, return the cooked acorn squash halves to the simmering water until they are reheated, about 3 minutes. You might want to place them in a colander before immersing in the water. Remove and drain.

8. In a separate bowl, combine the reserved vegetable mixture with the brown rice (reheat the rice if necessary) and cilantro. Mix well. Fill each acorn squash half with 1 cup of the rice mixture, mounding the mixture on top of the squashes.

9. To serve, place 1 cup of sauce on a heated plate and 1 stuffed squash half on top.

Stuffed Butternut Squash

Makes 4 servings
Beautiful colors, a variety of textures and flavor notes, and a "mouth feel" that satisfies you completely—what's not to like? The only slightly tricky step is poaching the squash shells, but it's not a problem if you take your time and watch them carefully so they don't overcook and become too soft.

3 butternut squashes
10 cups water
1 cup chopped onions, trimmings reserved
3 tablespoons unsalted butter
1 cup seeded and chopped red bell peppers
1 tablespoon finely chopped fresh garlic
1 tablespoon peeled and finely chopped
   fresh ginger
1 cup heavy cream
10 ounces baby spinach, washed well
4 cups hot cooked brown rice
½ cup coarsely chopped macadamia nuts

Seasoning Mix
2½ teaspoons salt
1½ teaspoons paprika
1 teaspoon dried basil
1 teaspoon onion powder
1 teaspoon ground dried New Mexico chile peppers
¾ teaspoon garlic powder
½ teaspoon fennel seeds
½ teaspoon dry mustard
½ teaspoon black pepper
¼ teaspoon white pepper

1. Combine the seasoning mix ingredients in a small bowl.

2. Peel the squashes and reserve the peelings. Cut the squashes in half lengthwise and, with an ice cream scoop or spoon, remove the seeds and membrane. Set aside 4 halves for poaching and cut the remaining 2 halves into ½-inch pieces.

3. In a 5-quart pot over high heat, bring the water to a full boil. Add the reserved squash halves, the onion trimmings, and the squash peelings. Reduce the heat so that the water is just simmering. Poach the squash halves until a knife penetrates easily into the center without resistance, about 5 to 10 minutes, depending on the size and hardness of the squash—don't overcook the squash because it can get very mushy very quickly. Drain the halves, run cold water over them to

stop the cooking, and set aside. Leave the water boiling—allowing it to reduce by up to half—while you continue the recipe.

4. Melt the butter in a 10-inch nonstick skillet over high heat. When the butter sizzles, add the chopped onions, bell peppers, garlic, ginger, and 1 tablespoon plus 2 teaspoons of the seasoning mix. Cook, stirring and scraping the pan bottom frequently, until the onions are golden and the bell peppers are darkened slightly and shiny, about 6 to 8 minutes. *At this time the mixture is salty with a deep roasted taste from the vegetables and a finish of fennel and ginger.*

5. Strain 1 cup of the squash water and add it, along with the reserved diced squash, to the skillet, then stir well and cover. Reduce the heat to medium and cook, uncovering to stir after about 7 minutes. Re-cover and cook until the squash is cooked and the water is reduced to a quarter of its original volume, about 15 minutes. When the squash pieces are cooked, remove the cover and stir the mixture vigorously, breaking up and mashing the squash until the mixture is thick. Remove and set aside ½ cup of the mixture. Add the heavy cream and ½ cup of the squash water. Increase the heat to high, stir well, and bring to a boil. Reduce the heat to low and simmer until the cream reduces slightly, about 4 minutes, then add the spinach. Increase the heat to high and cook until the spinach wilts, about 2 minutes. Makes 4 cups of sauce.

6. *This process is a great example of how flavors develop in a dish. When the squash is cooked, the flavor is broken into fennel (from the seeds), followed by squash flavors, then herbs and spices. The addition of the cream pulls the flavors together so that the taste is now complex with sweet highlights accentuated by the cream. The herb and spice flavors are much lower, as is the salt, and they are pushed back to the end of the taste. Reducing the cream slightly mellows the flavors and accentuates the sweetness and rich feeling in the mouth. Finally, the slightly cooked spinach reacts with the fennel seeds to produce a lingering finish that glows in the mouth. We New Orleanians think of this as Oysters Rockefeller flavor.*

7. In a large bowl, combine the hot cooked rice, macadamia nuts, and the reserved ½ cup of vegetable mixture and mix well.

8. Reheat the squash halves in the simmering water just until they are heated through and drain well. Fill each squash half with 1 cup of the brown rice mixture, mounding it up. Ladle 1 cup of the sauce over each stuffed squash half and serve immediately.

Stuffed Eggplant Pirogues

Makes 4 servings

Beautiful to look at and taste, these stuffed eggplants make a great light lunch or supper. A pirogue, for which the recipe is named, is a traditional flat-bottomed dugout wooden boat used by the Acadians (Cajuns) in south Louisiana for fishing and trapping. Sometimes we even fill real ones with boiled seafood and drape them with nets for large parties.

Two 1-pound eggplants
¾ cup unseasoned dried bread crumbs
6 tablespoons olive oil, in all
3 cups chopped onions, in all
1 cup seeded and chopped green bell peppers
1 cup seeded and chopped red bell peppers
1 cup seeded and chopped yellow bell
    peppers
2 cups peeled sweet potatoes cut
    into ¼-inch cubes
1 tablespoon plus 2 teaspoons minced fresh
    garlic, in all
2 cups vegetable stock, preferably,
    or chicken stock
2 teaspoons peeled and minced fresh ginger
One 15-ounce can diced tomatoes
One 15-ounce can tomato sauce
2 tablespoons chopped fresh thyme leaves
3 tablespoons chopped fresh basil leaves
2 tablespoons firmly packed light brown sugar

Seasoning Mix

1 tablespoon plus
    1 teaspoon salt
1 tablespoon paprika
2 teaspoons dry mustard
1½ teaspoons ground cumin
1½ teaspoons garlic powder
1½ teaspoons ground ginger
1½ teaspoons onion powder
1 teaspoon black pepper
½ teaspoon cayenne
½ teaspoon white pepper

1. Combine the seasoning mix ingredients in a small bowl.

2. Cut the eggplants in half lengthwise and hollow out the halves—a melon baller works well—reserving the pulp and leaving a shell about ½ inch thick. Dice the pulp and set it aside; you should have about 4 to 6 cups.

3. In an 8-inch nonstick skillet over high heat, toast the bread crumbs, stirring constantly, until they are light golden brown and have the aroma of fresh French bread. Set aside to cool.

4. In a heavy 12-inch nonstick skillet, heat 3 tablespoons of the olive oil over high heat just until it begins to smoke, about 3 to 4 minutes. Add 2 cups of the onions, all the bell peppers, the sweet potatoes, 2 teaspoons of the garlic, 4 table-spoons of the seasoning mix, and the reserved diced eggplant. Cover and cook, uncovering every 3 to 4 minutes to stir, for 12 minutes, then add the toasted bread crumbs. Stir just until the bread crumbs are moistened and remove from the heat. *The stuffing has a high-intensity seasoned flavor that leaves a tingle in your mouth. The middle flavors are the eggplant and sweet potato, with roasted, almost meaty, flavor highlights, followed by a toasted brown flavor from the bread crumbs and a lingering, faint taste of salt and residual heat from the seasonings.*

5. Preheat the oven to 350°F.

6. Sprinkle each pirogue evenly with 1 teaspoon of the seasoning mix and divide the stuffing evenly among the 4 of them, carefully mounding the stuffing. If the eggplant shells are too large, trim off the top edges a bit to make them shallower. Place the stuffed eggplants in a 9½ × 13-inch baking pan, gently pour the stock into the bottom of the pan, and cover the pan with a sheet of aluminum foil. Bake for 15 minutes, remove the foil, then bake until the tops of the stuffing are golden and the eggplant shells are tender, about 20 minutes more.

7. Make the sauce while the pirogues are baking. In a heavy 12-inch skillet, heat the remaining 3 tablespoons of olive oil over high heat just until it begins to smoke, about 3 to 4 minutes. Add the remaining seasoning mix, the remaining onions, the ginger, and the remaining garlic. Cover and cook, uncovering to stir 3 or 4 times, until the onions are caramelized, about 5 minutes. Uncover and add the diced tomatoes and tomato sauce. Re-cover and cook, uncovering to stir every 1 or 2 minutes, for 5 minutes, then uncover the skillet and cook until the tomatoes begin to thicken, about 8 minutes. Stir in the thyme, basil, and brown sugar. *The first taste is a high sweet taste from the brown sugar, together with a lower acid taste from the tomatoes. As the sauce cooks, the acid from the tomatoes becomes sweeter and the sweetness from the sugar lessens. Behind these tastes, the herbs and ginger provide a very gentle finish.* Reduce the heat to medium and sim-mer briskly, uncovered, stirring every 2 or 3 minutes, until the sauce is thick and gives off a rich, smoky tomato aroma, about 10 minutes.

8. Top each pirogue with one quarter of the sauce before serving.

Vegetables in a
Sweet Potato Cream

Makes 4 main-course or 8 side-dish servings

The taste of the sweet potatoes is critical to the appeal of this dish, so choose carefully. We like to use the Beauregard variety, a delicious Louisiana product that is available in many markets across the country.

2 medium-size sweet potatoes (about 1¼
    pounds total)
2 tablespoons unsalted butter
1½ cups onions cut into ½-inch pieces, in all
1 cup seeded red bell peppers cut into
    ½-inch pieces
1 cup seeded yellow bell peppers cut into
    ½-inch pieces
1 cup seeded green bell peppers cut into
    ½-inch pieces
1 cup carrots cut into ½-inch pieces
2 bay leaves
1 medium-size zucchini, peeled, cut into
    6 equal lengthwise wedges, then cut into
    ½-inch pieces (about 2 cups)
1 cup heavy cream
2½ cups vegetable stock, preferably, or chicken
    or beef stock, in all
3 cups cored cabbage cut into 1-inch pieces

Seasoning Mix

2 teaspoons salt
1 teaspoon dried basil
1 teaspoon garlic powder
1 teaspoon onion powder
½ teaspoon dillweed
½ teaspoon cayenne
½ teaspoon paprika
½ teaspoon black pepper
½ teaspoon dried thyme
    leaves
¼ teaspoon white pepper

1. Combine the seasoning mix ingredients in a small bowl.

2. Preheat the oven to 350°F.

3. Place the sweet potatoes on a sheet pan and bake until they are soft all the way through, about 45 minutes to 1 hour.

When they are cool enough to handle, peel and purée them in a food processor. If the purée is stringy, force it through a strainer. Set aside.

4. Melt the butter in a 14-inch skillet or 5-quart pot, preferably nonstick, over high heat. When the butter sizzles, add 1 cup of the onions, all the bell peppers, and the carrots. Stir well, then stir in the seasoning mix and the bay leaves. Cook, stirring frequently, especially as brown bits begin to form on the bottom of the pot, until the vegetables have a light golden coating from the seasonings but are still bright in color, about 6 to 8 minutes. *The vegetables will still have a little of their "raw" taste, but they have begun to pick up the subtle flavor of the dill and the heat of the pepper from the seasoning mix.*

5. Add the sweet potato purée and stir well, then add the zucchini and the remaining ½ cup onions. Cook, stirring frequently, until the mixture makes large slow bubbles, about 4 minutes. You will think that such a thick mixture will not "bubble," but it will. All of a sudden you will see very large amounts of the mixture slowly heave up from the bottom of the pot and pop open. It's an amusing sight, but you don't have time right now to stop and admire it! Immediately add the heavy cream and 1½ cups of the stock and stir well until completely blended in. Bring just to a boil, reduce the heat to medium, and simmer, stirring frequently, until the liquid is thickened and reduced, about 7 minutes.

6. Fold in the cabbage and continue to cook, stirring frequently, until the cabbage is cooked but still slightly crisp *(and it should be sweet-tasting)*, about 5 to 6 minutes. Add the remaining 1 cup stock. Stir well, then bring back just to a simmer—all the vegetables should be tender except the cabbage, which should still have a little crunch (if it's not tender enough, simmer a little longer and check again)—and remove from the heat. Remove the bay leaves and serve as you would a stew—in a bowl or over rice or pasta.

Yucca Casserole

Makes 6 to 8 servings *This is a great casserole! One of our tasters had never tried yucca before, and after sampling this dish said now it's his favorite vegetable. Not surprising, because its texture is similar to that of potato, and its flavor is sweet and a little nutty.*

Two 12-inch long yucca roots
6 cups water
1½ cups chopped onions, trimmings and peel reserved
1 cup chopped celery, trimmings reserved
6 tablespoons (¾ stick) unsalted butter
1 cup seeded and chopped red bell peppers
½ cup seeded and chopped fresh Anaheim chile peppers
½ cup seeded and chopped fresh poblano chile peppers
2 tablespoons peeled and minced fresh ginger
1 tablespoon minced fresh garlic
½ cup mirin
1 cup heavy cream
3 ounces Monterery Jack Cheese, freshly grated
3 ounces Cheddar cheese, freshly grated

Seasoning Mix

1 tablespoon salt
2½ teaspoons paprika
1½ teaspoons onion powder
1 teaspoon garlic powder
1 teaspoon black pepper
1 teaspoon ground dried Anaheim chile peppers
1 teaspoon dried rosemary
1 teaspoon dried thyme leaves
¾ teaspoon white pepper
½ teaspoon dry mustard

1. Combine the seasoning mix ingredients in a small bowl.

2. Peel the yucca, then cut each one in half lengthwise. Cut each half into lengths of about 3 inches each. Place the water in a 6-quart pot over high heat and bring to a boil. Add the yucca and the reserved onion and celery trimmings. Boil until the yucca is tender and a knife penetrates easily, about 40 minutes. Remove from the heat, then remove the yucca from the water and set it aside to cool. Strain and reserve the

cooking liquid. When the yucca is cool enough to handle, remove and discard the hard fibrous center—it pulls out easily by hand—cut the remaining yucca into ½-inch pieces, and set aside.

3. Melt the butter in a 10-inch nonstick skillet over high heat. When the butter begins to sizzle, add the chopped onions, celery, bell peppers, chile peppers, and 2 tablespoons of the seasoning mix. Stir well to coat the vegetables with the butter and distribute the seasoning mix evenly. Cover and cook, occasionally stirring and scraping the bottom to loosen any brown bits, until the poblano peppers are very bright and the onions are just beginning to brown, about 4 minutes. *The flavor at this point is dominated by a darkish taste from the peppers, overlaid by salt. This is followed by a rising sweetness from the onions, finishing with a hint of rosemary.* Add the ginger and garlic. Re-cover and continue to cook, stirring and scraping the bottom occasionally, until the onions darken, to a medium brown with a golden glow from the butter, about 7 minutes. *Now a rich brown flavor is developing that is both sweet and deep. The rosemary taste is quite fragrant, and there is a round mouth feel and flavor from the browned butter. Note the development of the different browned flavors as the vegetables continue to cook. When the vegetables are ready, the many tastes will have smoothed and blended into one continuous flavor of remarkable complexity and depth.*

4. Add 1 cup of the reserved yucca water to the skillet. Re-cover and cook, stirring occasionally, until the vegetables are well browned and breaking down, resembling a coarse purée, another 5 to 7 minutes. Add the remaining seasoning mix and stir until it is completely incorporated, then add the mirin and heavy cream and stir well. Bring to a boil and cook until the liquid reduces slightly, about 4 minutes. Makes about 2 cups sauce.

5. Preheat the oven to 350°F.

6. Combine the cheeses in a small bowl and mix well.

7. Place the reserved diced yucca in a 9½ × 13-inch casserole dish. The yucca should come about three quarters of the way up the sides of the dish. Pour the sauce over the yucca and stir to distribute the ingredients evenly and coat all the yucca. Top with the mixed cheeses and bake until the top is nicely browned, about 30 minutes.

Side Dishes
for Every Taste

You know, with cooking and meal planning, nothing is set in stone. If you want to use some of these dishes as appetizers or even the main course of a light lunch or supper, by all means go ahead! Take the Cheesy Jalapeño Skillet Corn Bread, for instance. (By the way, this recipe was one of the biggest favorites in the whole book!) It contains cheese and cornmeal, obviously, but also fresh chile peppers and chopped onions. You could add a green salad to a nice big wedge of corn bread, preferably still warm from the oven, and have a really great little meal.

Andouille Spicy Rice

Makes 8 or 9 side-dish servings *Everything in this wonderful dish, except some of the spices, can be found in traditional south Louisiana cooking. Everyone knows we eat a lot of rice, and andouille is one of our more spectacular contributions to good eating in this country. Especially great with roast pork, andouille spicy rice goes well with just about any strong-flavored meat.*

2 tablespoons vegetable oil
½ pound andouille, or your favorite
    smoked pork sausage, cut into
    ¼-inch cubes
2 cups chopped onions
2 cups peeled sweet potatoes cut into
    ¼-inch cubes
2 teaspoons minced fresh garlic
4 cups chicken stock, in all
2 cups uncooked long-grain rice

Seasoning Mix

1 tablespoon lightly packed
   dark brown sugar

2 teaspoons salt

1½ teaspoons ground
   coriander

1¼ teaspoons paprika

1¼ teaspoons ground cumin

1¼ teaspoons ground ginger

1¼ teaspoons onion powder

½ teaspoon ground dried
   chipotle chile peppers

½ teaspoon garlic powder

½ teaspoon ground dried
   pasilla chile peppers

¼ teaspoon cayenne

1. Combine the seasoning mix ingredients in a small bowl.

2. In a heavy 5-quart pot, heat the vegetable oil over high heat just until it begins to smoke, about 3 to 4 minutes. Add the andouille, onions, sweet potatoes, garlic, and the seasoning mix. Cover and cook, stirring and scraping the pot every 3 or 4 minutes, until the mixture begins to stick hard to the bottom, about 10 minutes. *The andouille will give its taste to the vegetables, especially the sweet potatoes, and everything will absorb much of the flavor of the seasoning mix.* Stir in 2 cups of the stock and scrape the bottom of the pot to loosen and dissolve the crust that has formed. This crust, by the way, is where a lot of good sweetness is found, and you're enriching the liquid by scraping up and dissolving the crust. Add the rice and stir, then add the remaining 2 cups stock and stir again. Bring just to a boil, then stir

briefly and reduce the heat to low. Cover the pot and simmer for 15 minutes, until most of the liquid is absorbed. Remove from the heat and gently stir the rice to redistribute all the ingredients evenly, then let sit, covered, for 5 minutes before serving. *When you taste this dish, you'll realize that the various ingredients can still be tasted separately, yet they somehow blend together to create a series of flavor sensations, all sparked by the chile peppers in the seasoning mix. As you chew and enjoy each bite, the flavors subtly but definitely change.*

Banana Corn Fritters

Makes 18 to 20 fritters; 4 to 5 servings *When you bite into
one of these crisp brown delights, your taste buds are going to think
they've gone to a party! The sweetness of the corn and bananas contrasts just perfectly with the tang of the onions.*

1 medium-size banana, yellow with green
    points, preferably, or ripe
5 tablespoons plus 1 teaspoon corn flour
5 tablespoons yellow cornmeal
5 tablespoons plus 1 teaspoon all-purpose
    flour
2 teaspoons baking powder
1½ teaspoons lightly packed light brown
    sugar
1 teaspoon cane vinegar, or your favorite
    vinegar
½ teaspoon pure vanilla extract
One 5-ounce can evaporated milk
One 11-ounce can Niblets corn, drained
¾ cup chopped onions
Vegetable oil for deep-frying
Confectioners' sugar for dusting (optional)

Seasoning Mix

¾ teaspoon salt

½ teaspoon cayenne

½ teaspoon ground
    cinnamon

½ teaspoon ground
    coriander

½ teaspoon ground dried
    New Mexico chile peppers

¼ teaspoon ground nutmeg

¼ teaspoon white peppers

1. Combine the seasoning mix ingredients in a small bowl.

2. Peel the banana, cut it in half lengthwise, then cut each
half lengthwise into 3 equal strips. Chop the strips into
¼-inch pieces and set aside.

3. In a large bowl, combine the corn flour, cornmeal, all-
purpose flour, baking powder, and the seasoning mix and
stir with a whisk until evenly combined. Sprinkle the
brown sugar over the flour mixture and work it in by rub-
bing the sugar and flour between your fingers until all the
lumps are gone, then stir with the whisk until combined.
Add the cane vinegar, vanilla, and evaporated milk and stir

just until the mixture is well blended. Gently stir in the banana, corn, and onions. Refrigerate until cold.

4. Pour enough vegetable oil into a large skillet to measure ½ inch deep. Place over high heat until the oil reaches 350°F, about 3 to 5 minutes. Use a cooking thermometer and adjust the heat to keep the oil as close to 350°F as possible, so the fritters will be nice and crisp, not soggy. An electric skillet works great for this. Using a soupspoon, spoon about 2 rounded tablespoons of the batter into the hot oil, pulling the batter sideways as you drop it in so that the fritter is stretched out into a thin oval shape. If the batter is the correct consistency, the fritters will be somewhat irregular in shape; also, be sure not to make the fritters too thick, or they will be doughy rather than crisp when fried. Repeat, forming as many fritters as will fit into your skillet without crowding. Fry the fritters, turning once, until they are a rich earthy brown, about 2½ minutes per side. Remove with a slotted spoon and drain on paper towels. Serve at once, sprinkled lightly with confectioners' sugar, if you like.

Candied Leeks

Makes 6 side-dish servings

Legend has it that the Roman emperor Nero thought leeks would improve his singing voice, so he ate enormous amounts of this wonderful root vegetable. It's been somewhat overlooked since then, and that's a shame! Besides in soup and salads, leeks are great as a side dish, and this sweet and tangy version can hold its own with beef or pork, even wild game.

6 large leeks
1 cup chicken stock
½ pound (2 sticks) unsalted butter
2 bay leaves
1 cup sugar
1 teaspoon finely chopped orange zest
1 teaspoon finely chopped lemon zest
1 teaspoon finely chopped lime zest

Seasoning Mix

¾ teaspoon salt

½ teaspoon ground allspice

½ teaspoon caraway seeds

½ teaspoon ground cinnamon

½ teaspoon ground nutmeg

1. Combine the seasoning mix ingredients in a small bowl and set aside.

2. Preheat the oven to 350°F.

3. Remove the bottoms and the dark green leaves from the leeks, leaving only the white and light green parts. Cut each leek in half lengthwise, then wash the leeks carefully under cold running water to remove any dirt or grit that may have lodged between the layers. Pat them dry and place them in a single layer in an 8 × 15-inch baking pan or casserole dish. Pour the stock over the leeks, then cover the pan with a sheet of aluminum foil.

4. Place the pan in the oven and cook until the leeks are soft, about 15 minutes. Remove from the oven and uncover, saving the aluminum foil for later use. Pour the stock that remains in the pan into a 10-inch skillet and set the pan of leeks aside.

5. Place the skillet over high heat and add the remaining ingredients and the seasoning mix. Cook, whisking constantly, until the mixture comes to a boil, about 4 minutes. Continue to cook, whisking constantly, until the mixture is thick and syrupy, about 2 more minutes. During this time the mixture will become very foamy, so be careful not to let it boil over. Remove from the heat and pour over the leeks, coating them evenly. Re-cover the pan with the aluminum foil. With a sharp knife, pierce about 12 small holes in the aluminum foil. Return the pan to the oven and bake, basting and turning the leeks over after 20 minutes, until the leeks are tender and beginning to brown in spots and the sauce is very thick, about 45 minutes in all. Serve hot, spooning some of the sauce over the leeks.

Cheesy Jalapeño
Skillet Corn Bread

Makes 8 servings

This may be the best recipe in the whole book! If you're an experienced baker of corn bread, you'll see that the basics are all here—flour, cornmeal, sugar, egg, baking powder, etc.—but what sets it apart is the judicious use of chile peppers: dried and ground in the seasoning mix, and fresh chiles as well. We might not have done that years ago, even here in Louisiana, where we love our peppers, but we're constantly learning new ways to pep up all our old recipes! To cook this wonderful corn bread, you really must have an ovenproof skillet, preferably one made of cast iron. Be sure to check the date of your baking powder, because if it's too old the rising action won't be sufficient and your corn bread might be heavy or gummy.

2 tablespoons unsalted butter

4 tablespoons cottonseed oil, preferably, or
    vegetable oil, in all

1½ cups chopped red onions

½ cup seeded and chopped fresh poblano
    chile peppers

½ cup seeded and chopped fresh Anaheim
    chile peppers

½ cup seeded and chopped fresh red
    (preferably, or use green) jalapeño chile
    peppers

¾ cup corn flour

1¼ cups all-purpose flour

¾ cup sugar

½ cup cornmeal

Seasoning Mix

2¼ teaspoons salt

1¼ teaspoons ground dried
New Mexico chile peppers

1 teaspoon onion powder

1 teaspoon paprika

1 teaspoon ground dried
chipotle chile peppers

¾ teaspoon ground cumin

¾ teaspoon garlic powder

1 tablespoon plus 2 teaspoons baking powder

1 large egg, beaten

1½ cups milk

5 tablespoons unsalted butter, melted and
    cooled to room temperature

1 cup Cheddar cheese, freshly grated, in all

1 cup Monterey Jack cheese, freshly grated, in all

1. Combine the seasoning mix ingredients in a small bowl.

2. In a 12-inch skillet over high heat, combine the butter with 2 tablespoons of the oil. As soon as the butter melts, add the onions, all the chile peppers, and 1 tablespoon plus 2 teaspoons of the seasoning mix. Stir well, then cook, stirring occasionally, until the vegetables begin to brown, about 6 to 8 minutes. Remove from the heat and set aside to cool to room temperature. The mixture should be a golden tan color, the onions a medium tan brown, and the peppers dark red and dark green. *The taste is first a bit salty, followed by a rich flavor of toasted cumin and chile peppers, combined with sweetness and roast pepper tastes from the vegetables.* The vegetables retain a slight crunch.

3. Preheat the oven to 350°F.

4. While the vegetables are cooling, make the corn bread batter. Combine the corn flour, all-purpose flour, sugar, cornmeal, baking powder, and the remaining seasoning mix in a large bowl. Add the egg, milk, melted butter, ½ cup each of the grated Cheddar and Monterey Jack cheeses, and the vegetable mixture. Mix until just combined.

5. Pour the remaining 2 tablespoons oil into a 12-inch cast-iron skillet. Make sure that the oil covers the entire bottom of the skillet—lift and roll the skillet if necessary. Heat the oil just until it begins to smoke, about 4 to 5 minutes. Add the batter to the skillet—the mixture will begin to sizzle right away. Remove the skillet from the heat immediately and sprinkle the top of the batter evenly with the remaining ½ cup each Cheddar and Monterey Jack cheeses.

6. Bake until a knife inserted into the middle of the corn bread comes out clean, about 30 minutes. Remove from the oven and let stand for 10 minutes before cutting.

Dirty Rice Fritters

"Dirty rice" is a favorite side dish in my part of the state, taking its name from the bits of meat that give it extra color and flavor. In this recipe we've increased the proportion of meat, so that the completed fritters are very much like pan-fried sausages. You can serve them any way you would serve little meat patties—for a hearty breakfast with eggs and grits, as an appetizer with a dollop of savory sauce on the side, or as the main course for lunch or supper. This is one of the few recipes in which I don't specify Converted rice. To help the fritters hold together, you want the rice to be very starchy and sticky, so after it's cooked according to package directions, check the texture. If it's fluffy and the grains are easily separated, add ½ cup water, cover, and cook another 4 to 5 minutes. Remove from the heat but leave covered until you're ready to add it to the other ingredients.

Seasoning Mix
2 teaspoons salt
2 teaspoons onion powder
1½ teaspoons cayenne
1½ teaspoons garlic powder
1½ teaspoons dry mustard
1 teaspoon ground cumin
1 teaspoon black pepper
¾ teaspoon white pepper

1 tablespoon plus 1½ teaspoons vegetable oil
1 cup chopped onions, in all
¼ cup seeded and chopped green bell peppers
¼ cup seeded and chopped red bell peppers
¼ cup seeded and chopped yellow bell peppers
¼ pound freshly ground beef
¼ pound freshly ground pork
2 bay leaves
1½ teaspoons minced fresh garlic
1 cup plus 1 tablespoon plus 1½ teaspoons
    all-purpose flour, in all
2½ to 3 cups pork or chicken stock, in all
2 cups cooked long-grain rice
1 teaspoon baking powder
Vegetable oil for frying

1. Combine the seasoning mix ingredients in a small bowl and set aside.

2. Heat the oil in a heavy 4-quart pot, preferably nonstick, over high heat just until it begins to smoke, about 3 to 4 minutes. Add ½ cup of the onions and all the bell peppers, and cook, stirring occasionally, until the onions are brown on the edges, about 4 to 6 minutes. Add the ground beef, ground pork, 3 tablespoons of the seasoning mix, and the bay leaves. Cook, stirring frequently and breaking up the meat with your spoon, until the meat is lightly browned, about 8 to 10 minutes. *The vegetables, which were bright and crisp at the beginning of this cooking time, will have caramelized enough that you can now detect a wonderful sweetness, while they still maintain their distinctive flavors underneath.* Stir in the garlic and 1 tablespoon plus 1½ teaspoons of the flour and cook, stirring constantly, until the white is no longer visible, about 1 minute. Continue to cook and stir for 2 more minutes, allowing a crust to form on the bottom of the pot. *By now the vegetables are richly sweet, with an added "darkness." The cumin, previously an outstanding note in the seasonings, is now more subtle, helping to hold together the other spices.* Add 1 cup of the stock and scrape the bottom and sides thoroughly, loosening the crust and dissolving it in the stock. Continue to cook, stirring and scraping frequently, for 5 minutes, then add the remaining onions. Cook, stirring and scraping frequently, for 5 minutes. If the mixture is very thick, stir in up to ½ cup of the stock now. Cook for 5 more minutes, then add another ½ cup stock. Continue to cook, stirring and scraping frequently, until almost all the liquid evaporates and the mixture is very thick, about 6 to 8 minutes. Remove from the heat, remove the bay leaves, then thoroughly mix in the cooked rice. *You'll notice that the onions added the second time retain more of their distinctive "onion" flavor, giving a nice contrast to the well-caramelized onions previously added.* Cool to room temperature.

3. In a mixing bowl, combine the remaining 1 cup flour, the baking powder, and the remaining seasoning mix. Whisk until combined, then add 1 cup stock and whisk until the batter is smooth. Combine the batter and rice mixture and stir until fully blended. Refrigerate until very cold.

4. Pour ¼-inch oil into a 12-inch skillet. Place over high heat just until the oil begins to smoke, about 3 to 4 minutes. Working quickly so the heat of your hands doesn't warm the batter, form about ⅓ cup of the batter into patties—as many as will fit easily in your skillet—each 2½ to 3 inches long and about 2 inches wide. Cook, turning once, until brown on both sides, about 3 to 5 minutes in all. Drain on paper towels and keep warm while you cook the remaining fritters. Serve hot.

Double Mustard
Stuffed Onions

Makes 4 servings *You might not have thought of using radicchio leaves in anything but a salad, but why not? We're using a small amount—only ½ cup—just enough to add a little zing to the more traditional flavors of the two potatoes, greens, and onions.*

4 large onions
10 cups water

Stuffing

¼ cup (½ stick) unsalted butter
1 cup chopped celery
8 cups mustard greens, stemmed, washed
well, and torn into 1-inch pieces
½ cup chopped radicchio leaves
2 cups peeled sweet potatoes cut into
½-inch pieces
2 cups peeled white potatoes cut into
½-inch pieces
3 cups cored cabbage cut into ½-inch pieces
10 ounces baby spinach, washed well

Sauce

3 tablespoons unsalted butter
3 tablespoons all-purpose flour
3 tablespoons Creole mustard, or your favorite
mustard
2 tablespoons lightly packed dark brown sugar
1 cup sour cream or heavy cream, or the
water used to poach the onions

1. Combine the seasoning mix ingredients in a small bowl.

2. Peel and remove the tops from the whole onions. With a spoon or a melon baller, hollow-out the onions, leaving a

Seasoning Mix

2½ teaspoon salt

2 teaspoons paprika

1½ teaspoons dry mustard

1 teaspoon dried basil

1 teaspoon garlic powder

1 teaspoon black pepper

¾ teaspoon white pepper

½ teaspoon dried oregano

½ teaspoon dried thyme
leaves

thickness of about ¼ inch. Save the pulp and chop it coarsely for use in the recipe. You should have about 4 cups.

3. In a 5-quart pot over high heat, bring the water to a full boil. Add the hollowed-out onions—start the timer now—and blanch them briefly, about 5 minutes. Drain the onions, run cold water over them to stop the cooking, and set them aside. Leave the water boiling while you prepare the rest of the recipe, allowing it to reduce by up to half.

4. Melt the butter in a 14-inch skillet or a 5-quart pot over high heat. As soon as the butter sizzles, add 3 cups of the onion pulp and the celery. Cook, stirring frequently, until the onions are brown and sweet, about 10 minutes. Add 2 tablespoons of the seasoning mix and stir well. Cook for 2 minutes, then remove and reserve 1 cup of the vegetables for use in the sauce. *Note the very sweet and rich flavor of the onions and how the seasonings accent and complement the onion flavors.*

5. Add the mustard greens, radicchio, sweet potatoes, and white potatoes to the skillet. Add a little of the onion cooking water and deglaze the skillet if the vegetables are browning too much and sticking. Cover and cook, uncovering to stir every few minutes, until the white potatoes are about half cooked and the greens are wilted, about 12 minutes. Add the cabbage and stir well, then add the spinach and 2 teaspoons of the seasoning mix. Re-cover and continue to cook, stirring and scraping the skillet bottom, for 8 minutes. Add 1 cup of the onion cooking water, re-cover, and continue to cook, stirring and scraping the skillet bottom, for 8 minutes longer. Add 1 cup of the onion cooking water, scrape the bottom well, and cook, stirring, for 2 minutes more. Remove from the heat. *Medium herb and spice flavors predominate throughout the taste, with the flavors of the different greens arranging themselves from front to back in the mouth.*

6. Preheat the oven to 350°F.

7. Divide the stuffing among the onion shells, mounding it up on top—a custard cup or 1-cup measuring cup works well for this. Place the onions in a baking pan with a little of the onion cooking water. Bake until the onions are touched with gold and heated through, about 20 to 30 minutes.

8. While the onions are baking, make the sauce. Melt the butter in a 12-inch nonstick skillet over high heat. When the butter sizzles, add the reserved onion mixture and the remaining seasoning mix. Stir well, then add the flour and whisk constantly until completely dissolved. Add 2 cups of the onion cooking water, the mustard, and brown sugar and stir well until blended; then add the sour cream (or heavy cream or onion cooking water). Bring just to a boil, stirring constantly, then remove from the heat. If it gets a little too thick, thin with an additional ½ cup of onion water.

9. Drizzle a little sauce over the onions before serving and pass the rest.

Fluffy Fried Vegetables

This recipe is great to prepare with your company either watching or participating. You can have the batter and oil ready, then let your guests fry their favorite vegetables. We developed the sauce especially to complement the vegetables, but by all means offer one or two other kinds if you like. Just be sure to have the sauces ready before you heat the oil.

Dipping Sauce (makes about ¾ cup)

- 1 teaspoon crushed sweet red bell peppers
- ½ teaspoon ground dried Anaheim chile peppers
- 1 tablespoon lightly packed light brown sugar
- 1 tablespoon dried cilantro
- 2 tablespoons rice salad vinegar
- 2 tablespoons tamari
- 2 teaspoons dark sesame oil
- 2 teaspoons minced fresh garlic
- ¼ cup mirin (sweet rice wine)
- 1 tablespoon peeled and minced fresh ginger
- 2 tablespoons dried shrimp, powdered

Vegetable oil for frying

Batter

- 6 large egg whites
- 2 cups all-purpose flour
- 1 cup corn flour
- ½ cup cornmeal
- 2 cups milk

Seasoning Mix

- 2½ teaspoons paprika
- 2½ teaspoons salt
- 2 teaspoons onion powder
- 1¼ teaspoons garlic powder
- 1¼ teaspoons ground dried New Mexico chile peppers
- 1 teaspoon ground dried ancho chile peppers
- 1 teaspoon ground ginger
- 1 teaspoon black pepper
- ¾ teaspoon dry mustard
- ¾ teaspoon white pepper

Vegetables for Frying

  1 medium-size onion, cut into ¾-inch-thick slices and separated
    into rings
  1 medium-size zucchini, ends trimmed but left unpeeled and cut
    diagonally into ½-inch-thick slices
  1 medium-size eggplant, stem trimmed but left unpeeled and cut
    into ¼-inch-thick slices
  1 medium-size sweet potato, peeled and cut into ¼-inch-thick slices
  1 medium-size mirliton, peeled, cored, and cut into ½-inch-thick
    slices

1. Make the dipping sauce first. Combine all the sauce ingredients in a small jar or pitcher and mix well.

2. Combine the seasoning mix ingredients in a small bowl.

3. Fill a deep fryer with a thermostat with vegetable oil to a depth of 3 inches and heat the oil to 350°F. Or use a 6-quart pot over high heat and a cooking thermometer. Adjust the heat as necessary to keep the temperature of the oil as close to 350°F as possible. If the temperature falls too much (25°F or more), the vegetables will be soggy instead of crisp.

4. Beat the egg whites in a large bowl with an electric mixer until they form stiff peaks. In another large bowl, combine the all-purpose flour, corn flour, cornmeal, and the seasoning mix. Stir until well combined, then add the milk and whip until completely blended. Gently fold in the beaten egg whites just until they are incorporated—be careful not to overfold, which would deflate the egg whites and cause the batter to lose its lightness. Use immediately or refrigerate until ready to use.

5. When the oil reaches 350°F, dip the vegetable pieces in the batter, turning to coat them lightly but evenly, and immediately place them in the hot oil. Fry until the pieces are nicely browned, about 2 to 4 minutes. Remove with a slotted spoon, drain on paper towels, and serve immediately, accompanied by the Dipping Sauce.

Green Tomatoes
with Stilton Cheese

Makes 4 main-course or 8 appetizer servings *The richness of Stilton cheese and the sweetness of coconut milk, plus the tad of brown sugar, nicely balance the chile peppers, making these stuffed tomatoes a happy surprise for family and friends. Serve them as an accompaniment to broiled or grilled meat or fish, as the highlight of a vegetarian meal, or, singly, as an unusual appetizer.*

Choose the best quality Stilton cheese you can find, but an excellent blue cheese would be infinitely preferable to a mediocre Stilton.

8 green tomatoes, each about 3 inches in
diameter
4 tablespoons (½ stick) unsalted butter, in all
2 cups chopped onions
2 cups peeled parsnips cut into ¼-inch pieces
1 cup plus 2 tablespoons vegetable stock, in all
3 cups seeded mirlitons (chayotes) cut into
½-inch pieces
2 cups seeded and chopped red bell peppers
8 ounces Stilton cheese, crumbled
One 13.5-ounce can unsweetened coconut
milk
1 tablespoon lightly packed dark brown
sugar

Seasoning Mix

1 tablespoon plus ½
teaspoon dried oregano

1 tablespoon plus ½
teaspoon salt

1¾ teaspoons ground cumin

1¾ teaspoons garlic powder

1¾ teaspoons ground ginger

1¾ teaspoons onion powder

1¾ teaspoons ground dried
Anaheim chile peppers

1¾ teaspoons ground dried
New Mexico chile peppers

1½ teaspoons ground
cinnamon

1½ teaspoons ground dried
guajillo chile peppers

1 teaspoon ground dried
ancho chile peppers

1 teaspoon ground dried
chipotle chile peppers

1. Combine the seasoning mix ingredients in a small bowl.

2. Peel the tomatoes, then cut the tops off, creating an opening about half as wide as the tomato. Save the tops. Cut a small slice off the bottom if necessary to keep the tomato upright. Using a spoon or melon baller, scoop out the pulp, leaving the outer shells intact. Chop the pulp and set it aside.

3. Place a 6-quart pot over high heat and add 2 tablespoons of the butter. When the butter begins to sizzle, add the onions. Cook, stirring every 2 minutes, until the edges begin to brown, about 6 to 7 minutes. Add the parsnips and cook, stirring every 2 minutes, until the mixture is dry and the parsnips start to brown and soften and the taste becomes quite sweet, about 6 to 10 minutes. Add 2 tablespoons of the stock to deglaze the pot if necessary to keep the mixture from burning. Add the mirlitons, bell peppers, the reserved tomato pulp, and 5 tablespoons of the seasoning mix. Stir well, then cover the pot—covering the pot helps to keep the mixture moist and the flavors locked in—then cook, uncovering to stir and scrape every 2 minutes, until the mixture just begins to stick, about 8 to 10 minutes. *Now there's a strong taste of the tomato, with the seasonings in the front of the mouth. In the back of the mouth is the sweetness of the other vegetables.* Uncover, add ½ cup of the stock and 1 tablespoon of the seasoning mix, and scrape the bottom of the pan well, loosening any brown bits. Re-cover and cook, uncovering every 2 to 3 minutes to stir and check to make sure that the mixture is not sticking. When the mixture begins to stick hard, about 8 to 10 minutes, add the remaining ½ cup stock, scrape the pot well, and remove it from the heat. Combine the mixture with the crumbled cheese. *At this point the tomato acid is down, the sweetness is up, and the seasoning is fairly intense with a good strong build.*

4. Preheat the oven to 350°F.

5. Fill each tomato shell with ½ cup of the stuffing, mounding the excess on top of the opening. Top the mounded stuffing with the reserved tomato cap. Reserve the excess stuffing. Place the tomatoes in a baking pan large enough to hold them with least 1 inch between them. Bake for 12 to 13 minutes and remove from the oven.

6. To make the sauce, scrape the brown crust and drippings from the pan in which the tomatoes were baked, and combine them in a food processor with the remaining stuffing and the coconut milk. Process until smooth and set aside.

7. In a 10-inch skillet over high heat, place the remaining 2 tablespoons of butter, then top with 2 teaspoons of the seasoning mix. As soon as the butter melts, add the brown sugar. Shake the pan to combine the seasonings, then add the puréed stuffing and whisk it into the butter. Bring the sauce just to a boil, whisking constantly, then remove from the heat.

8. For each main-course serving, top 2 tomatoes with ¾ cup sauce. Serve 1 tomato with ⅜ cup sauce as an appetizer or side dish.

Penne Pasta with
Lemongrass Basil Pesto

Makes 4 to 5 servings

Pesto, a traditional Italian sauce that is very popular here in Louisiana as well as in the rest of the country, usually contains fresh basil, garlic, pine nuts, olive oil, and grated cheese. As you can see, our recipe uses both dried and fresh basil, garlic, and olive oil, but we use good old Southern pecans instead of pine nuts, and we've given it added zip with chile peppers and fresh lime juice. The name comes from an Italian word that means "to pound," because it was originally made with a mortar and pestle—aren't you glad we can use a blender?

Not that you're likely to have any left over, but you should know that a fresh pesto sauce does not keep more than a day or so, and it's much tastier the next day if you serve it at room temperature, rather than chilled or reheated.

Shelled nuts are very much like filleted fish, in that the oils extrude easily and then are attacked by oxygen and spoil. So be sure your nuts are very fresh and keep them well packaged.

Seasoning Mix

1½ teaspoons dried basil

1½ teaspoons ground cardamom

1½ teaspoons onion powder

1½ teaspoons salt

1 teaspoon garlic powder

1 teaspoon ground ginger

1 teaspoon dry mustard

---

10 cloves fresh garlic, peeled
¾ cup pecans
3 stalks lemongrass
1½ cups olive oil
2 tablespoons seeded and chopped fresh red
  jalapeño chile peppers (mild heat)
¼ cup seeded and chopped fresh green
  jalapeño chile peppers (medium heat)
2 cups gently packed fresh basil leaves with
  stems removed

2 large shallots, quartered

¼ cup cider vinegar

Juice of 3 small limes

1½ teaspoons dark sesame oil

12 to 15 cups cooked penne pasta

1. Combine the seasoning mix ingredients in a small bowl.

2. Preheat the oven to 350°F.

3. Roast the garlic and pecans on a sheet pan until the pecans turn dark brown and the garlic cloves are tinged with brown, 10 to 15 minutes. Set aside.

4. Peel the tough outer leaves from the lemongrass and slice the fragrant inner portions into ¼-inch-thick rounds. You should have about ½ cup.

5. In a blender, combine the sliced lemongrass with the olive oil and process until the mixture is a smooth paste, about 1 minute. Strain the mixture through a fine-mesh strainer and discard the lemongrass pulp.

6. In a food processor, combine the roasted pecans, garlic, lemongrass oil, and the seasoning mix with all the jalapeño chile peppers, the fresh basil, shallots, vinegar, lime juice, and sesame oil. Process until the pesto is a smooth purée, about 2 to 3 minutes, scraping down the sides of the container as needed.

7. For each serving combine 3 cups of the cooked pasta with ½ cup of the pesto. You can serve the dish right now while it's warm, or let it cool to room temperature.

Penne Pasta with Tarragon Pesto

Makes 4 servings

Pasta and pesto are popular these days, and our carefully balanced seasoning mix makes this version unlike any you've tasted. There are four types of pepper in the mix—a combination that gives the dish a pleasant "bite"—so if you'll be serving someone who can't take the heat, simply reduce the amount of each pepper type, not the number of types.

I grow tarragon in my own herb garden, so I can pick it fresh whenever I want some, but if you're not so fortunate, you should be able to find it easily at the supermarket. Examine it closely as you remove the stems, and don't use any bruised or wilted leaves. Add Italian bread and maybe a mixed green salad, and you have a great lunch or light supper.

Seasoning Mix
2 teaspoons onion powder
1½ teaspoons garlic powder
1½ teaspoons salt
1½ teaspoons dried tarragon
1 teaspoon ground coriander
1 teaspoon paprika
1 teaspoon ground dried ancho chile peppers
¾ teaspoon cayenne
¾ teaspoon white pepper
½ teaspoon ground cumin
½ teaspoon black pepper

½ cup raw pumpkin seeds
1 cup olive oil
2 cups gently packed fresh tarragon leaves
    with stems removed
2 large shallots, quartered
3 tablespoons white balsamic vinegar
½ cup mirin (sweet rice wine)
12 cups cooked penne pasta

1. Combine the seasoning mix ingredients in a small bowl.

2. Preheat the oven to 350°F.

3. Roast the pumpkin seeds on a sheet pan in the oven until they are tinged with brown, about 10 to 15 minutes. Remove from the oven and let cool.

4. In a food processor, combine the pumpkin seeds, the seasoning mix, and all the remaining ingredients except the pasta. Process, scraping down the sides of the bowl as needed, until the pesto is a smooth purée, about 2 to 3 minutes.

5. For each serving, combine 3 cups of the cooked pasta with ½ cup of the pesto. Serve at room temperature or cold, or combine the pasta and pesto in a nonstick skillet and heat, tossing constantly, until the pasta is heated through.

Delightful Desserts

Just look at the desserts in this chapter and you'll see that every recipe seems familiar. That's because each is based on a dessert idea that's been popular in south Louisiana for ages. But wait till you taste what we've done with these traditional favorites! Can't imagine chile peppers with apple pie? One bite of this pie and I'm sure you'll agree it turns out to be a happy combination. Another example—the fresh ginger in the gingerbread. It produces a flavor spark that takes the dessert way out of the ordinary. You'll find a unique touch in each of these palate-pleasers.

Apple Pie with
Chiles and Cheese

"This is not the kind of pie my Aunt Mary used to make!" whined one of my helpers. "Well," I told her, "this is what my Tante Marie would do with her old apple pie recipe if she had a modern frame of mind and access to chile peppers!" For best results, buy crispy, moderately sweet eating apples—we used Galas. Also, because pie tins vary considerably in size and capacity, you may find you have too much filling for yours. If that happens, simply remove some of the liquid so that the level falls slightly below the top of the crust. I like to use 9-inch cake pans, with straight sides, for my pies.

Chile Pepper Pie Crust

4 tablespoons (½ stick) unsalted butter, softened
½ cup sugar
1 small egg
½ teaspoon ground dried Anaheim chile peppers
½ teaspoon ground dried New Mexico chile peppers
¼ teaspoon ground dried árbol chile peppers
¼ teaspoon ground cinnamon
½ teaspoon cream of tartar
½ teaspoon pure vanilla extract
¼ cup plain yogurt
1¾ cups all-purpose flour

Apple Filling

1 small lemon
2¼ cups water, in all
5 medium-size apples (about 7 ounces each)
3 tablespoons cornstarch
3 tablespoons unsalted butter
½ teaspoon ground cinnamon

½ teaspoon ground dried Anaheim chile peppers

½ teaspoon ground dried ancho chile peppers

½ teaspoon ground dried New Mexico chile peppers

¾ cup sugar

¼ cup cane vinegar, or cider vinegar

1 teaspoon pure vanilla extract

10 ounces smoked Gouda cheese, freshly grated

½ cup black currants

1. Make the crust by processing all the crust ingredients together in an electric mixer fitted with a dough hook until just combined; then refrigerate until very cold, preferably overnight, but at least 8 hours. Leave in the refrigerator while you make the filling.

2. Add the juice of the lemon to a large bowl of water, and place 2 cups of water in a 1-quart saucepan. Peel and core the apples, placing the peels in the saucepan (to make a stock) and the peeled apples into the bowl of lemon water to prevent discoloration. When all the apples are peeled, remove them, one at a time, from the lemon water, quarter them, then cut the quarters into 4 or 5 slices, depending on size, and place the slices back into the lemon water until ready to use. You should have about 5 cups of apple slices.

3. Place the saucepan with the peels and water over high heat and bring to a boil. Reduce the heat to medium and simmer for about 20 minutes. Discard the peels and reserve 1 cup of the stock.

4. Dissolve the cornstarch in ¼ cup water and set it aside.

5. Melt the butter in a 3-quart pot over high heat until it begins to sizzle. Add the cinnamon and all the ground peppers and cook, whisking constantly, for 2 minutes. Slowly and carefully, to prevent splashing and possible burning, add the sugar and the reserved 1 cup apple stock. Cook for 2 minutes, whisking constantly, then add the vinegar and vanilla. Cook, whisking frequently, until the mixture begins to reduce, about 5 minutes. Add the cornstarch mixture and whisk constantly and quickly until the mixture is evenly distributed and thickens to the consistency of a very thick gravy. Don't worry that the mixture doesn't have a real sweet fragrance at this time—the natural sweetness of the apples will make the end result delicious and plenty sweet! Add the cheese and whisk thoroughly until melted. Drain the apples, discarding the lemon water, and add them along with the currants. Stir until all the fruit is evenly coated with the mixture. Cover the pot, reduce the heat to medium-low, and cook for 8 more minutes, then remove from the heat. *continued*

6. Preheat the oven to 350°F.

7. Form the chilled dough into a ball and liberally flour the dough, your work surface, and a rolling pin. Roll out the dough to ¼ inch thick. This dough is very tender, so you'll need to handle it gently and carefully. Line a 9-inch pie tin with the dough, then fill it with the apple mixture—the currants will tend to gravitate to the bottom of the pot, so be sure to reach down with your spoon to get them all—and use the scraps of dough to make an attractive lattice or other decorative topping.

8. Bake until the crust is golden brown, about 35 to 45 minutes. Serve warm or at room temperature.

Banana Bliss

Makes about 4 cups sauce; 8 servings

We developed this sauce for ice cream, but it's also great over pound cake, gingerbread, or pudding. Be sure to use bananas that are fully ripe but not over-ripe—bright yellow flecked with brown.

4 large bananas (see headnote above)
½ cup pecans, halves or chopped
½ cup water
½ pound (2 sticks) unsalted butter, cut into pieces
1 cup lightly packed dark brown sugar
1 teaspoon pure vanilla extract
2 tablespoons banana liqueur
2 tablespoons Bailey's Irish Cream Liqueur
1 tablespoon Cognac
1 teaspoon dark sesame oil

Seasoning Mix

1½ teaspoons ground cinnamon

½ teaspoon ground anise seeds

½ teaspoon ground ginger

½ teaspoon ground nutmeg

½ teaspoon salt

1. Peel the bananas and cut them into diagonal slices about ½ inch thick. Set aside.

2. In a small nonstick skillet over medium heat, roast the pecans, stirring constantly, until they begin to darken and give off a rich toasted aroma. Remove from the heat and set aside.

3. In a 10-inch skillet over high heat, whisk together the water, butter, and brown sugar. When the butter melts, add the seasoning mix and bring to a boil, whisking frequently. Whisk in the remaining ingredients, then add the reserved bananas and pecans. Continue to cook, stirring gently, for 4 minutes. Remove from the heat and serve warm.

Chocolate Chocolate Bars

If you want to make this appealing dessert when fresh cherries aren't available, you can use one 16½-ounce can of dark sweet cherries. Drain them well and pat dry before adding to the other ingredients.

Bottom Layer (milk chocolate)

6 ounces Baker's German's sweet chocolate
12 tablepoons (1½ sticks) unsalted butter, softened
1 teaspoon pure vanilla extract
½ cup confectioners' sugar
1½ cups all-purpose flour
¼ teaspoon salt
Vegetable oil cooking spray

Top Layer (white chocolate and fruit)

12 ounces Baker's Premium white chocolate
2 large eggs
½ cup all-purpose flour
1 teaspoon pure vanilla extract
1 cup fresh Bing cherries, stemmed, halved, and pitted
6 ounces fresh raspberries
½ cup unsalted raw sunflower seeds

1. Preheat the oven to 350°F.

2. Melt the German's sweet chocolate in the top of a double boiler over boiling water just until it's mostly melted—you don't want it to get too hot or it will melt the butter to which you're going to add it. There will still be some lumps in it. Remove from the heat and whip until the lumps melt and the chocolate is completely smooth.

3. Place the butter, vanilla, confectioners' sugar, flour, and salt in the bowl of a kitchen mixer fitted with a paddle attachment and mix at a very slow speed, turning the mixer on and off quickly to avoid spilling, just to combine the ingredients. Add the melted chocolate and beat, scraping down the sides of the bowl as necessary, just until the batter comes away from the sides of the bowl, about 3 minutes.

4. Lightly and evenly oil a 9-inch square cake pan.

5. Place the bottom layer batter into the prepared pan and press it down evenly—a smooth metal spatula works well. Bake until it is dark around the edges and the bubbles there have set—it will still be a bit runny in the center—15 to 20 minutes, then remove from the oven and let cool on a cake rack while you prepare the white chocolate layer.

6. Melt the white chocolate in the same way as you did the sweet chocolate.

7. In a bowl of a kitchen mixer fitted with a wire whisk, beat the eggs until they are frothy. Add the flour, vanilla, and the melted white chocolate. Beat slowly for 20 to 30 seconds to blend thoroughly, then stir in the cherry halves and raspberries, making sure they are evenly distributed. Pour over the baked chocolate layer and sprinkle evenly with the sunflower seeds. Bake until the center is firm, the edges are lightly browned, and the seeds are lightly toasted, about 40 minutes. Let cool before cutting into squares.

Cupcakes with
Papaya Sauce

Semolina flour is usually used to make pasta, and it will probably be labeled "pasta flour" or "flour for pasta." It is found near the dry pasta products. I like to use it in other recipes because of its distinctive flavor and the bit of crunch it adds.

Papaya Sauce

2 ripe papayas
½ cup granulated sugar
½ cup heavy cream
4 ounces cream cheese, softened
2 tablespoons unsalted butter
1 teaspoon pure vanilla extract
2 tablespoons freshly squeezed lime juice
½ teaspoon ground cinnamon
¼ teaspoon salt

Cupcakes

¼ pound (1 stick) unsalted butter, softened
½ cup granulated sugar
½ cup firmly packed dark brown sugar
3 large eggs
½ cup all-purpose flour
½ cup semolina flour
Vegetable oil spray

1. Peel the papayas, discard the seeds, and process the papaya flesh in a blender until smooth. Add the remaining sauce ingredients to the blender, one at a time, processing between additions. Refrigerate the sauce until ready to use.

2. Preheat the oven to 375°F.

3. Cream the butter and sugars together until smooth in a large bowl. Add the eggs, one at a time, beating well between additions. Add the flours and beat until completely combined—the batter should look like butter cream frosting.

4. Lightly and evenly spray the cups of muffin tins—a total of 16 cups—with vegetable oil spray (or use paper liners) and spoon enough batter into each cup to come up even with the edge. Because the batter doesn't contain baking powder, the cupcakes will not rise above the edges of the cups. Bake until the cupcakes are lightly browned and set, about 15 minutes. Serve with a dollop of sauce on the side or drizzled over the top of each.

Fresh Ginger
Gingerbread

Makes 12 servings

I think you're really going to like this light and tender gingerbread. When we developed the recipe, it occurred to us that this is probably pretty much how gingerbread tasted back in the days before you could buy little jars of ground dried gingerroot in the store. Although related and both have their uses, the flavors of fresh and dried ginger are very different.

1 cup water
¼ cup peeled and minced fresh ginger, in all
3 large eggs
½ cup sugar
1 cup cane syrup, or your favorite syrup (fruit or
    pure maple syrup)
½ pound (2 sticks) unsalted butter, softened and
    cut into pats about 1 tablespoon each
One 8-ounce container sour cream
2½ cups all-purpose flour
2 teaspoons baking soda
Vegetable oil spray

1. Preheat the oven to 325°F.

2. In a small saucepan over high heat, make a ginger tea as they do in the Orient: Bring the water to a boil and add 2 tablespoons of the ginger. Reduce the heat and simmer for 10 minutes, then add the remaining 2 tablespoons ginger and continue to simmer until the liquid is thick and syrupy and reduced to about ½ cup, 20 to 25 minutes. If too much water evaporates, add a little more as necessary—try to gauge the amount so that you end up with ½ cup syrup. Adding the ginger at different times during the simmering will give 2 different ginger tastes. Set aside to cool to room temperature.

3. In a blender, whip the eggs for 30 seconds, then add the sugar and whip until they are well mixed and frothy, another 30 seconds.

4. In a bowl of a kitchen mixer fitted with a paddle attachment, place the cane syrup and butter and mix at slow speed until combined. Add the egg/sugar mixture and sour cream and mix until combined. Slowly beat in the flour and baking soda, then beat in the ginger syrup.

5. Lightly and evenly spray a 9 × 13 × 2-inch baking pan with vegetable oil spray and spread the batter in it. Bake until a knife inserted in the center comes out clean, about 40 minutes. Let cool slightly on a cake rack before cutting into 12 rectangles to serve.

Islands in the Sunset

Makes 4 servings *A tropical variation of a traditional French dessert, floating island, this uses the wonderfully compatible flavors of sweet potatoes and mangoes. Their golden colors—reminiscent of islands glowing in the late evening sun—inspired the fanciful new name. Try to find Louisiana sweet potatoes, called Beauregards, for they are far more flavorful than other varieties. If you use Beauregards, then 1 large potato will be enough, but if you use some other kind, you'll need 2 large potatoes.*

Custard

1 to 2 large sweet potatoes, or 1 large Beauregard sweet potato
3 cups heavy cream
3 large eggs
½ cup sugar
1½ teaspoons pure vanilla extract

Meringue

1 cup sugar
1 cup water
4 large egg whites
2 ripe mangoes, peeled, seeded, and puréed
Milk for poaching

Caramel Sauce (makes 1¼ cups)

1 cup sugar
4 tablespoons (½ stick) unsalted butter
½ cup heavy cream

1. Preheat the oven to 350°F.

2. Don't wrap the sweet potatoes, though you may want to place a sheet of aluminum foil or a sheet pan under them in case they drip—if they do, it will be the sugar in the potatoes dripping—but place them right on an oven rack and bake

until they are soft all the way through, 50 to 70 minutes. When they are cool enough to handle, remove the skin and press the meat through a fine-mesh strainer. You'll need 1 cup strained potato if you used a Louisiana potato, or 2 cups if you used another variety. Set aside.

3. Heat the heavy cream over low heat until it's very warm, 140°F to 160°F.

4. In the top section of a double boiler, whisk the eggs just until they're frothy, about 4 to 5 minutes, then place over rapidly simmering but not boiling water. While whisking constantly, slowly add the sugar and continue cooking and whisking until the mixture forms a solid thin "string" when you place some in a spoon, lift it out of the pan, and let the liquid fall back in, about 6 minutes longer. While continuing to whisk constantly, slowly add the warm cream and the vanilla. Continue whisking until the liquid forms a more solid, thicker "ribbon" when poured back into the pan from a spoon. This stage can take anywhere from 15 to 25 minutes, depending on the speed of your whisking and the temperature of the cream when you add it. You can use a hand electric mixer if it's lightweight enough for you to hold that long. When the custard reaches ribbon stage, fold in the strained sweet potato and blend gently but completely. If your kitchen is very hot, you may want to refrigerate the custard while you make the meringue and sauce.

5. Make the meringue: Combine the sugar and water in a small saucepan and bring to a boil, whisking until the sugar dissolves. Boil until this sugar syrup reaches the stringy stage, about 7 to 8 minutes. Keep it hot, but don't let it simmer, while you begin the next step.

6. In a large bowl with an electric mixer, beat the egg whites until they form soft peaks. Very slowly pour the hot sugar syrup in a thin stream into the beaten egg whites—if the syrup is too cool, it will break down the whites, but if it's hot it will stabilize the meringue. Beat just until all the syrup is incorporated, then fold in the mango purée.

7. If you haven't poached meringue before, read this section once or twice, visualizing exactly what you're going to be doing, before proceeding. Pour enough milk to reach a depth of 1 inch in a large skillet over high heat. When tiny bubbles form around the outside edge of the milk, reduce the heat just enough so that it stays at a gentle simmer. With a large cooking spoon or a pastry bag with a ½-inch opening, slowly place some of the meringue—about ¾ cup—on top of the milk. The "island" will hold its shape well if you allow a little bit of the meringue to cook for a few seconds before adding more—this technique forms a base upon which you can build. If you're experienced and confident, you can

poach more than 1 meringue at a time. Let cook until the base appears set, then, with a slotted spoon or slotted curved spatula, carefully turn over the meringue and cook until set all the way through. Carefully drain and transfer the islands to a platter as they are completed. This recipe makes enough meringue for you to practice a little until you master the technique.

8. Make the sauce: Place the sugar and butter in a heavy 8-inch skillet over medium-low heat and cook without stirring until about one third of the sugar melts and begins to brown. Now stir or whisk gently to keep the ingredients moving so all the sugar caramelizes but nothing burns. As soon as all the sugar is melted and the mixture reaches a good caramel color, remove it from the heat and whisk in the heavy cream.

9. To serve, place 1 generous cup of the custard on a dessert plate or in a shallow bowl, top with a meringue island, and drizzle some of the caramel sauce on top. Leftover sauce can be refrigerated, but it will harden, so simply soften in the microwave or in a saucepan set over hot water.

Sweet Potato Custard

Makes six 4-ounce custards *Who says I can't create simple recipes? You can turn these into a holiday dessert by topping each with a little whipped cream and chopped toasted pecans or a rich praline sauce.*

Try to find Louisiana sweet potatoes, called Beauregards, as they pack a lot more flavor per ounce than other types. If you use Beauregards, then 1 large potato will be enough, but if you use some other variety, you're going to need 2 cups of strained potato, so use 2 large potatoes. In this case, your yield will be six to eight 6-ounce custards.

1 to 2 large sweet potatoes (see headnote above)
1 large egg
2 large egg yolks
¼ cup sugar
¼ teaspoon salt
1 cup milk
1 cup heavy cream
2 teaspoons pure vanilla extract

1. Preheat the oven to 350°F.

2. Don't wrap the sweet potatoes (though you may want to place a sheet of aluminum foil or a sheet pan under them in case they drip—if they do, it will be the natural sugar in them), but place them right on an oven rack and bake until they are soft all the way through, 50 to 70 minutes. When they are cool enough to handle, remove the skin and press the meat through a fine-mesh strainer.

3. In the large bowl of an electric mixer fitted with a wire whisk, beat the egg, egg yolks, sugar, and salt until fluffy and lemon-colored, then whisk in the milk, heavy cream, vanilla, and 1 cup (or, if you're not using Beauregards 2 cups) of the strained sweet potato and whisk until thoroughly blended.

4. Divide the mixture among six 4-ounce custard cups. Place the cups in a baking pan large enough to hold them without touching and add enough hot water to come about halfway up the sides of the cups. Bake until the custards are set, about 40 minutes. If they are not completely firm when you remove them from the oven, they will set up as they cool. Serve warm, at room temperature, or chilled.

Rice Pudding with
Cranberries and Raisins

Makes 9 servings   *If you've cooked or even read many of my recipes, you've noticed that I often specify "processed" or "Converted" rice, but in this case we don't want to use processed rice because we do want the rice to be sticky, which processing reduces. Think about it— when you're serving rice as a side dish with meat or chicken, you want it fluffy, with every grain separate, not sticky. But for a rich, sweet dessert, stickiness just adds to the fun on your palate!*

Not that this delicious pudding needs a thing, but if you really want to go all out, you could make a fresh berry sauce to decorate the plate or pour over the top of the dessert.

5 cups milk
1 cup uncooked long-grain rice
¼ cup dried black currants
¼ cup raisins
½ cup dried cranberries
2 large eggs
¼ teaspoon salt
6 tablespoons sugar
1 teaspoon pure vanilla extract
One 12-ounce can evaporated milk
1 teaspoon ground cinnamon

1. In a 4-quart pot, heat the fresh milk over medium heat just until bubbles form around the edge. Once you add the rice, you must watch the pot very carefully to be sure the mixture does not burn or boil over. We cooked ours over medium heat, but if your pot is not as thick-bottomed as ours, or if your stove puts out more BTUs than ours does, you may need to reduce the heat to medium-low or even low. Stir in the rice, cover the pot, and cook, stirring gently every 5 minutes to keep the rice from sticking to the bottom of the pot, until the rice is tender and sticky, about 25 to 30 minutes. Remove from the heat and stir in the currants, raisins, and cranberries. Set aside.

2. Preheat the oven to 350°F.

3. In a medium-size bowl, whisk together the eggs, salt, sugar, vanilla, evaporated milk, and cinnamon just until well combined. Stir this mixture into the rice mixture until the ingredients are evenly distributed. Pour the batter into an 8-inch square baking pan or casserole dish and bake until the top is lightly browned and a knife inserted into the middle of the pudding comes out clean, about 45 minutes. Let cool slightly before serving.

Spicy Pear Pie

Homemade pie is one of those pleasures that we'll always enjoy, no matter how far we travel or how many exotic dishes we taste. This rich crust is still delicious even after a couple of days—if it lasts that long.

Pie Crust

1 cup plus 3 tablespoons all-purpose
   flour, in all
½ teaspoon salt
7 tablespoons cold unsalted butter,
   cut into small pieces
¼ cup ice water

Filling

6 ripe pears (about 6 ounces each)
¼ cup freshly squeezed lemon juice
1½ cups water
5 large egg yolks
½ cup sugar
¼ cup heavy cream
One ¼-ounce packet unflavored gelatin
1 cup raisins
1 tablespoon white balsamic vinegar

Seasoning Mix

1 teaspoon ground
   cinnamon

1 teaspoon ground ginger

1 teaspoon ground nutmeg

½ teaspoon ground allspice

½ teaspoon salt

1 cup firmly packed dark
   brown sugar

---

1. Make the pie crust. Sift 1 cup of the flour and the salt in a large bowl. Add the butter and, working quickly and with a light touch, cut the butter into the flour with a spoon and your fingertips (or use a pastry cutter or a fork) until the mixture has the texture of coarse cornmeal. Add the ice water and stir just until blended—the less you handle it, the more tender the crust will be. Form the dough into a ball, wrap it in plastic wrap, and refrigerate until it is very cold, at least 1 hour.

2. When the dough is very cold, sprinkle your work surface with the remaining 3 tablespoons flour, using some of it to coat the rolling pin. Roll out the dough to an even circle about ⅛ inch thick. Place an ungreased 10-inch pie pan over the dough and cut around the pan, leaving a ¾-inch border. Lightly flour the top of the dough and fold it into quarters. Carefully place the dough in the pie pan with the points of the folded dough centered. Unfold the dough and arrange it in the pan, gently pressing it into place and draping a little over the rim. Flute the edges or trim them and refrigerate the shell until ready to fill.

3. Make the filling. Peel the pears, reserving the peels, then quarter each pear and cut each quarter crosswise into ½-inch-thick slices. Sprinkle the pear slices with the lemon juice and toss gently to coat—this prevents browning—and set them aside. Place the peels in a small saucepan and add the water. Bring to a boil, reduce the heat to low, and simmer while you continue the recipe.

4. Preheat the oven to 350°F.

5. In a large bowl, beat the egg yolks until light and lemon-colored, then beat in the sugar. Stir in the heavy cream, then sprinkle evenly with the gelatin and stir gently to combine well.

6. Combine the seasoning mix in a medium-size bowl and mix thoroughly. Set aside ½ cup of this mixture for the topping and the remaining amount for the filling. Add the raisins to the remaining seasoning mix, then add 1 cup of the pear stock and the vinegar. Stir to mix well, then pour into the egg/cream mixture. Stir well to combine the ingredients, then add the pear slices. Stir gently but well to be sure all the pear slices are coated and the raisins are evenly distributed. Pour the filling into the prepared crust, sprinkle evenly with the reserved ½ cup seasoning mixture, and bake until the edges are nicely browned and the liquid is bubbly, about 1 hour. Refrigerate until cold before serving.

Sweetie Magic®
Bread Pudding

Makes 6 to 8 servings   *Traditional cooks in south Louisiana would have used herbs like sage and dill only with meat or vegetables, but I wanted to try them with fresh fruit. And you know what? I was not the slightest bit surprised that they added an appealing note to the sweetness of this pudding. I never use unconventional combinations just for the shock value of doing it—that seems pointless to me, because my goal is a better-tasting dish, not a weird one—but somehow I suspected these flavors would work well together. This dessert takes its name from a spicy and sweet mix that we sell on-line through our home page at http://www.chefpaul.com. Visit us there some time!*

One loaf day-old French bread
   (about 6 to 8 ounces)
5 large eggs
Two 12-ounce cans evaporated milk
1 ripe peach (about 7 ounces), peeled, pitted,
   and chopped
1 ripe pear (about 6 ounces), peeled, cored,
   and chopped
1 cup seedless white grapes, halved
1 cup fresh blueberries, picked over to
   remove stems

Seasoning Mix

2 cups sugar

1 tablespoon ground cinnamon

1 tablespoon rubbed sage

2 teaspoons ground coriander

¾ teaspoon dillweed

1. Mix the seasoning mix ingredients together in a 1-quart bowl.

2. Cut the bread into pieces about 1 × 1 × 1½ inches. If it is not day-old and dry, dry it in a preheated 300°F oven, checking frequently to be sure it doesn't burn, for up to 1 hour.

3. In the large bowl of an electric mixer fitted with a wire whisk, beat the eggs until they are frothy and very fluffy, about 6 to 7 minutes. Stir in the evaporated milk.

4. Set aside ½ cup of the seasoning mixture for the topping and add the rest to the egg/milk mixture. Stir well to combine, then add the bread pieces, then the fruit, and let sit, stirring well every 30 minutes or so, until the bread absorbs most of the liquid, at least 2 hours.

5. When the bread is thoroughly moistened, preheat the oven to 325°F and transfer the pudding to a 9 × 13-inch baking pan or casserole dish. Sprinkle the top of the pudding with the reserved ½ cup seasoning mixture. Bake until the top is nicely browned and the liquid is bubbly, about 40 minutes. Serve warm, at room temperature, or cold, and it's even better the next day!

Tender Pear Cake

Makes six 4-inch-square servings *I developed this recipe using Louisiana pears, but you can use any good cooking variety, such as Bosc or Comice. Buy your pears just before you plan to make the cake, because they can become overripe very quickly, and you want firm ones for this dessert. Pears that are soft and sweet, such as Bartlett, are wonderful to eat fresh, but don't hold up well in baking.*

½ cup pecan halves
1 cup all-purpose flour
½ cup semolina flour
½ teaspoon baking soda
½ teaspoon baking powder
½ cup granulated sugar
¼ cup lightly packed dark brown sugar
2 large egg yolks
12 tablepoons (1½ sticks) unsalted butter, softened
1 teaspoon pure vanilla extract
¼ cup sour cream
3 medium-size ripe but firm pears (about 6 ounces each), peeled, cored, quartered, and each quarter cut crosswise into ½-inch-thick slices
4 large egg whites
Vegetable oil cooking spray

1. Preheat the oven to 325°F.

2. Place the pecans in a pie pan and roast them in the oven until they darken slightly and give off a toasted aroma, 11 to 12 minutes. Set aside.

3. Place the all-purpose flour, semolina flour, baking soda, baking powder, granulated sugar, and brown sugar in the large bowl of a kitchen mixer equipped with a paddle attachment. Mix at the lowest speed, turning on and off quickly if necessary to keep from spilling, just until the ingredients are combined—be sure to break up any lumps of brown sugar. Add the egg yolks, butter, and vanilla and blend on low speed until well mixed, then add the sour cream. Beat on medium speed, scraping down the sides of the bowl as necessary, until very smooth and creamy, about 2 to 3 minutes. Add the pears and roasted pecans and stir to distribute them evenly throughout the batter.

4. Beat the egg whites in a medium-size bowl with an electric mixer until they form firm peaks, then gently but thoroughly fold them into the batter, turning the bowl to incorporate the whites evenly.

5. Spray an 8 × 12-inch cake pan lightly and evenly with the cooking spray. Spread the batter evenly in the pan and bake until golden brown and a knife inserted into the middle of the cake comes out clean, about 30 minutes. Let cool on a rack before cutting into squares to serve.

Notes from My Kitchen

Freshness

The single most important aspect of wonderful food is, of course, its taste, achieved partly by the freshness of the ingredients, whether seafood, meat, or poultry, dairy products, or herbs and spices. Baking powder and yeast must be absolutely fresh or their proper rising action will not take place. When choosing produce and meat, you can make your selection according to their odor as well as their appearance—fish, poultry, beef, tomatoes, apples, and shrimp, especially, develop a very unpleasant smell—and packaged products display "sell by" dates.

Sometimes you just can't get quality, flavorful fresh produce. Have you ever noticed stacks of tomatoes that are all exactly the same size and shape? I suspect that they were grown for their appearance and ease of shipping rather than for flavor, although sometimes I'm surprised to find that they're fragrant and tasty. If you can't get delicious fresh toma-toes, Hunt's Choice-Cut Diced Tomatoes make a good substitute.

Measuring Herbs and Spices

These recipes were developed, tested, and retested using carefully measured seasoning mixes, so if you want to duplicate the tastes we obtained, you'll need to measure accurately. Scoop up the spice or herb with the correct size measuring spoon, then level it off with the back of a knife. We've found that it goes quickly if you keep a dry paper towel handy to wipe off both the spoon and knife (to prevent cross-contamination), for the paper towel cleans them quickly without getting them wet. With some herbs, such as whole dried leaves, you may need to level off the spoon gently with your fingers, as a knife may remove too many of the leaves.

Measuring is easy when the product is in a widemouthed container. Some brands use jars that will allow you to use a measuring spoon up to 1 teaspoon, but others have openings too small for anything larger than a quarter teaspoon. Some of my assistants save widemouthed small jars—ones that originally held mustard, jam, and so forth—and transfer the seasonings to them, identifying the contents with a marking pen or stick-on label. This really saves a lot of time with seasonings you use often, such as salt and paprika.

Another time-saver is to have more than one set of measuring spoons—use one for dry seasonings and the other for oil, vinegar, soy sauce, etc.

Measuring Liquids and Solids

A cup is a cup—1 cup of water will measure the same whether you use a glass or plastic measuring cup, but the different types have different purposes. Liquids are easier to measure in clear glass cups that are marked in increments, whereas solids such as flour and sugar should be measured in the kind of cups that have handles and come in sets of 1 cup, $\frac{1}{2}$ cup, $\frac{1}{3}$ cup, and $\frac{1}{4}$ cup. With sugar or cornmeal, you can simply scoop the ingredient with the cup and level it off with a knife, but flour should be added to the cup with a big spoon (which avoids air bubbles and keeps the flour from compacting down, either of which would make the measurement inaccurate), then leveled off. When adding liquids to the clear measuring cup, be sure to look at the markings from the outside of the cup, rather than through the glass with the markings away from your sight, for the glass distorts the reading. Test this yourself if you don't believe me!

Measuring Dairy Products

An ounce may not always be an ounce—there are ounces of weight and there are measured ounces that comprise cups. When we give the amount of a dairy ingredient in ounces, that ingredient should be weighed. When we mean for you to use a measuring cup to determine the correct amount, we will list the measurement in cups. For instance, the recipe might say "3 ounces sharp Cheddar cheese," which indicates that you should weigh the cheese (or use three quarters of a 4-ounce package); another might list "1 cup freshly grated Monterey Jack cheese," for which you should use a measuring cup. If a recipe should call for 1 cup sour cream, and you have a 16-ounce container, don't assume that you'll need half the container, for the "16 ounces" refers to weight, and we're calling for 1 cupful, which measures 8 ounces of volume, but not necessarily 8 ounces of weight.

A handy table:

3 teaspoons = 1 tablespoon
4 tablespoons = $\frac{1}{4}$ cup
2 cups = 1 pint
2 pints = 1 quart
4 quarts = 1 gallon

Chile Peppers

I like to use both dried and ground, and fresh chile peppers in my cooking, and thank goodness they're easier to find these days than they used to be. When you shop, you may not be able to find the exact varieties we used in developing the recipe, but you should be able to make a good substitution from what is available if you know a few of the basic types.

The heat in chile peppers comes from capsaicin, a liquid found mostly in the seeds and membranes of the pepper. The level of heat is measured in Scoville units, named for Wilbur Scoville, the pharmacist who developed the rating in 1912— the larger the Scoville number, the hotter the pepper. Mild peppers—such as bells, banana peppers or wax peppers, and pimentos—are rated at zero Scoville units, whereas a habanero pepper can register a whopping 300,000 units!

An actual fresh chile pepper that you buy at the supermarket may be more or less hot than another of the same variety, because peppers vary according to where they're grown, the weather there, and even the time of year they're harvested. To make matters even more confusing, crossbreeding has produced some unusual results, including a very mild jalapeño.

I like to use ground dried chile peppers, too. In fact, my company distributes nine kinds of chile peppers, rated by degrees of heat on a level from 1 to 10, with 5 being the level I like. Lower than 5 on this list would indicate a pepper with less heat than I like, and a higher rating would mean a hotter level than I enjoy. Now, this doesn't mean that I don't use all these chiles—I simply use less of the hotter kinds. Remember, too, that the other ingredients in a dish have an effect on the heat of the chiles; foods that have a natural sweetness will particularly reduce the perception of heat. By the way, paprika, which is a pepper, on a scale of 1 to 10 would have a rating of 0, which means no heat at all.

Anaheim	1–2
Ancho	5
Árbol	6–7
Cayenne	7–8
Chipotle	7–9
Guajillo	4–5
New Mexico	3–4
Pasilla	5

If you can't find chile peppers already dried and ground, you can dry them yourself in a preheated 200°F oven until they're dark and crisp, then grind them in a coffee grinder. The darker the skins become, the more taste that will develop, but be very careful, because if the peppers actually burn, the taste will be bitter. Most supermarkets and ethnic markets sell whole dried peppers, so all you have to do is grind them. Store them in the pantry, away from light and humidity, with your other seasonings, in a tightly closed jar labeled with the variety and date. You can also order our ground dried chiles by calling 1-800-457-2857.

When handling fresh chile peppers, always wear latex or vinyl gloves if your skin is sensitive or if you have a cut on your hand. We buy inexpensive disposable ones at the pharmacy.

Why do we like chile peppers? Especially in hot climates? Two scientists at Cornell University have studied the subject and give us two primary reasons. First, spices add an emotional appeal to food and make it taste better (big surprise there!), therefore making us more likely to eat nutritious foods that may not taste wonderful in their unseasoned state. Secondly, spices naturally preserve the foods. In warm climates, bacteria and fungi multiply faster than in cold climates, and food spoils faster. Potent spices—such as chile peppers, as well as garlic, onion, allspice, and oregano—attack these microbes, making the food last longer and therefore more readily available.

Although with modern refrigeration, we don't have to worry so much about rapid spoilage, we still like our hot peppers. Why? Well, according to Cornell's Paul W. Sherman, writing in the *Quarterly Review of Biology*, in the distant past, "Traits that are beneficial are transmitted both culturally and genetically, and that includes taste receptors in our mouths and our taste for certain flavors. People who enjoyed food with antibacterial spices probably were healthier, especially in hot climates. They lived longer and left more off-spring. And they taught their offspring and others: 'This is how to cook a mastodon.' We believe the ultimate reason for using spice is to kill food-borne bacteria and fungi."

Sounds reasonable to me. It would explain why the cuisine of southern Louisiana, India, and Mexico, for instance, is spicier than the food in Scandinavia and Germany.

Scalloping Meat

To scallop meat, start with the meat in front of you on a firm surface, with the grain running from left to right. With a sharp, heavy knife held at a 45° angle to the meat, cut off an oval of meat that measures about 2 by 3 inches and about $1/_2$ inch thick. Continue removing thin ovals down the length of the meat, working from side to side and down the middle, until all the meat has been scalloped.

Stock

In almost all cases, I suggest using stock rather than water in my dishes. Making a good stock is simple to do, and doesn't take much time. In fact, in most cases if you start your stock as you begin the recipe, it will be ready by the time you need it. Simmer as long as possible, adding water only if the quantity drops below 1 quart. If you have time to let your stock cook for 4 or 5 hours, great, but even stock that simmers for no more than 30 minutes is better than water.

Use a stockpot if you have one,

for its tall sides and small diameter mean there is less liquid surface, which slows evaporation. No stockpot? No problem—you can make stock in any pot large enough to hold it. For 1 quart stock, start with 2 quarts of room temperature water in the pot over high heat.

For vegetable stock, add all the trimmings from the vegetables in the recipe (except don't add any bell peppers or chile peppers; their flavors are too strong) or a few celery leaves, an unpeeled quartered onion, and two unpeeled chopped garlic cloves.

For poultry stock, to the water and vegetable trimmings add 1 to 2 pounds chicken backs, necks, and/or bones that have been roasted in a 350°F oven, turning once, until thoroughly browned, about 30 minutes.

For meat stock, to the water and vegetable trimmings add 1 to 2 pounds shank or meat bones that have been roasted in a 350°F oven, turning once, until thoroughly browned, about 30 minutes.

For seafood stock, to the water and vegetable trimmings add rinsed shrimp heads and/or shells, or crawfish heads and/or shells, or crab shells, or rinsed fish carcasses (heads and gills removed), or any combination of these.

Bring to a boil, then reduce the heat and simmer, adding water only if the liquid falls below 1 quart. Cook the stock as long as possible and strain it through several layers of cheesecloth. The recipe can be doubled or tripled if your stockpot is big enough.

If you reduce your stock, it will be much richer and take up less storage space. To reduce stock, after straining it, pour it into a clean stockpot and bring it back to a boil over high heat. As soon as it boils, lower the heat and simmer the stock until it is reduced to the desired level. After cooling, refrigerate or freeze. This produces a very rich stock that can be used as is or, if you don't want stock with so concentrated a flavor, diluted before use.

To freeze stock, first reduce it, then let it cool and pour it into ice cube trays. Freeze, then wrap in three layers of plastic wrap. Take out a cube anytime you want to add a wonderfully rich flavor to your cooking.

Unusual Ingredients

Andouille Pronounced *ahn-doo-ee,* this is the most popular Louisiana smoked pork sausage. It's highly seasoned and is not only wonderful in jambalaya, beans, soup, pasta, and other dishes but is great cut into lengths and grilled. If you can't find authentic andouille, use the best quality smoked pork sausage you can find, or order it by calling 1-800-457-2857.

Bok choy We can thank our Asian friends for introducing us to this member of the cabbage family. It resembles a fat, smooth bunch of very white celery, and its leaves can be used as a green. Both stalks and leaves are chopped and used in some of my recipes, and are also great in stir-fry cooking.

Broccoflower As its name implies, broccoflower is a hybrid, a combination of broccoli and cauliflower, with the latter's firm, round shape and a brilliant yellow-green color instead of off-white. It's wonderful cut into large florets and served raw with a dip, or steamed just until tender-crisp, with a bit of lemon juice and melted butter, as well as in recipes. Broccoflower can be substituted for either broccoli or cauliflower and, if you can't find broccoflower, use cauliflower instead.

Cane syrup A by-product of cane sugar production, cane syrup is thinner than molasses. Around this part of the country, most people serve it on their pancakes and waffles instead of maple syrup. I like it on cornbread, and it adds a great sweetness to many of my recipes. You can substitute any sweet syrup, such as a fruit syrup or pure maple syrup, in these recipes, or order it from C. S. Steen Syrup Mill, Inc., P.O. Box 339, Abbeville, LA 70510, or by calling 1-800-457-2857.

Cane vinegar This Louisiana product is made from sugar cane juice and has a wonderful sweetness that complements the vinegar's natural acidity. Because it's so delicious, it's available far beyond this state; if you can't find it where you shop, you can order it from C. S. Steen Syrup Mill, Inc., P.O. Box 339, Abbeville, LA 70510, or by calling 1-800-457-2857. Or you can substitute your favorite sweet vinegar.

Chayote See Mirliton.

Coconut milk This delicious liquid is made by steeping or boiling freshly grated coconut in milk, and is not obtained by draining off the liquid found in coconuts. It's available in cans in many supermarkets, and almost always in Hispanic and Asian markets. For our recipes, be sure the label says "unsweetened"; the sweetened varieties are used in drinks such as piña coladas.

Daikon A large Asian radish, daikon is wonderful peeled and grated raw into salads, thinly sliced and deep-fried, or chopped and added to stews and soups. Its flavor is mild and slightly sweet, and the creamy white flesh is crisp and firm.

Dark sesame oil The rich fragrance of the dark variety of sesame oil is just what you would expect if you're familiar with the taste and fragrance of toasted sesame seeds, which is why we specify it instead of its pale, practically flavorless cousin.

Drum This is a family of fish noted for the odd drumming or croaking sounds it makes by pressing muscles against its air bladder. The group includes Atlantic and black croaker, black drum, California corbina, hardhead, kingfish, redfish (also called red drum), spot (because many have one or more dark spots near the tail), weakfish, and white seabass. There are fresh and saltwater varieties, and most are popular with commercial and recreational fishermen.

Elephant garlic This wonderful vegetable is not actually a garlic, but is more closely related to leeks. However, onions of all kinds and garlic are kissing cousins, all having delicious bulbs that grow underground, and long, slender leaves. Elephant garlic is somewhat milder in flavor and fragrance than true garlic, so if you use one for the other, be sure to make the appropriate adjustment in quantity.

Fennel Fennel has a pale green bulb that looks a bit like the bottom of a celery stalk, and bright green feathery leaves. Both bulb and stems are great raw or cooked, and the leaves can be added at the last minute of cooking to give a delicate sweet flavor that will remind you of anise.

Japanese eggplant Also called Asian eggplant, this vegetable can be solid purple or striped with a lighter shade. Its flesh is tender and slightly sweet, and its shape is thin and fairly straight. If you cannot find it, you can substitute common eggplant, although you may need to adjust the cooking time because of the difference in texture.

Jicama Once found only in Hispanic markets and recipes, this great vegetable boasts a crisp, off-white flesh encased in a very hard brown skin. It's good peeled, then grated raw into salads, cubed and cooked (some people call it the Mexican potato), or thinly sliced and deep fried. Its mild flavor and crunchy texture have been compared to those of water chestnuts.

Kohlrabi A member of the turnip family, this vegetable tastes a little like its cousin, but it's a bit milder and sweeter. The bulb and leaves are edible, and you can use either the green or purple variety. The bulb is usually fairly large—4 to 5 inches in diameter—and each has several stalks growing from it.

Lemongrass I was introduced to lemongrass because of my fondness for Thai cooking, in which it's an important seasoning, and have since found that it works really well in many of the dishes I like to cook. It's usually available in larger supermarkets (if not, ask the produce manager to order it for you), and certainly in Asian markets. It's long and thin, with pale grayish green and very tough outer leaves wrapped tightly around almost white inner leaves, and has a tough inner core. It gets its lemon-like fragrance and flavor from citral, an oil also found in lemon peel. If you absolutely can't find it, you can substitute a similar amount of finely chopped lemon peel, but, as lemongrass has its own unique taste, the result won't be exactly the same.

Mango This delicious fruit was originally cultivated in India, but now is grown all over the world. They're ovoid (egg shaped) and, when ripe, are very soft and have bright yellow skin tinged with red. The flesh is a brilliant yellow orange. The examples most often seen in this country are 6 or 7 inches long. Mangoes are wonderful eaten raw, perhaps sprinkled with a bit of lime juice, and they make a great contribution to fruit salads. I've also discovered that they're incredible with chicken and seafood. We used to think of mangoes as exotic, but now they can be found in just about any supermarket, and certainly in Latin American markets. If your mangoes aren't quite ripe, place them in a paper bag at room temperature for a few days. Do not refrigerate them. Some people's skin is sensitive to an enzyme in mangoes, so if that's the case, you may want to wear plastic gloves to handle them.

Mirin Available in Japanese markets and the international section of most larger supermarkets, mirin is a sweet, golden wine made from glutinous rice. It's similar to sake, also a rice wine, but somewhat sweeter, so if you must substitute, you'll need to add a bit of sugar.

Mirliton Popular in dishes around the world, the mirliton is also known as chayote in Latin America, christophene in France and parts of the Caribbean and Africa, and as alligator pear in many New Orleans households. It is about the size of a pear, with crisp, very pale green flesh and a slightly deeper green skin. Its mild flavor requires a good bit of seasoning to make it interesting, but it adapts well to a variety of uses—raw in salads, stuffed with seafood or meat, or chopped into casseroles, soups, or stews. Let me tell you one way we prepare mirliton in my restaurant. We peel it, halve it, then scoop out and discard the seed. Next we scoop out the crisp flesh, leaving about $1/4$-inch thickness to make a shell or cup. We set aside the scooped flesh while we batter and deep-fry the shell, then sauté the flesh with andouille and seasonings to make a stuffing. We place the stuffing into the fried shells and top the whole thing with fried oysters or shrimp, then with tasso Béarnaise or Hollandaise sauce. Looking at one humble little mirliton, you might never guess it can be turned into such a great dish.

Mushrooms

Enoki mushrooms are usually sold still in the clumps in which they grow, a cluster of long, slender stems, each surmounted by a round cap, all snowy white. Their flavor is mild and slightly fruity, and their texture tender but crunchy.

Portobellos are basically overgrown white mushrooms, often 5 or 6 inches across. They're so meaty in flavor and texture that they can substitute for meat in sandwiches or as the main course of a meal, and I think they're great grilled.

Shiitake mushrooms are nice-looking, with slightly curled caps and a creamy brown color, and delicious, with a rich meaty flavor. They can be cooked just about any way you can think of—sautéed, chopped and added to sauces or casseroles, baked, or broiled.

Papaya We think of the papaya as very exotic, but it actually is native to North America, though now it is grown around the world. Most of the papayas you'll see in the United States are about 6 inches long and weigh from 1 to 2 pounds. They're somewhat pear-shaped, and ripe ones are bright golden yellow. The delicious bright yellow flesh surrounds a multitude of shiny black seeds. We usually throw these seeds away, but in some cultures they're also eaten; if you decide to try them, check with a reliable source to find out if there are any secrets to their preparation. Like mangoes, papayas contain an enzyme to which some people are sensitive, so if you are, wear plastic gloves when handling them.

Pepperoncini This Italian word actually refers to small, thin, bright red chile peppers, but the ones we specify are the pickled ones sold in jars. Look for them in the pickle, olive, and relish section of your supermarket.

Plantain A very large, firm variety of banana, the plantain is not eaten raw, but used in the cooking of many different cultures, especially in Latin America, the West Indies, and parts of Africa. Its texture is somewhat starchy, particularly when not fully ripe, and its flavor is mild, more like that of a squash than a typical banana.

Rutabaga Some botanists think the rutabaga is a cross between a turnip and a cabbage—it certainly looks like a large turnip, but with yellow-orange flesh that is firm and slightly sweet. Delicious by itself, rutabaga also combines well with other ingredients.

Spices and Herbs

Anise This black-gray powder is the ground seed of a plant in the parsley family; its licorice flavor is distinctive and popular in Greek and Southeast Asian dishes. In China, however, the star anise, a brown powder from seeds of a tree related to the magnolia, and somewhat more bitter than regular anise, is more often used. I prefer star anise also.

Cardamom The ground seeds of a member of the ginger family, cardamom boasts a sweet and spicy flavor that does wonders for sauces and meat dishes.

Chervil This herb is a member of the parsley family, wonderful when fresh and great if carefully dried. Its delicate flavor, with just a hint of anise, can be lost if overcooked, though, so watch the heat after adding it.

Coriander Another parsley cousin, coriander seeds are dried to add a mild fragrance and flavor that may remind you of a combination of lemon and sage. This spice is often used in baked goods, as well as stews and soups. The leaves of the plant are sometimes called cilantro, sometimes called coriander, and look a lot like flat-leaved parsley, but be sure to sniff the leaves before buying to be sure you're getting the right one. Its pungent flavor makes it popular in Asian and Latin American cooking.

Cumin If you've ever traveled by car through the Mexican countryside you'll recognize the fragrance of cumin, for it's a staple of many dishes in that country. And it's popular in the Middle East, Asia, and the Mediterranean. There are three colors—black, white, and amber—of which the white and amber are very similar, whereas the black seeds and powder are somewhat more peppery.

Fenugreek This is one spice you may have a hard time finding already ground, but the seeds should be available at health food shops or perhaps in the tea section of the supermarket. The flavor, between bitter and sweet, is distinctive, so there really isn't a substitute. Fenugreek is a common ingredient in curry mixes.

Turmeric A member of the ginger family, turmeric's use has been documented for some 2,600 years. Its bright golden yellow color—it's what makes American prepared mustard so vivid—and exotic fragrance and flavor are welcome additions to many Asian and East Indian foods. It's made by grinding the root of a lily like plant native to Southeast Asia.

Sugar snap peas Like their slightly smaller cousins the snow peas, sugar snap peas are bright green and crisp and can be eaten pod and all, adding a fresh, springlike touch to dishes. Their delicate texture and flavor are best when cooked for only a very short time (or served raw!), so be sure to add to the dish at the end of the cooking time.

Tamari Richer and more complex in flavor than regular soy sauce, tamari is made with more soybeans and aged much longer. It should be readily available in the international section of your supermarket or at an Asian market, but if you can't find it, use the very best quality of soy sauce available.

Tasso This air-dried ham, heavily coated with spices, is a staple of country cooking in south Louisiana. If you can't find it in your part of the country, you can order it by calling 1-800-457-2857.

White balsamic vinegar A blend of white wine vinegar and the boiled-down musts (unfermented juice, pulp, and seeds) of grapes, white balsamic vinegar is somewhat lighter in color and less intense in flavor than darker balsamic vinegar. Both were originally produced only in Italy.

Yucca root Also known as cassava, or manioc, yucca is used to make tapioca, but I like to chop and add it to various dishes (five in this book alone!), because it adds a good texture and blends well with other, stronger flavored ingredients. It's also great thinly sliced and deep fried. Although generally smaller, the root can be up to 1 foot long, and usually is about 3 or 4 inches in diameter. The skin is rough and dark brown, and the flesh is white, firm, and crisp.

If you have a hard time finding certain ingredients, in spite of the fact that in several cases we offer appropriate substitutions, try our own order service by calling 800-457-2857.

Roasting

Roasting chile peppers, bell peppers, onions, or garlic gives them a wonderful smoky flavor that cannot be achieved any other way. If you have a gas stove, place the vegetable directly in the flame and let it roast, turning frequently with tongs, until the skin is blistered and charred all the way around and gives off a distinctively roasted aroma. Hold the vegetable under cold running water to stop the cooking, then remove the black skin, which slips off very easily.

Chief Chris Pasia, who works with me in the Research and Development Kitchen, discovered that you can get the same result with less mess by wrapping the vegetable loosely in aluminum foil before placing in the fire.

If your stove is electric, you can roast vegetables in a preheated 500°F oven, turning them so they roast evenly, then hold under running water to remove the skins.

Marinating

Marinating changes the color and sometimes the texture of the food, because the food's juices are being exchanged with the marinade liquid.

We marinate food for two reasons—to tenderize and to add flavor. The essential difference between the two is the length of time. Simply adding flavor to food doesn't take very long—a few hours at most—but if we're marinating meat to tenderize it, we'll need to let it sit in the marinade for a longer period of time, usually overnight. It's important to remember this, because if the purpose is to add flavor to meat, be careful not to let it sit in the marinade longer than the recipe specifies.

A Cast-iron Skillet

We don't use cast-iron cookware as much now as we did when I was growing up. But a good heavy iron skillet is a wonderful addition to your kitchen, and one of these recipes, the Cheesy Jalapeño Corn Bread, requires one to come out right.

A well-seasoned iron skillet is naturally nonstick, and it's no big deal to season one. Make sure it's clean, then rub it on all surfaces with vegetable oil. Place it in a preheated 200°F oven for three or four hours, perhaps with a cookie sheet on the shelf below to catch any oil that might drip. And that's all there is to it! When it's cool enough to handle, wipe it with a paper towel, then store away from moisture. After use, you should be able to remove any sticking food particles with a scrunched-up paper towel, a plastic scrubber, or a clean cloth towel dipped in vegetable oil. You can wash it in warm soapy water if you absolutely have to. Dry it immediately and thoroughly—the best way to be sure it's completely dry is to place it over high heat for three or four minutes. If your washing is frequent or vigorous, you may have to re-season the skillet. The very best place to store your skillets is in the oven of a gas stove with a pilot light, but if that's not possible, keep them in the driest place of the house.

Deep-Frying

One secret to successful deep-frying is to keep the temperature of the oil as close to 350°F as possible, because if the temperature drops more than 25°F, the food will be oily instead of crisp. If this becomes a problem, try frying smaller batches. Use a cooking thermometer and adjust the heat as necessary, or use an electric appliance with a reliable thermostat.

Let me define a few terms. We talk about a dry coating, which could be plain flour, a mixture of flour with some other dry ingredient, such as cornmeal or corn flour, and either seasoned or unseasoned. A wash is a mixture of egg with milk or water. And a batter is a fairly thick mixture of dry and wet ingredients, such as milk, corn flour, all-purpose flour, and seasonings.

Before you start to fry using a dry coating, remember that, for best results, the food should not sit in the coating. If the recipe calls for an egg/milk or other wash as well as a dry coating, it's okay for the food to sit in the wash as long as necessary, but don't transfer the food to the final coating until you're actually ready to fry. If you're dexterous, you can use one hand for the wash and the other hand for the dry coating. When you place the food to be fried into the dry coating, quickly cover it with a generous handful of the coating and press down gently, coating the food completely, then shake off any excess coating before proceeding with the next step.

When you're frying with a batter, place the food in the batter, then quickly hold it up to drain off as much excess batter as possible, and quickly transfer it to the hot oil.

Unless you're experienced at deep-frying, it might be a good idea to fry one or two pieces, then check to be sure they're done on the inside. If the food browned too quickly, lower the heat slightly—your thermometer may not be entirely accurate. And if the food takes a lot longer than the recipe says to brown sufficiently, you may want to raise the heat. It's much more important to pay attention to the food than to the thermometer or the clock.

And always, repeat *always,* use fresh oil.

Cooking over High Heat

Almost all of my recipes are cooked over high heat for at least part of the time. I don't want you to burn your food—there's a tremendous difference between caramelizing the ingredients and scorching them. Your stove may give off a lot more BTUs than the one in the Research and Development Kitchen does, or your pots and pans may have thinner bottoms than ours do. Therefore, it's important that you watch the food and if it seems to be cooking too quickly, reduce the heat. If the food is right on the verge of burning, act quickly and remove the pan from the heat completely, let it cool for a few moments, then return to lower heat.

Cooking is not an exact science—not only stoves and cookware but ingredients vary considerably. Your potato may weigh exactly the same as the one we used to develop the recipe, but it may contain less moisture than ours, so it cooks differently. I'd like to help you develop your instinct to be a real cook rather than a directions follower, which is one reason we've included tasting notes in many of these recipes. Look at the food, sniff it, sample it, and use your good judgment to know when to raise or lower the heat and when to turn it off completely.

Stirring and Scraping

I often tell you to stir and scrape up the flavorful brown bits on the bottom of the pot because they add richness and an incredible flavor to the dish. Be sure to turn the pot several times as you stir so that you reach all sides of the pot.

I hope that these notes will add to your knowledge of my style of cooking, as well as indicate the enormous variety of seasonings and ingredients that are just waiting for you to try them.

Index

leek(s):
    candied, 280–81
    potato, and tasso soup, 48–49
    in roasted oxtails with vegetables,
        112–13
    in stuffed veal flank steaks, 170–71
lemongrass, 327–28
    basil pesto, penne pasta with, 292–93
    in chicken Palawan, 188–89
liver, calf's, with fire-roasted pepper
    sauce, 110–11
Louisiana crawfish tails, in stuffed
    flounder, 217–19

mackerel, smoked, in Bucktown soup,
    32–33
Magazine Street pork stew, 150–51
mango(es), 328
    caraway mayonnaise, 83
    chowchow, 92
    in fruit salad with poppy seed
        dressing, 64–65
    honey sauce, blackened stuffed ham
        with, 142–44
    in islands in the sunset, 308–10
    shrimp bisque, 37–39
    in shrimp in tropical fruit cream,
        248–49
    in tropical fruit salad with bronzed
        chicken, 204–5
manioc, 331
marinated lamb chops, 130–31
marinating, 331
mayonnaise:
    caraway mango, 83
    fire-roasted, crab claws vinaigrette
        with, 2–3
    guajillo, 91
    sweet vinegar, 214–15
measuring:
    of dairy products, 322

of herbs and spices, 321–22
    of liquids and solids, 322
meat, scalloping of, 324
meringue, for islands in the sunset,
    308–11
mint jelly, jalapeño, lamb chops in a
    black iron skillet with, 124–25
mirin, 328
mirliton(s), 328
    in clam and pasta salad, 62–63
    in fluffy fried vegetables, 288–89
    glazed, and other good vegetables,
        88–89
    in green tomatoes with Stilton
        cheese, 290–91
    in shrimp chowchow with mixed
        vegetables, 24–25
    in stellar lamb pouches, 134–35
    in stuffed Anaheim chiles, 162–63
    in vegetables and chicken olé!, 206–7
Monterey Jack cheese:
    in bronzed steak enchiladas with a
        New Mexico pepper sauce, 104–6
    in cheesy jalapeño skillet corn
        bread, 282–83
    in chicken with a green and white
        taste, 186–87
    in eggplant with a tomato filling,
        261–63
    in stuffed Anaheim chiles, 162–63
    in veal-stuffed poblano chiles,
        167–69
    in yucca casserole, 272–73
mousse, smoked trout, 26–27
Muenster cheese:
    in crabmeat au gratin, 4–5
    in eggplant with a tomato filling,
        261–63
mushroom(s), 328–29
    in Bayou Teche potato pirogues, 107–9
    caps, salmon-stuffed, 20–21
    crawfish-stuffed, 6–8
    enoki, sauce, veal cutlets with,
        174–75